– athirst is my soul
for God – Psalm 42

"Your brother will rise again... I am the resurrection and the life... Do you believe this?" "Yes, Lord, I have come to believe that you are the Messiah."

THIRSTING FOR THE LORD

ESSAYS IN BIBLICAL SPIRITUALITY

CARROLL STUHLMUELLER, C.P.

Edited by Sr. M. Romanus Penrose, O.S.B.

Drawings by Lillian Brulc

Introduction by Alcuin Coyle, O.F.M.

ALBA · HOUSE NEW · YORK

SOCIETY OF ST. PAUL, 2187 VICTORY BLVD., STATEN ISLAND, NEW YORK 10314

ACKNOWLEDGMENTS

America Press, Inc., *Documents of Vatican II* (1966), Walter M. Abbott, S.J., Ed., for use of scattered quotations.

Scripture texts used in this work are from *The New American Bible*, copyright © 1970 by the Confraternity of Christian Doctrine, Washington, D.C., and are used by license of copyright owner. All rights reserved.

Library of Congress Cataloging in Publication Data

Stuhlmueller, Carroll.
 Thirsting for the Lord.

 Includes index.
  1. Spiritual life--Biblical teaching. 2. Spiritual life--Catholic authors. 3. Liturgics--Catholic Church. I. Title.
BS680.S7S78   248'.4   76-51736
ISBN 0-8189-0341-4

Imprimi Potest:
Roger Mercurio, C.P.
Provincial

Nihil Obstat:
Daniel V. Flynn, J.C.D.
Censor Librorum

Imprimatur:
✠ *James P. Mahoney, D.D.*
Vicar General, Archdiocese of New York
January 7, 1977

Designed, printed and bound in the United States of America by the Fathers and Brothers of the Society of St. Paul, 2187 Victory Boulevard, Staten Island, New York, 10314, as part of their communications apostolate.

2 3 4 5 6 7 8 9 (Current Printing: first digit).

DEDICATION

With devoted gratitude to my four sisters:
Mary (+ 1972) and Louise, Sisters of Notre
Dame de Namur; Janet, wife of Daniel J.
Kuebel; and my youngest sister Vera, wife
of Joseph M. McCune, II.

—Carroll Stuhlmueller, C.P.

Gratefully, to all those who have led me to
joy in the Word, especially: CS, JB, JC, MT,
PC, PQ, and to my brother, whose namesake,
the great St. Jerome, was scholar of the Word.

—M. Romanus Penrose, O.S.B.

To the many people whose lives have
interwoven with mine and in some way
have become part of what is expressed
in my work.

—Lillian Brulc

PREFACE

One evening about two years ago Father Carroll Stuhlmueller was visiting with us at our convent in St. Louis. In a chance conversation, I asked when he was going to write his next book. His rejoinder, a reminder about his over-crowded schedule and preoccupation with many things, was superfluous. Just teasing, I said, "Well, why don't you just compile a collection of your lectures and articles and make them available for a wider audience in book form?" I should have known better. We were soon into the area of readership and related topics. This book is a result of that conversation.

As I began collecting and revising the material, I tried to keep the audience we had spoken about in mind. It was not to be a book for those not yet acquainted with the Scriptures; nor, on the other hand, was it to be for the scholars. Instead, I aimed primarily to reach a large number of people in between these two groups: educated people who were not biblical scholars, those who had some biblical study but would like to have more enrichment in this area, educators and catechists who would like to have more background for their work. For these and all who were *thirsting for the Lord* (Ps 42:3) and would like to "taste and see how good the Lord is" (Ps 34:9) by supplementing their ongoing life of study and meditation, this book was written.

Naturally, as I worked with the text, I also kept thinking in terms of updating the material I had on hand. Periodically, however, I ran into the paradox of finding some sections particularly pertinent even though the papers had been written several years ago. One of the most obvious examples dealt with the Israelites who, in allowing themselves to be conquered culturally by other nations, transformed these same nations with their own unique prophetical insights. Father Stuhlmueller suggests that some of the fiascos we moderns have experienced through our own refusal to adapt to other cultures whose land we have invaded in one way or another was an object lesson the biblical ancients learned to avoid long ago. There are other examples.

As I began editing and revising the work, I realized I was in touch once more with rich insights and characteristic ways of expressing them. It was my hope that the vast number of readers around the globe who are familiar with Fr. Stuhlmueller's thought and style would be able also to share that experience again. For this reason I have tried, whenever possible, to retain his own patterns of expression.

A great deal of gratitude is owed to Sister M. Salome Komar, O.S.B., who typed the final draft of the manuscript and to Sister Maureen Truland, O.S.B., who proof-read the text in its final stages. Without the time and effort they spent on it and without their encouragement, the book would not have been completed.

We also wish to thank the following for permission to use articles, all of which have been thoroughly revised and edited for this book: St. John's University Press, New York (ch. 1); Liturgical Press, Collegeville, Minn. for articles published in *Worship*, *The Bible Today* and *Sisters Today* (chs. 2, 4, 10, 11, 12, 21); The Catholic University Press, Washington, D. C., for an article in *The American Ecclesiastical Review* (ch. 3); America Press, New York, for the article, "Women Priests" in *America* Vol. 131 (Dec. 15, 1974) 385-7 (ch. 6); *The Homiletic and Pastoral Review* (ch. 8); McGraw-Hill Book Company for an article which first appeared in *The Revival of the Liturgy*, edited by Frederick R. McManus and published by Herder & Herder (ch. 9); Trinity College, Burlington, Vt., for an article published in *Biblical Studies in Contemporary Thought*, edited by Miriam Ward, R.S.M. (ch. 13); The Catholic Theological Society of America (ch. 14 & 15); Catholic Charities of Brooklyn, N. Y. (ch. 16); *Communio* (chs. 17 & 18); Franciscan Herald Press, Chicago (ch. 19); *The Living Light* (ch. 20).

Sister M. Romanus Penrose, O.S.B.

CONTENTS

LIST OF ABBREVIATIONS

Documents: all taken from THE DOCUMENTS OF VATICAN II,
Walter M. Abbott, SJ (General Editor), The America Press,
1966.

LG = *Lumen Gentium* (Dogmatic Constitution on the
Church)

GS = *Gaudium et Spes* (Pastoral Constitution on the Church
in the Modern World)

DV = *Dei Verbum* (Dogmatic Constitution on Divine
Revelation)

OS = Opening Speech—Pope John XXIII (October 11, 1962)

MH = Message to Humanity—Fathers of the Council to all
men (October 20, 1962)

Others:

CS = Carroll Stuhlmueller's translation

QS = Qumran Scrolls

INTRODUCTION

This new book of Fr. Carroll Stuhlmueller, C.P., is a presentation of essays and images in biblical spirituality, and is in response to the great desire on the part of the Church that religious leaders should be versed in the Bible, prayer and the apostolate. The book draws its life and imagery from the Bible, and represents the teaching and preaching of a very gifted scholar and a seasoned apostle of the Word.

Fr. Stuhlmueller has been a Professor of Biblical Studies in a number of seminaries and universities, including those of his own Passionist Congregation. The author serves as Professor of Old Testament Studies at the Catholic Theological Union of Chicago, and is presently Chairman of the Biblical Department. As an apostle of the Word, the author has also conducted many workshops and retreats in mission areas of Asia and Africa. He presently lectures in the World Mission Department of Catholic Theological Union, a school which numbers fourteen nations among its student population.

The author's teaching career reaches back to the establishment of the Graduate School of Theology for Women by Sister Madeleva Wolff, C.S.C., at St. Mary's College, Notre Dame, Indiana, where he taught during the summers of 1957 to 1964.

The editor of this book, Sister Romanus Penrose, O.S.B., studied under Fr. Carroll Stuhlmueller at St. Mary's Graduate School of Theology and has cooperated with him on other publishing ventures, among them, *The Bible Today Reader* (Liturgical Press: 1973). Her life as a Benedictine Sister of Perpetual Adoration and her work as editor of *Spirit and Life* keep her in contact with a strong liturgical life and the world of contemporary writers. The book combines Fr. Stuhlmueller's biblical scholarship and pastoral concerns with Sister Romanus' reflections upon his thought from her contemplative stance.

The contemplative quality of this book has been further enhanced by the art of Ms. Lillian Brulc, a faculty member of the Chicago Academy of Fine Arts. Ms. Brulc has contributed on occasion to Fr. Stuhlmueller's teaching at CTU, as well as to some of his published works. Her interest in the apostolate eventually led to an invitation to join a mission team in Panama as resident artist. In 1965 and 1966, she completed the San Miguelito murals which express biblical images according to the hopes and struggles of Panamanian people today. These were used as illustrations in *The Bible Today*, October, 1974. The universal appeal of the drawings of Ms. Brulc's art fits naturally into this book, complemented as it is by Fr. Stuhlmueller's experiential knowledge of the world-wide concern of the Church in the world today.

The origins of this book are deeply rooted in the ancient scriptures, as well as in the liturgical, cultural and historical mission of the Church. Hopefully, readers of this book will experience for themselves a new "thirsting for the Lord" and will be compelled to plunge their own roots into the Bible, thereby absorbing the strength and direction of the Holy Spirit.

Alcuin Coyle, O.F.M.
President, The Catholic Theological Union
          at Chicago

THIRSTING FOR THE LORD

• PART ONE
BEGINNINGS

fire, smoke, visions, dreams –
"Moses, Moses"

Chapter One
Catholic Spirituality in a Post-Vatican II World

The clue for understanding Catholic spirituality in a post-Vatican II world can be found only by searching for it in the light of Vatican II itself. The words *in the light of* point out the role of Vatican II. Light illumines what is already present but in danger of being overlooked. More than that, light by its warmth energizes the growth potential of presently living organisms and attracts them to turn communally in a single direction. Using this analogy, we see that though Vatican II did not necessarily insert anything new into the world, it did spread a light of charity. In this light, we were enabled to recognize what we may have been blind to up until then, or what we may have been seeing only with a hazy or distorted vision. Vatican II, by the warmth of its light of charity, drew all persons to look and seek in the same true direction.

That direction, or rather, that place where all people are united in a genuinely "catholic," that is, world-wide spirituality, is the person of Jesus. "I am the light of the world" (Jn 8:12). The "light" seen from this evangelical perspective, is not primarily a word found in a statement nor a descriptive expression of the most orthodox form of doctrine. It is the *person* of Jesus-savior. The love of Jesus exudes a light so bright as to blind us in long moments of ecstasy and prayer; yet in this mystic darkness the warmth of his goodness attracts, unites and induces the greatest growth in spirituality.

Those biblical saints most distinguished for their wisdom were also persons whose spirituality was rooted in charity, a charity which precipitated intense suffering and enduring darkness. We think of the patriarch Joseph who forgave his brothers for selling him into slavery and who, out of imprisonment, became the counselor of Pharoah and the savior of his family (Gn 27-50); or the prophet Hosea who, each time with ever greater agony, received back again his adulterous wife and thus knew the Lord and the full import of Yahweh's espousal with Israel (Ho 2:22). In each case, charity generated wisdom by sweeping the person beyond the clear formulations of his intellect into the dark but glorious ecstasy of love.

This identification of charity as the light of true wisdom, a light which enables all people to recognize what God's goodness has already achieved in the world and which unites everyone in cooperating more effectively in God's dream of final paradise, comes to our attention repeatedly in the documents of Vatican II. "The theme of light is the key theme of the Second Vatican Council; and its motto, as he [Pope John] suggested, was *Lumen Christi, Lumen Gentium*—'Light of Christ, Light of the Nations'" (MH, p. 3, fn. 5).

In *Gaudium et Spes*, the Council's pastoral statement on "The Church in the Modern World," we read: "The Council brings to mankind *light kindled from the Gospel* . . . This sacred Synod proclaims the highest destiny of man and champions the *godlike seed* which has been sown in him" (GS #3; italics added). It is evident that the Council does not create humankind's destiny; God imparts the seed of his own life within the community of men and women. The light is Christ, and in reflecting this light the Council hopes to alert all people to what God as savior has already initiated but which can be fully accomplished only through their obedience to the gospel and their love for God and others.

GOD-SAVIOR WITHIN THE COMMUNITY

In an attempt to appreciate Catholic spirituality in the light of Vatican II, we need to explore the personal presence of God-savior within the community. God is present as savior, according to the biblical intuition, in the person of his son Jesus, who instructed all people "for their eternal salvation." When Jesus taught, however, he did not intend primarily to impart knowledge nor to give the clearest or the most orthodox statements; at the same time, he always spoke the truth (cf. Jn 8:44-46). His purpose was always "for their salvation." This clarity of purpose is enshrined in the Conciliar affirmation about truth in the Bible: ". . . the books of Scripture must be acknowledged as teaching firmly, faithfully, and without error that truth which God wanted put into the sacred writings for the sake of our salvation" (DV #11). The final words just quoted emphasize the pastoral ministry of the Church; here is where the main competency of the Church lies; here, too, is where the bishops receive their special charism in guiding and in directing the deliberations of theologians.

The salutary or redemptive character of truth means that genuine Catholic spirituality continually challenges the surface achievements of persons and of society. Humankind at its best still remains in need of further purification. And God as savior is pressing everyone to seek within their own depths still further goals of goodness and prayer, goals which will not be reached until the prayer of Jesus receives its final "Amen":

> I pray . . .
> that all may be one
> as you, Father, are in me, and I in you;
> I pray that they may be [one] in us . . .
> I living in them, you living in me
> that their unity may be complete (Jn 17:20-23).

To study Catholic spirituality in the light of Vatican II then, we must consider the initial impulse of Pope John in calling it: ". . . such is the aim of the Second Vatican Ecumenical Council, which, while bringing together the Church's best energies and striving to have men welcome more favorably the good tidings of salvation, prepares, as it were, and consolidates the path toward that unity of mankind which is required as a necessary foundation, in order that the earthly city may be brought to the resemblance of that heavenly city where truth reigns, charity is the law, and whose extent is eternity" (OS, p. 718).

Pope John enunciated this goal of unity only at the end of his discourse. He first expressed the necessity of responding to God as savior, urging us to greater charity and more profound prayer and to seeking primarily the kingdom of God in all of life's activities. Such redemptive work must be personal and interior, by means of individual reform as well as the reform of the Catholic Church (MH, pp. 3-4). It is in this way that we will be directed by the light of a personal God.

Redemption draws attention away from the past and even away from the present. It projects us into the future where hopes are realized, where God, according to St. John,

> shall wipe every tear from their eyes,
> and there shall be no more death or mourning . . .
> for the former world has passed away.
> The one who sat on the throne said to me
> 'See, I make all things new!' (Rv 21:4-5)

The Council Fathers, with an eye to the future, titled chapter 7 of the Constitution on the Church, "The Eschatological Nature of the Pilgrim Church and Her Union with the Heavenly Church." This future Church, however, the Council perceives as already present: "The final age of the world has already come upon us (cf. 1 Cor 10:11). The renovation of the world has been irrevocably decreed and in this age is already anticipated in some real way" (LG, #48).

Through the Church, Jesus saves by bringing the demands of heavenly existence to bear upon the contemporary world. These expectations for purity of heart, for responsiveness to the least as well as to the strongest impulses towards goodness, are far more compelling for growth and development than any past ideal or former paradise. Those who think otherwise, in the immortal phrase of Pope John, are "prophets of gloom" with whom "we feel we must disagree" (OS, p. 712). We always have something greater to look forward to than ever happened in the past. Even Jesus told his disciples at the end of his life, "I solemnly assure you, the man who has faith in me will do the works I do, and greater far than these" (Jn 14:12).

This direction towards the new creation fully accords with the Bible's primary intuition of God as *savior* rather than as *creator*. It can be argued that not even the first three chapters of Genesis are mainly concerned with first creation at the beginning of time but rather are directing attention to the re-creation of the world—in Genesis 1:1–2:4a through obedience to God's word, and in Genesis 2:4b into chapter 3 by realizing the sorry consequences of sin. If we go beyond the introductory chapters of the Bible (Gn 1-11), and begin where biblical history began (Gn 12), we find that the Israelites always met God in moments of great need as their savior: Abraham, homeless and childless (Gn 15:1-6); Israel, enslaved in Egypt (Ex 3:16-17), or continually threatened in the days of the Judges (Jg 3:1-8), or at the point of extinction during the Babylonian exile (cf. Book of Lamentations); sheep without a shepherd in the days of Jesus (Mt 9:36; Jn 10).

And the early Church was no exception. In the Church, through the Spirit of Jesus, God was present as savior, never predictable but always faithful and dependable, always responding to a prayer which expressed one's total need of him. Total need meant that nothing in human beings could predict or determine the future: the eschaton can only be measured by God's goodness, which is immeasurable. This theology of biblical faith presenting God as savior has important consequences for Catholic spirituality.

The first of these is total dependence on God as savior. Sometimes it is those moments when we have done our best that our human weakness becomes most sharply manifest and we experience the need for further purification and redemption. A theology of God as savior expects energetic human endeavor, but also a continuing attitude of faith. At any moment God can cut across human achievements with a shattering experience of what still awaits to be done in the future. And the incipient advance is possible only by humbly submitting to further correction and change.

A second consequence for Catholic spirituality follows upon the importance of time in salvation history. Redemption is not a process of patching up the pieces of a paradise lost, but a striving towards a new creation and a bodily resurrection. The Bible announces the future, not by predicting external details, but rather by forming interior attitudes. Time, therefore, becomes a matter of great concern: God acts in time and we must wait and grow into God's supreme moment and his great hopes. No one can hurry or delay God's time. The psalmist repeated convulsively in a shout of agony, "How long, O Lord?" (cf. Ps 13).

The disciples put the same question to Jesus on one of his appearances after the resurrection, "Lord, are you going to restore the rule to Israel now?" (Ac 1:6). And this after Jesus had just said, "Wait, rather, for the fulfillment of my Father's promise" (1:4). His reply is clear: "The exact time is not yours to know. The Father has reserved that to himself" (1:7). That word *wait*, in fact, is among the most significant ones of the Hebrew language for *faith*. The basic meaning of *hîl* (to wait) is to have labor pains (childbirth). Its derived meaning reaches out to include: painful expectation, to tremble, to writhe in fear, to await (cf. Is 13:8; Jr 4:19; 5:22; Mi 4:10; Pss 55:5; 97:4). Biblical faith, then, includes all of these elements so closely related to perseverance through difficult moments of time.

In considering spirituality today, it is important to understand the biblical notion of eschatology. In doing so, we are forced to accept the slow, grinding, at times seemingly directionless path of history as the way to salvation. Throughout it all, religious leadership must possess a sense of peace and strength, born of faith in Jesus, before it can be a light to such faith within the Church. At times the dark, meandering path of the Christian life— and the moments are truly those of *kairos*—brings us into a vital concern of contemporary persons, that of mysticism.

The religious leader who demands instant fulfillment and immediate eschatology wants the vision of heaven already on earth. Mysticism, the ecstasy of earth, is overwhelmingly different from the eternal wonder and the time-less ecstasy of heaven. Earthly mysticism presumes a surrendering of an imperfect, sinful society, the longing gasp of time, the unfulfilled striving of love. One cannot be lifted by faith beyond words and images unless one starts with clear ideas and strong sentences, nor can one be borne ahead by the Spirit unless a strong confidence in the goodness of God be present. If one demands a heavenly set of realities for life now and for the ministry now, then psychological barriers already block genuine Christian mysticism.

PROFESSIONAL LIFE

A third important consequence for Catholic spirituality derives from the Gospel imperative: "Seek first his kingship over you, his way of holiness, and all these things will be given you besides" (Mt 6:33). The Christian leader must move within "all these things" of education, counseling, hospital work, programs for racial equality, poverty programs and other services answering private and social needs. Yet, the minister of the Gospel is present not as an organization person, that is, not primarily as a professional educator, nurse or doctor, qualified counselor or social worker, but as one who seeks first of all the presence of Jesus and the challenging demands of his goodness, forgiveness and expiatory suffering.

Have Christian leaders over-stressed their professional life? Or do they appear first and above all as ministers of the Gospel? Do they challenge all these institutions and professions with the words of Jesus, "Seek first his kingdom over you, his way of holiness"? Christian leaders do need to be qualified and professionally trained. Nevertheless, as men and women who are ministers of the Gospel and mediators of Jesus Christ, they must ask themselves whether they truly represent him. After all, he came from the socially unacceptable town of Nazareth, never belonged to any of the major religious parties like the Pharisees or the Essenes. He lived poor and died naked and abandoned even by his heavenly Father. Ministers of the Gospel bear the imperative to be conformed to their master, Jesus.

This brings us to a fourth consequence for Catholic spirituality: the Christian witness to poverty. It is possible for the Church as well as her ministers to make the claim that she is world-wide. She can create all kinds of social and educational institutions; she can undertake massive propaganda campaigns for new recruits and converts; she can sway civil authorities and even control the news media. But without denying the value of such approaches and human resources, it is imperative to ask if the Church is forgetting to put first the kingdom of God, to rely totally in faith upon the spirit of Jesus, and to be mediator and image of Jesus today. It even might be claimed that because the Church can muster mighty human power she can not only predict the future but she can even fulfill it! But is such an attitude conducive to an evangelical spirit?

The Council Fathers presented a different value system when they admitted, "We are lacking in human resources and earthly power" (MH, p. 6). In *Lumen Gentium* they stated, "Thus although the Church needs human resources to carry out her mission, she is not set up to seek earthly glory, but to proclaim humility and self-sacrifice, even by her own example" (LG #8). At this moment in her history, the Catholic Church has been forced to become poor. The departures she has suffered and the severe curtailment of some of her missionary activities are two of the more obvious examples of such poverty.

But these facts need not be discouraging or fearsome. They are simply announcing a great moment for Catholic spirituality, that moment when religious leaders can resonate with Paul's glorious tribute to faith: ". . . to live for God. I have been crucified with Christ, and the life I live now is not my own; Christ is living in me. I still live my human life, but it is a life of faith in the Son of God, who loved me and gave himself up for me. I will not treat God's gracious gift as pointless. If justice is available through the law, then Christ died to no purpose" (Gal 2:19-21). Jesus alone is savior; we are only his mediators who respond to his Spirit who is powerful and transforming. This is true Christian mysticism and it is through such an experience that the Church acquires a spirituality based on the poverty of Jesus.

OUR RESPONSE

These consequences following upon a true Catholic spirituality would be incomplete if we did not consider spirituality in the light of our own personal response to God's love and initiative: "We, for our part, love because he first loved us" (1 Jn 4:19). It is only when we personally respond to his love that we become aware of his presence. And personal interaction is not possible if confined to an exclusively interior, non-visible relationship. In everyday life a person projects his or her unique personality in such seemingly insignificant things as clothing, hair style, arrangement of furniture, and even through recipes. At the same time, people are extremely sensitive to criticism about these very things. Similarly, God is never content solely with interior locutions or with mystic expressions of his presence. In the Bible he is a God of space and time. In the Old Testament he gave himself the name *Yahweh,* which means, "He who is always there." In the New Testament, "The Word became flesh and made his dwelling among us" (Jn 1:14). He was so caught up in the details of daily life and the psychology of human existence as to be hungry and lonely, to be tempted, to suffer and to die.

God, then, saves us personally. He does not save us primarily by creeds and statements of doctrine, but by his personal presence as savior. He saves us not so much through orthodoxy and intellectual exactitude as through the light of charity. However, external circumstances are also a necessary part of human existence, and some external details which are vital to a personal expression of religion and prayer are doctrinal formulations, creeds and liturgy. All of these factors need careful consideration by leadership in the Church so that they can be easily understood and peacefully executed by its members. Anything else would be a personal violation of one another in the name of religion. Understandably enough, Catholics are very sensitive regarding changes in these areas. These problems have always been existent in the Church (cf. 1 Cor 11:22 ff.).

External details, on the other hand, must not be allowed to degenerate into idols according to the sacred writers. They must symbolize the interior mystery of God's personal presence rather than be substitutes for God or be considered as imperfectible as he is. And when it is a matter of doctrines and creeds, though words and phrases are absolutely necessary for accurate communication, they must not be mere formulas; they must be significant symbols conveying the mysteries beneath them, mysteries rooted in the person of God. Christian faith and spirituality is not even directed so much to events, undeniable and as important as they may be, but to the person of Jesus. For this reason, Pope Paul, in the opening discourse at the second session of Vatican II, September 29, 1963, declared, "The Church is a mystery. It is a reality imbued with the hidden presence of God. It lies, therefore, within the very nature of the Church to be always open to new and greater exploration" (LG, p. 14, fn. 1).

Not only is the risen Jesus personally present at the heart of all activity—that fact would be mysterious enough—but he is there as savior: challenging, sweeping forward, allowing the heavenly reality to break through the earthly surface, engulfing it in a mystery of love beyond human comprehension. Certain additional implications for Catholic spirituality flow from this consideration. If Jesus is personally present always and everywhere, then our approach to persons and events ought to be marked with reverence and concern. Faith should actuate the poet in each of us, enabling us to look at everything with awe. Such personal concern should lead us not only to a God-mindedness punctuating the small moments in between the various activities of our day, but it should lead as well to longer stretches of prayer when the full impact of God's presence penetrates our whole consciousness. A blueprint for such a stance can be found in Philippians 4:4-9. An apostolic worker truly conscious of the sacredness of life and the mystery of personal union with Jesus-savior everywhere in life can hardly be satisfied with less than an hour of silent contemplative prayer daily. And this should lead to dignified liturgical prayer.

If liturgy reflects life, then life ought to be influenced and challenged by liturgy. Families, parishes, religious communities and rectories ought to reflect, like worship, the charity of heaven in hope and desire. Such hopes precipitate suffering and a sense of sin; they make each one aware of much selfishness and narrow ambition. The "liturgy of daily life," like the liturgy of worship, presumes a knowledge of many arts and sciences: music, language, sociology, architecture, psychology, history, nutrition. All of these resources must converge harmoniously and effectively in the moment of liturgy, whether this liturgy be worship in church or in family life at home. Ideally, the home, the community and the rectory should project an image of what it means to be consecrated to God, devoted to prayer and committed to charity and peace so as to draw all people into union with them in Jesus.

If unity is to be achieved interiorly where people think, ponder, judge and form ideals, then it will be a slow process. Quick salvation tends to make idols out of externals. In order to achieve outward conformity, externals must be imposed from without. This instant salvation is an ever-present temptation. Jesus' own temptations, whether described more realistically as scattered throughout John's Gospel (Jn 6:15, 30; 7:1-5) or in a more concentrated fashion as found in the midrashic accounts of Matthew and Luke (Mt 4:1-11; Lk 4:1-13), spring from the desire to accomplish a beautiful goal quickly by miraculous signs. We find that what Jesus himself endured later became a community temptation in the Nazareth episode: "Do here in your own country the [marvelous] things we have heard you have done in Caphernaum" (Lk 4:23). Jesus refused and was rejected, and so commenced the long, slow ministry, leading inexorably to his death and glorification.

The Church, too, has been projected into a long journey of faith in darkness, daily carrying the cross of Jesus until the day of glorification. True unity is never the product of force or violence nor does it come quickly. It can be achieved only through the continuous, interior, energetic presence of the Holy Spirit. It was to this Holy Spirit that Pope John addressed his prayer for the success of the Ecumenical Council. Genuine unity is the final result of the long personal purification of all individuals. And it will be complete only when it is achieved everywhere.

Today, those apostolic workers who give ultimatums to God or to the Church—such and such must happen in one, two or five years' time, or else I quit—are not guided by the God of the Bible. They have not read the message of the long, tedious, repetitious

debate of Job, which led to no conclusion other than the confession, "I disown what I have said, and repent in dust and ashes"
(Jb 42:6). Nor are these workers praying with the greatest prophet, Jeremiah, whose dialogue with God indicated he must persevere longer, suffer more, and be purified more fiercely (Jr 12:5;
15:10-21). Though unity achieved through interior renewal is
slow, arduous and painful, it does have genuine and lasting results.
This lesson is evident if we look, for example, at what the Catholic
Church attempted at Vatican II or at what leaders in racial equality asked of the United States a few years ago. A genuine Catholic
spirituality will teach the lesson of the cross: never appeal to
charity and unity unless you are ready to suffer.

More than anyone else, leaders in spirituality receive the most
pressing call to suffer. As leaders, they are persons plunged within
the community, so that they can enter into its hopes and possibilities. They are at the same time persons beyond the community,
for they see these ideals and dream these dreams more vividly,
with more urgent demand on conscience, than anyone else. Such
tension induces mental suffering. As in the case of Jesus, there is
the temptation to evade the issue through some quick messianism,
some marvelous display, some immediate individual fulfillment.

SUMMARY

Catholic spirituality in the light of Vatican II must maintain
the pastoral thrust of the Council. Just as God in the Old Testament times and Jesus in the New Testament era never forced
holiness upon anyone, not even by miracles, so also the Council
sounded a call for interior renewal. God accomplishes salvation
personally. God as savior acts as a personal God. And personal
renewal or redemption within community is complete only when
all are one in Christ Jesus. Unity, the final goal of redemption in
the Bible, prompted Pope John to call the Council. Yet, he foresaw
the possibility of its glorious achievement only after the Catholic
Church had gone through the struggle of interior renewal.

• PART TWO
PROPHECY

– a prophet to the nations I appointed you –
Jeremiah 1:5

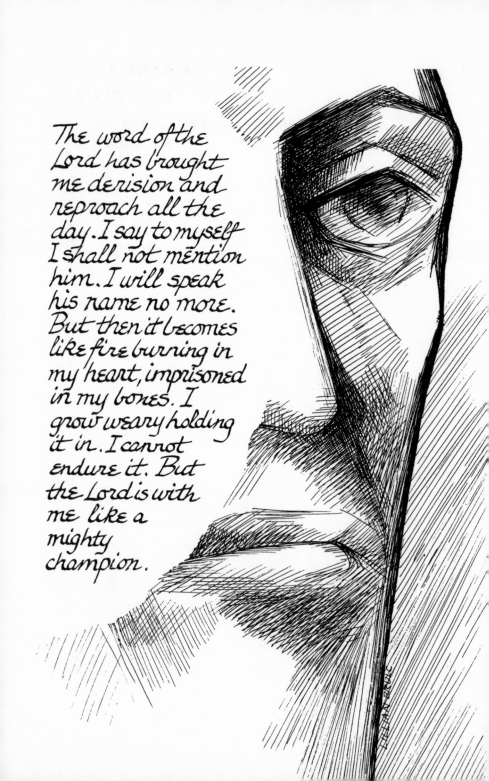

The word of the Lord has brought me derision and reproach all the day. I say to myself I shall not mention him. I will speak his name no more. But then it becomes like fire burning in my heart, imprisoned in my bones. I grow weary holding it in. I cannot endure it. But the Lord is with me like a mighty champion.

Chapter Two
The Community Assesses its Prophets

How should a community respond to the challenge of new ideas? To express the same question differently, how can a community entertain and absorb new, significant ideas without destroying itself? What qualities must a community possess so that new ideas reform and even transform it without obliterating its identity or breaking its continuity from the past into the future?

Parishioners, religious and other groups in the Church have asked themselves these questions repeatedly since Vatican II. Granted that the idea-people in a given group—we will call them *prophets*—rightly confront the community with the pure sound of conscience, we should not forget that the majority of non-prophets *must* exercise their adult right and obligation to assess and evaluate their prophets. In fact, unless a community performs this duty, it will no longer possess any prophets. Only strong, reliable persons with a clear sense of identity and an integral style of putting the parts together can peacefully entertain new ideas. Weak individuals without consistency and integral wholeness in life react defensively and negatively to new prophetic ideas. The application to community is clear, but it is also too important not to spell it out in more detail.

The Scriptures force a re-examination of what is meant by prophet. This task is no simple one with an obvious answer. So thoroughly does prophet belong to the Sacred Scriptures that the English word is simply a transliteration of the Greek *prophetes*. The Hebrew form *nabi* (pronounced nah-vee) seems to be distinctively Israelite because scholars are not certain how it derived from more ancient semitic languages. A definition drawn from several studies tells us that a prophet is that person 1) so fully and consistently a member of his or her community and 2) so perceptive and articulate that 3) as a result, he or she can bring the *internal* challenge of the community's conscience—its hopes and ideals—to bear upon the *external* form of the community's life-style and work.

A prophet speaks *for* and *to* the community. The success of the prophet, therefore, depends upon the community's response to an absorption of the prophetic message. A prophet does not set out to form a new community but works to purify and enrich what has existed and continues to exist with its own identity. The prophet, therefore, is destined to lose his or her identity within the new, reformed community just as Moses seems to be buried within the *Torah* of Israel, and Jesus must be found within the gospels according to Matthew, Mark, Luke and John or what Saint Paul called "*his* gospel" (Rm 2:16; 16:25). Let it be stated clearly that a prophet who refuses to be buried within the community disqualifies himself or herself from the prophetic office. Only the Christian, according to Paul, who dies with Jesus and is buried with him, can be united with him in his glorious resurrection (Rm 6:5; Col 2:12).

In the Bible, Old as well as New Testament, the community response to the prophet can be seen within a five-stage process:

1) Israel or the Church already exist before prophetical leaders appear.

2) Prophets like Jeremiah or Jesus presume the existence of Israel, and each seeks to reform by reviving the voice of the Spirit within the external form of the community.

3) The "school" of Jeremiah or Jesus develops among their disciples; oral traditions more and more take a definite shape and at times are written down; experimentation occurs.

4) From the traditions, documents and experience of the stage just mentioned, organizational leaders within the community edit a book, usually under a dominant theme. The *prophecy* of Jeremiah now becomes the *book* of Jeremiah;

Jesus the prophet evolves into the theology of Jesus Christ according to Matthew, Mark, Luke and John.

5) The books of Jeremiah, Matthew and so on, as part of the Bible, provide guidelines, norms and laws for the community. This final step becomes, in time, stage one again and a new development gets under way.

DIFFERENT GIFTS BUT THE SAME SPIRIT

The community's response to the prophet is identified chiefly with stage four. In biblical language, the community discusses, amends and formalizes a proposal by *editing* the prophet's ideas which then become the book of Jeremiah or the gospel of Matthew. The prophet's message was inserted within the pages of the Bible because the community reacted to the living presence of the prophet—pro and con—and because the community found in the prophet's preaching and activity a mirror of its own hopes and struggles for living in God's presence. It was only when the people of Israel could honestly declare, "Yes, you speak the meaning of ourselves before God, our God-inspired hopes and ideals, our God-strengthened and divinely fibered courage" that the inspired message of the prophet was canonized within the community's Bible.

This literary work, moreover, was not accomplished simply by a group consensus normally, but by an individual editor or evangelist. The community, therefore, edits the prophet's message through its leaders: this fact presumes a well-knit, organized group of men and women. In the history of Israel, anonymous heroes performed great wonders, yet their words and exploits are not recorded in the Bible. The Epistle to the Hebrews calls these people our "cloud of witnesses" (12:1). If, on the other hand, other prophets, kings and sages were represented in the Sacred Scriptures, sometimes in biographical accounts (Elijah and Elisha in the two Books of Kings), and at other times in a record of their preaching (the great "classical" prophets: Amos, Hosea, Isaiah), the reason lies primarily because of and within the dynamism of the community of Israel. The community through its leaders took upon itself the preservation of the Prophet's word and work.

Today the task of editing the prophetical message is identified ordinarily with religious superiors, provincial and general chapters, bishop's conferences and Ecumenical Councils. Their work is to provide a practical norm for mustering the resources of the community into a fervent home life and a zealous apostolic response. The role of these leaders, then, is not to be prophetic, but courageously to pass judgment upon the prophets. They must be strong enough to avoid the popular stance of appearing before the community with the prophet's mantle. Prophets, on the other hand, must be sturdy enough in their dedication to the community not to rebel when their magnetic voice is rolled out flat within a program of action for all the non-prophets within the community. Variety of talents is the key phrase in the Bible. No individual person can do everything.

No one in the Bible returned more often to this theme than the expert apostle Saint Paul. Repeatedly in the Corinthian correspondence he writes against jealousy. A typical chapter occurs in First Corinthians: "There are different gifts but the same Spirit; there are different ministries but the same Lord; there are different works but the same God who accomplishes all of them in everyone. To each person the manifestation of the Spirit is given for the common good. . . . If the body were all eyes, what would happen to our hearing? If it were all ears, what would happen to our smelling? . . ." (12:4-7, 17). Even in God there is a distinction of person—Spirit, the Lord Jesus and God the Father—which Paul carefully called to the attention of the Corinthians when discussing their own distinction of gifts.

The prophetical charism to challenge the conscience of Israel would have evaporated like water flowing into desert sand had the Jewish priests of the postexilic age not utilized their organizational charism to edit the prophetical books. Their purpose was not just to preserve a memorial script, but to provide a continuous guide to life in the prophetic books. Today's prophets, the Jeremiahs and Isaiahs and Hoseas of our age, also disappear in a dry wadi if today's organizational leaders do not act to preserve their words—again, not as an inscription on a tombstone but as an effective norm for thinking, judging and acting in unity.

Within this context of different gifts, two principal charisms are noted: that of organizational leadership, to sustain unity in the contemporary moment and foreseeable future; and that of prophetical leadership, to enliven that unity in order to lead the community into the different future. Only a community with strong organizational leadership provides the life-setting conducive to prophets. Only a mature, steady person entertains new ideas from others; the immature person at once takes on a defensive stance. Powerful leaders, we must sadly admit, can and do kill the prophets; and yet only where such leadership exists do prophets appear! What are the dangers and losses threatening a community which is swept into either extreme?

SUPPRESSION OF PROPHECY: COMMUNITY EXTREMES

In a no-leadership community, everyone is tempted to do "his or her own thing." In this situation a series of problems lurk in ambush: little or no concern for community or parish property or finances; indifference to the public image of the community; preference for individual careers and personal satisfaction; less and less healthy competition and mutual advice in common tasks of the apostolate. Such excessive individualism compels each one to emphasize aspects of home-life or ministry not visible in the group as a whole. Everyone, it seems, has to be a prophet and so all set out to proclaim themselves prophets. Like it or not, society always suspects the self-styled prophet who must be different from the rest. Moreover, the leaderless community forces too many members to sustain too many tensions for too long a time without group support. Every aspect of life tends to become an individual project. Few persons can endure such continuous demands every day.

In such leaderless groups, non-conformism, selfishness and idiosyncrasies can be confused with prophetism. All are whittled down into a classless society where no one challenges anyone else. In religious houses if someone is greatly devoted to prayer, that is "their thing," no one else's. If another is talented with liturgical celebration, others in the community can remain unaffected, for each is working out his or her own career. If social enterprise rather than individual prayer happens to be the "thing" of others, there may be too many in a community who pray too little. In this case, the community may have little or no community prayer and liturgy because so many are either psychologically or geographically not at home most of the time. The result is quite obvious. When few, if any, are interested in community image before the public, in the name of sincerity and openness, then the mediocrity of this religious group becomes all too evident to all the world.

The other extreme, of course, is dictatorship, where leaders within the community tolerate no prophetical variations from routine. In such a group numbers tend to keep up and there are fewer defections, but there is less and less room for the genius, poet and saint. Externalism protects the minimal expectations of the spirit. For example, in religious houses, the community looks prayerful, because all have been corralled into the chapel for prayer. The community appears to be zealous and apostolic because everything is done on schedule and everyone is kept busy.

If one must choose between sins—between the classless society where everyone must pretend to be prophetical and the rigid society where no one is—the latter situation at least allows for the possibility of true prophetism. Whether we study the times of Amos and Hosea, Isaiah and Micah, or Jesus and John the Baptist, each prophet appeared at a moment characterized by rigid conformism. Where there is forced unity, at least everyone will be affected by the voice of the prophet; where there is little or no unity, everyone can ignore the prophet. For a prophet to appear, then, there must be a unity strong enough that no one can shield himself or herself from the challenge of the spirit in anyone else. Such a community results only where there are organizational leaders. Unity, like a happy marriage, just does not happen among sinful persons.

THE PROCESS

A prophet cannot be born except in community. New ideas, like new life, spring out of the tension of love between different types of persons. A prophetical idea, like a baby, will never develop to maturity unless the community be stable and permanent. The prophet who challenges community must himself or herself be challenged by the same community, in order to further purify, enrich, strengthen and apply the idea. Only in community is there enough cohesive strength for a new idea to be born. Many biblical examples can be cited.

From the Mosaic heritage there developed the idea of a "chosen people." Moses had led the people out of Egypt, separating them from all other nations. Moses' military successor, Joshua, brought them across the Jordan River. After establishing this beachhead, he directed the conquest of the Promised Land, again rejecting foreigners that there be room for God's elect people. The concept of "chosen people" presumed a community identified as different from all the non-chosen people. Community strength led up to the concept of a chosen people, and that idea precipitated the problem of non-election. What about the non-chosen gentiles? Israel had arrived at the moment of prophetic response.

First, however, a different kind of prophetic message was heard in Israel. The prophet Amos had inherited the sense of a personal God who had chosen the people Israel. He expressed this in his desert shepherd way:

> Do two walk together
> unless they have agreed?
> [obviously not in a desert]
> Does a lion roar in the forest
> when it has no prey? . . .
> [to roar too soon scares away the prey]
> Is a bird brought to earth by a snare
> when there is no lure for it?
> [Not in a desert where food is scarce]
> If the trumpet sounds in a city
> will the people not be frightened?

[like the Israeli on October 6, 1973]
If evil befalls a city,
has not the Lord caused it?
Indeed, the Lord God does nothing
without revealing his plan
to his servants, the prophets (Am 3:3-7).

The God who has chosen Israel is a personal God who loves each Israelite individually and controls each moment of life. Somehow or other, to be an Israelite is more than to be born; it means to be loved by Yahweh and to respond with love. Election, then, is not to be associated with externals like birth in a family as though all Israelites are automatically true Israelites.

In Amos, only a few, *the remnant*, are saved during the terrifying experience of foreign invasion and exile. He does not declare that the external experience of exile necessarily begets the authentic Israelite spirit. The interior sense of loss and the desperate cry for meaning must be directed and entrusted to Yahweh, the God of Israel; this point of life, so insignificant and so feeble as to be almost without life, becomes the source of all life in faith. This prophetical message of the remnant threads its way through the Old Testament and becomes something of the warp and woof of Jesus' message: the tiny mustard seed . . . Oh, little flock . . . narrow is the way and few there are who go by it . . . unless you lose your life. . .

Before the prophetical idea of remnant reached the mind of Jesus and there stirred extraordinary intuitions, it begot another prophetical notion, that of *universal salvation*. Not only did Second Isaiah (the unknown prophet whose preaching is recorded in Chapters 40-55) announce the return of the remnant from exile, but he recognized that Israel's personal God was summoning the gentile Cyrus to achieve this wonder for Israel.

If God's love reaches so favorably to the gentile, then we are not surprised that Second Isaiah should announce the salvation of the gentiles in his Suffering Servant Songs. "My servant," God announced through the prophet, "neither cries out nor shouts [so meek is this remnant, yet] . . . he establishes justice on the earth and the coastlands await his teaching" (Is 42:1-4). This new idea of universal salvation is born from a union of remnant, personal God and chosen people, but such a union of prophetical intuitions was possible only because in Israel there existed an identity before God, sustained over a long period of time.

Sensitive interaction within a community must exist for the prophet's mission to be complete. Prophets need community and its tensions if they are ever to come up with prophetical ideas. New prophetical ideas must be integrated into the wholeness or unity of the group. Prophets do not undertake their mission simply for personal satisfaction or for the relief of having spoken their mind. Once a community accepts and responds and agonizes over the prophet's idea, then the prophet must recognize that the new idea is community property, and no longer a pet reserve of his or her own. For example, once a proposal is introduced into group discussion, parliamentary law prevents the initiator from retracting the idea without group consent. Furthermore, the group can add amendments to the initial idea and approve something different than what was originally proposed.

The obligation to take the difficult, somewhat unpopular and, therefore, courageous act of passing judgment upon the prophets on the part of the community's leaders is not a prophetic action but a pragmatic one. The leaders address themselves not so much to the truth of the prophet's words but to their effectiveness in bringing about community peace, joy and love. The community is not seeking truth for truth's sake. The leaders' task, consequently, is not to arrive at the purest statement on peace, for example, but rather to achieve strong and cooperative unity in a divergent group. Nor is it the leaders' task to present the most accurate exegesis of a biblical passage, but the most effective application of that passage to community prayer, social justice, forgiveness, and so on. It is for these practical reasons that leaders preserve the prophet's words.

None of us could survive the pressure if prophets were on our backs all the time, correcting and challenging each action of the day: informing us how we can and ought to pray more fervently, eat and drink more salubriously, recreate with more relaxation, study and work with more serious dedication. When Moses anxiously requested of God, "Do let me see your glory," God declared, with the practical realism of the organizational leader, "No one can see me and still live" (Ex 33:18, 20). No community can survive the onslaught of all its prophets at once. A religious superior has to moderate, compromise, harmonize and unify all the varied, prophetical voices of his or her community. New ideas must be synthesized with older ones so that the large majority of persons within the community know how to arrange their weeks and days in a realistic, cooperative way for prayer, work, recreation, liturgy, political and social concern.

This program of life will not have the zest and lustre of the prophetic message. The strong, even sarcastic, rebuttals of Amos will be dulled when united with the political *savoir-faire* of Isaiah; Jeremiah's piety will lose its personal poignancy when joined with the liturgical expectations of Haggai or Zechariah. The community always seems to "compromise" in correlating individual prophetical ideas within its pre-existing synthesis. Yet, only in this way can a balanced spirituality be attained, and the unity of many members in the one body manifest heroic charity, the greatest of all gifts (1 Cor 13).

REALISTIC SPIRITUALITY

Pragmatic realism seems to be evidenced all through the Bible. The "way" proposed by the Scriptures does not drift through clouds, nor does it tunnel beneath the earth. It wanders across the earth so that the dirt of this earth gets into the toes of each wayfarer. The Bible includes war songs, soldiers' ballads, the "Wall Street" response of Proverbs and Sirach and the poor man's challenge in Amos and Micah. The Bible brings two practical reminders to our attention. Let us look at them in the context of a modern community in its work of editing its prophetical books.

First, the charism of leadership, whether among bishops, religious superiors, parish priests or teachers in a classroom, differs from the charism of prophecy. A priest or teacher may be prophetic, but to be a clear teacher or effective parish priest, he or she must be other than a prophet. At the end of the school year the students must have been more than challenged; they must have also acquired a body of information and a style of good judgment, so that they can make a mature, independent response to new problems. A parish must be much more than a center of correct biblical interpretation. A parish combines many activities as harmoniously as possible: devotions of piety, social concern and help, loving perseverance in marriage and family life.

Second, organizational leaders must take active control of the prophetical intuitions. This action must be taken in such a way that religious superiors remain within their own competency and charism. As a result, a bishop of the Magisterium will not dictate the exact sense of a biblical passage to a biblical scholar unless he is trained in ancient languages, Semitic thought and literary patterns, international politics of the Fertile Crescent and so on. However, the Magisterium can and must tell the biblical scholar that such and such an interpretation, true as it may be, is not sanctifying and unifying in their parish, diocese or in the Church at large. This latter judgment is the special charism of the apostolic leader.

Similarly, it is within the special competency of the teacher, once he or she has become experienced in the classroom and well acquainted with a group of students, to determine what books or articles, how much discussion and what style of testing will become a profitable learning experience for the students. In the classroom the yardstick for judging material is not simply truth for truth's sake, but truth for the sake of being absorbed and integrated by students who are becoming ever more mature in their response to life and to their own career in life.

That prophet, therefore, is to be followed more readily who speaks from a wide background of experience, especially of experience within community. For this reason, a community ought to ponder more carefully in all its aspects the prophetic voice heard from outside the community or from the young who have had only a few years of "suffering" ideals within the group. The young certainly can speak more purely and more forcefully; their prophetic message of moral righteousness and just anger can ring out more movingly. The role of organizational leaders, in response, lies in a different area, that of integration. The new idea must be interrelated with older ideas into a workable program for the large majority of members.

In making a response to the prophets, organizational leaders must be courageous enough to state:

1) what prophetical ideas are to be rejected, not because they are false nor because they are wicked, but perhaps because they are too true, too holy, too abrupt and sudden for a profitable, mature, unifying and strengthening action within a community.

2) what prophetical ideas are only partially acceptable and therefore must be partially rejected. Leaders must announce what activities are still on the fringe, tolerated for special individuals for personal reasons. These prophetical activities need more experimentation before they can be absorbed into a community program of action. As a matter of fact, these fringe ideas or actions are often enough the source of new vitality and direction for the community in the future.

3) what prophetical ideas are fully accepted and formed within the synthesis of community spirituality and activity.

CONCLUSION

The topic of this chapter has examined prophetical voices heard within single restricted communities: individual dioceses, religious communities, parishes and so on. But each of these communities can take on a wider prophetical role: the priesthood and married state to the whole Church, one religious order to other orders, the parish and diocese to the Church, the Church to the world at large, and so on. When they do so, the same principles already elucidated apply. The prophetical voice must be heard as clearly as possible. The religious order or diocesan priesthood must present itself with a strong sense of identity. No biblical prophet speaks in large generalities. And the community which responds must take control of the prophetical idea. The prophetical priesthood or the prophetical religious order must allow its idea to be realistically integrated within the Church and by the Church. If any of the groups mentioned above have become uncertain of their own identity, they project no clear image to the Church at large and they are no longer prophetic.

To sum up the program for the community which will enable prophetic vision to flourish in the Church, the following points need to be recapitulated:

1) Just as prophets are necessary for community, lest it become dull, formalistic and mechanistic, community is necessary for prophets to appear. New ideas are born and develop to maturity only in the tension of close relationships. Only in a strong community where superiors avoid the temptation to be prophetical themselves and, instead, fulfill their proper charism of uniting and integrating the new ideas within a viable synthesis with old ideas can a healthy tension exist, so necessary for new prophets to appear.

2) Prophets and community must suffer new ideas together, for only in the *pleroma* of Jesus are truth and sanctity united.

3) In the process towards such a *pleroma*—the Bible calls it a "way"—the community through its organizational leaders must courageously recognize and legislate how and to what extent prophetical ideas are accepted within the program of life and apostolate. Their decision must hinge on a careful discerning of what will sanctify and unify the community. Such action means that some "true" prophetical ideas are totally rejected, others are declared to be on the fringe, tolerated with permission, and still others are fully accepted.

A final question might be asked: have we lost prophets within religious orders and the diocesan priesthood, not because the strong, integrated community killed them, but because they could not get attention in a weak, splintered, unidentifiable group of people? The true prophet is martyred because he or she gets attention, and so the seed of new life could develop from the blood of the martyr. The most disheartening factor today is not the killing of the prophets by the community which cared to take action, no matter how misdirected that action, but rather the failure of would-be prophets to persevere long enough within their community to become martyrs. If this is a harsh judgment against prophets and ever-demanding in its expectations of them, then the Bible is at fault for cutting the prophet's mantle to such heroic size!

Chapter Three
Priests as Prophets

The topic of priest and prophet is a difficult one for many reasons. For one thing, we begin from a position of confusion. The nature of the Catholic priesthood itself is being discussed seriously in theological circles. Is the priesthood characterized chiefly, as traditional theology would say, by a qualitative mark or character on the soul? Or, is it, as a newer theological position is suggesting, a special relationship to the Christian community?

Not only do we begin with a certain amount of perplexity on the nature of the Catholic priesthood, but a haze of confusion also blurs the clear lines of prophetism. The word *prophet* takes on various meanings in the Old Testament and in the New Testament. The office is not clearly definable, at least in the details of a job description. The prophet does not set out to be a prophet. In fact, in some cases the role is denied. The Old Testament persons, whom we think of immediately when the word *prophet* comes to mind, seldom called themselves prophets.

Amos, as we read in chapter 7 of his book, denied that he was a prophet. He was emphatic when Amaziah, high priest at the king's sanctuary of Bethel, told him to go back to Judah to prophesy. Amos spit back his reply almost into the very eyeballs of Amaziah, as he shouted in Hebrew: *lō' nabi' 'anōki welō' ben-nabi"anōki.* The English dulls the stinging barb of the original language: "I am no prophet, nor am I a member of any prophetic guild."

The supreme prophet, Jeremiah, hardly ever called himself a prophet. Moreover, he is involved repeatedly in a battle against false prophets (Jr 26-28). Only in the book of Ezekiel do we meet someone frequently calling himself a prophet. So far as the

earlier men are concerned—Amos, Hosea, Isaiah and Jeremiah—
the title of *prophet* usually occurs in the introduction or in other
biographical sections, inserted into the book by a later editor.
This fact alone makes self-styled prophets suspect.

This confusion about the exact nature of prophetism carries
over when we study the relationship of prophet and priest in the
Bible. Amos was expelled from the sanctuary of Bethel by the
priest Amaziah. Ezekiel was a priest before joining the prophetic
movement. It seems he destroyed the prophetic movement by
joining it. After Ezekiel, the prophetic movement quickly
changed its form. Haggai, Zechariah and Joel of the post-exilic
age hardly measured up to the stature of Amos, Hosea and Jeremiah. Jeremiah brought the prophetic movement to its apex
and supreme expression. He was a member of the priestly family
at Anathoth.

Despite this cloudiness, however, we can draw up at least a
working, non-technical definition of priest and prophet. While
the priest is distinguished as an anointed leader of an institutional
organization, the prophet has no official status within the institution. Priests can be defined in an unsophisticated way as those
members of a religious group or organization whose first duty
involves them as leaders in community worship and prayer; secondly, they are committed to a traditional instruction about God
and divine ideals; and thirdly, they are expected to apply God's
will and interpret God's law for the people. As priests they are
a unifying force between the past and the future, between those
living their life together as a community, between the people
and their God.

Prophets, on the other hand, are persons whom God raises up
individually out of the ranks of the community to champion a
personal interior response to God at a time when the community
is endangered by external formalism and is tending towards
miraculous or automatic forms of divine intervention. Unlike
the priest, the prophet *as prophet* has no official standing.

Nonetheless, if the priest is differentiated as an institutional
leader and the prophet as a non-institutional person, prophets cannot be understood and, in fact, cannot exist, outside of the insti-

tution. They are continually reacting to, with or against the institution or the society. The emergence of prophets, moreover, depends essentially upon certain conditions within the institution. When an institution tends toward excessive rigidity and over-concern for externals, the hour has struck for the prophet to arise. Yet prophets never set out to destroy the institution nor do they isolate their own ultimate goals from the good of the institution.

DISCERNMENT OF THE PROPHETIC SPIRIT

Who determines who the prophets are in a community? Only the institution at a later date can make this judgment. It is the community of the future—as it is one with the community of the prophet and one with the community before the prophet—which determines who are its true prophets. It was Israel, after the death of the prophets, who put their writings into the sacred body of literature called *prophetic*. This relationship of prophet to the community and, particularly, this necessity of being accepted as prophet by the later community, presents many difficulties.

Prophets were rejected very often by the community of their own times. They were stoned and crucified. If they were accepted, it was not in their own country, nor in their own time. The greater prophets died before the community had the time or the courage to edit their words. Some prophetic ideas, we must admit, are so immense and their repercussions so overwhelming that the community requires a great deal of time—more time, in fact, than the prophet's life span permits—before it can assimilate them. Jeremiah and Jesus both died before their ideas were realized within the community.

On the other hand, the dictum, "a prophet is stoned by his community," presumes that the prophet stays within a community long enough to die there. Jeremiah would not have died, hounded and persecuted by his own people down in Egypt (Jr 42-43), had he accepted the offer of Nabuzaradan, speaking on behalf of Nebuchadnezzar, of preferential treatment in Babylon or any place of his own choice (Jr 40:4-6). If Jesus had fled with his chosen disciples to a *Shangri-La*, he would not have been crucified. True prophets are willing to take full responsibility for the ideas which they release within the community. They persevere in loyalty to those ideas even if they are momentarily rejected by the community. If the prophets' ideas cause Jerusalem to come crashing down, they and their ideas are with and beneath the city as it comes crashing down. And though prophets die at times, their ideas raise up a new Jerusalem for a new generation.

False prophets are like illegitimate parents who desert the babies they beget. It is not such a challenge to go through the physical motions of begetting children, but only true parents can muster the strength, wisdom and persevering patience to rear them. True prophets do more than beget the hopes and life of the future; they also stand by loyally suffering and continuing to hope, while the community gradually grows up to the full stature and fulfillment of these hopes.

TRUE PROPHETS

Prophets of any sort, in any kind of community—political, social, or whatever it may be—are those who are so much at the heart of the community that they can think deeply, purely, at the heart of what the community is all about. Thinking deeply at this level they clarify and bring to the surface the ideals and goals found there. Then, out of loyalty to the community, they articulate these ideas—the prophetic intuition. This in turn results in prophets being shoved to the outer edge of the community, because articulating the ideals, the goals and the purest hopes of a community challenges its conscience and usually results in rejection of the prophets. This is hard, but prophets have to have the strength to be at the heart of the community and be rejected by that community.

To maintain this kind of tension is the prophetic role. Out of the tension comes a strength and a purity which the community can resist no longer. Then, at the proper moment, when it comes to recognize the truth and can no longer live with its troubled conscience, the community says, "Come back to the heart of us. You are articulating our ideas. You are the best of us; you are our heart. Articulate, expound and implement in our midst. We want to stabilize you in our midst." At that moment, the prophet or prophetic word is accepted and stabilized within the community.

True prophets operate within the traditions of the people. They do not set out to create a new community, nor do they do so, even though it may seem that this is happening. Rather, they purify that community. They are not dealing with externals but with ideas and hopes. Jesus can be considered truly prophetic only if the post-Pentecostal Church authentically continues the life and hope of that Israel in which Jesus passed his earthly days. Biblically, it is impossible to separate prophetic words from the prophet who speaks them.

True prophets remain, interacting with the community, sustaining community interest and maintaining a practical concern for the community's welfare. No true biblical prophet, certainly not Jesus, ever deserted Israel. Loners or the hermits who cut themselves off from the community or who over-antagonize the group, or who are unwilling to let go of their ideas as the group adds its amendments and modifications, or who walk out in a huff if another amendment is offered, disqualify themselves from the role of prophet.

True prophets do not approach the community as though already rejected and martyred. Such persons, whether or not they realize it, harbor a very low estimate of the community. They are prophets of doom who presume the group to be obdurate, dull, spiritless. They give evidence of a persecution complex and a better-than-thou attitude of mind. Such proud pessimism is hardly reflected in the initial preaching of the biblical prophets. Jesus' first sermon announced that, "Today this Scripture passage is fulfilled in your hearing" (Lk 4:21). Jeremiah's initial preaching is contained in the glorious, melodic passages of chapters 3-31, where he announced the "new covenant" and admonished Rachel mourning and bitterly weeping:

> Cease your cries of mourning,

wipe the tears from your eyes. . .
There is hope for your future. . . (Jr 31:16-17).

On the other hand, true prophets do not tailor their ideas to
what the community wants to hear. Prophets announce truths
which their consciences compel them to articulate, sincerely
hoping that truth will liberate the community from over-organi-
zation, rigidity and formalism, and free them to reflect the living,
personal God in their midst. Truth must be spoken with independence. Truth is not enunciated to make a living or to get an
advancement. The great classical prophets like Amos or Isaiah
or John the Baptist usually had another way of making a living;
prophecy was not their bread and butter job. Amos was a shepherd, Isaiah was a court official, and John the Baptist lived off
desert produce. Prophets, consequently, must be a part of the
community, yet always able to exercise independent judgment.

Prophets also practice what they preach—they wait upon the
Lord. The detachment resulting from being rejected violently
from the community and environment of their own time serves
to contribute to their own mystical prayer and their being alone
in God. Second Isaiah complained in a speech about the weariness
and timidity of the people declaring, "Those who wait upon the
Lord renew their strength" (Is 40:31). Prophetic prayer springs
from intuitions and hopes rather than from accomplished works
and goals. It does not bask in the glory of the past, nor does it
strut the gaudy feathers of present achievement.

The past and present, in this context, can be compared to the
scrub bushes which Moses saw daily in the deserts of Sinai. His
hopes and ideals for the future struck a flame within these bushes
(Ex 3). Actually, Moses was the scrub bush himself; his impossible dream the fire. How could he be so foolish as to think of
freeing his people from Egypt? This dream never destroyed him.
He persevered until death, always the mystic, never the achiever.
He died without entering the Promised Land. Several centuries
later, the prophet Isaiah saw not only scrub bushes but the marble
walls of the Jerusalem temple melt away and disappear as the
glory of the Lord summoned him to a new ministry (Is 6).

FULFILLMENT OF PROPHECY

Ultimately, then, the prophetic spirit is determined by the prophet's ability to enunciate the hopes and ideas already simmering inside the community, actual membership of the prophet in the community and his heroic perseverance in prayer and suffering within the community. These hard and cold facts bring up a serious question: does God want every good desire to be fulfilled—at least on the terms of the one possessing the desire? An emphatic "NO!" is the answer shouted back at us in the Bible; yet it is not heard by many would-be contemporary prophets. The prophecy of Jeremiah is strewn with the debris of unfulfilled prophecies, that is, unfulfilled on Jeremiah's terms.

Some prophetical ideas are so great that several generations are too soon for fulfillment. Each new idea must be a carrier onward until the day of eschatological fulfillment arrives. The complete fulfillment of the prophetic word comes about only when all men and women, of all time, are united in Jesus. Until that moment comes, no truth is completely true, for it will lack the full perspective or balancing factor of other truths. A prophetic statement on liturgy requires a prophetic statement on social harmony; social harmony depends upon the prophets of justice and forgiveness; forgiveness is impossible without the prophetic message of the cross; and the cross presumes the hope of resurrection; and hopes, like ideals, raise whole new series of problems.

Fullness, or *pleroma* in this case, does not consist in a well-balanced and nicely nuanced statement, but rather, on Jesus who declared he was "Truth" personified. Truth, then, is not for truth's sake, but for its sanctifying effectiveness, the union of all men and women in Jesus. Truth that divides is not prophetic. The biblical words for truth—*emeth* in the Hebrew Bible or *aletheia* in the Greek Scriptures—refer primarily to fidelity within a community and only secondarily to a correct statement.

> I will espouse you to me forever;
> I will espouse you in right and in
> justice,

> in love and in mercy;
> I will espouse you in fidelity [=Hebrew
> word for truth],
> and you shall know the Lord (Ho 2:21).

Truth here is Israel's experience of total unity in charity, not only among themselves, but also, as Hosea expresses it, "with the beasts of the field, with the birds of the air, and with the things that crawl on the ground."

> Bow and sword and war
> I will destroy from the land,
> and I will let them take their rest
> in security (Ho 2:20).

How, then, do prophets respond to community? By staying within it until death no matter how violent the life or death may be; by speaking and acting to transform community; and as a result, taking the consequences following upon the community's taking possession of the prophetic word. Finally, the prophet responds by not seeking truth for truth's sake, but for its sanctifying and unifying power.

PROPHETIC PRIESTS TODAY

When we consider the prophetic role of contemporary priests, we must presume they are persons who ponder seriously and allow their minds to rest long in the goals and hopes of God for the community of the Church. In this interior depth they are strengthened to challenge the surface type of priestly life and activity and to condemn the stereotype, the excessively rigid, the stiff and formal, the automatic and superstitious. The external life-style and the apostolic activity of priests are godly, never in and by themselves, but only to the extent that they pulsate with the interior presence of God.

This interior, prophetic challenge reaches even to the sacramental actions of priests. True, sacraments do not depend for their validity on the holiness of the minister. A sacrament, validly administered, always imparts grace and blessing. But to what degree is another question and is perhaps the crucial question. The strength of the grace and the abiding power of the blessing can be so minimal as to evaporate almost immediately, or can be so overpowering as to transform the believer. The difference may depend on the interior holiness animating the prophetic spirit of priests.

More than anything else, prayer is the absolute *conditio sine qua non* of priests as prophets. Prayer embraces those moments when priests think deeply. By thinking deeply, they are being prepared to make their prophetic challenge to the surface details of life. By pondering long before God, the priests avoid the pitfall of cliches and platitudes and so arrive at a speech manifesting strong, personal conviction. Their prophetic words, sustained by prayer, can inject the fresh vigor of new life into the stereotype answers of orthodoxy.

The prophetic prayer of priests must be a persevering prayer, even a mystical form of contemplation, because it trains them to do much more than repeat what has already been said. Prophetic prayer deals with hopes and dreams not yet visible on the surface. As such, it cannot repeat the obvious but it sweeps far beyond it, where the light is so blinding that a long time is needed to accustom the eyes of faith and still more time is necessary to enable one to speak about it intelligently. Because the future comes slowly, the prophetic prayer of priests will necessarily be tempered with persevering strength.

Priest-prophets, sustained long by dreams and hopes without fulfillment and without compromise, are absorbed in this mystical prayer. The fire is within the scrub bushes which are themselves. The glory of the Lord is within the walls of their churches. The prophetic role of priests emerges when their interior spirits challenge with new freshness whatever tends to become stiff, formal and automatic on the surface of priestly or church activity. No wonder, then, that the inner attitude of priests requires prayerful hearts, residing long, even mystically, in hopes which are centered in God.

The interior quality of prophetic priests shows up in still another way: in their uniqueness and singularity as persons. We all know that when another person comes close within the circle of our friendship, everything about us must somehow be rethought and reshaped. A new child makes a great difference in the rearrangement of all the little details of family life. Each priest has the opportunity to respond to the priestly institution in a very unique way, and each priest also brings a certain prophetic character of singularity which forces a rethinking of the priesthood.

There is, consequently, a prophetic character about all priests. Whether or not priests become great prophets, however, depends upon many factors outside of themselves and beyond their own control. One of these factors, though absolutely essential, is simply a convergence of external circumstances. Pope John XXIII, for instance, never might have been considered a prophet by anyone if he had lived in 1920 or 1925. If he had made a ripple in society, it would have been no more than a yawn. A problem or a hope must be simmering beneath the surface for a prophet to get a response. Prophets, it seems, do not light the fire; they turn up the heat.

Initially, there has to be a convergence of circumstances in the culture of the Church as in the world at large, for prophets to be formed, much less heard. Their spirit comes to birth from a seed already stirring with life within the womb of society itself. And then God, breathing hopes deeply within the Church, impregnates the Church with its future prophets. And when the Church arrives at the time of her labor pains, prophets are born. For priests to become prophets depends thoroughly upon the times and circumstances of the Church: its needs and its readiness to respond to hopes and challenges. Priests cannot dictate that moment nor determine the impact of their prophetic role any more than children can dictate their conception, the time of their birth or even their sex.

There is still another factor, beyond the control of priests, which may limit their initiative in becoming prophets. If the great prophets seldom called themselves prophets, and if the prophetic mission of priests flows from that unique point of themselves where they are singularly unique persons, we can raise some crucial questions. Does there exist a plaster-cast model of the priest-prophet so that they can climb into the role and become one? Priesthood does have an institutional model. It is a standard office. Persons, consequently, can decide whether or not to become priests. Can the same be said of the role of prophecy?

No, there is no yardstick by which priests can measure their potentiality toward prophetism, much less great prophetism. All they can do in order to become prophets is to be their unique selves as priests. They can be themselves if they truly exist at the heart of their existence in God's presence, and in that deep, prayerful, even mystical sense of union with God, respond to all the needs and the demands within the institution of the priesthood. Realizing all this, is it surprising that self-styled prophets might be considered suspect?

THE PROCESS

When the priests respond to the institution, they must not demand that the community fulfill all the *details* of their prophecies of hopes. To be effective, priests, like the earlier prophets, address themselves to specific problems and get down to practical points. But their crucial role is stirring up hopes and ideals. They are releasing a spirit. They inject adrenalin into the heart of the institutional structure. At times it can happen that the details of fulfillment will be very different from those details emphasized by the prophets initially. During his lifetime, not even Jesus dictated the details of future Church life and Church structure; he did impart the spirit which enabled the Church gradually to structure herself into a viable community.

Like Jesus, priest-prophets persevere in hopes and dreams and possibilities. They thereby keep the external form of the institution of the Church living and warm. Never do they seek automatic, miraculous or quick redemption for the Church. These priests as prophets enable other people to think; they never do the thinking for them. Their prayer enables others to join them in prayer; they never substitute their own prayer for others. The priest-prophets do not dictate the details of life but transform these details by their hopes and dreams.

As prophets they never seek to destroy the external structure of the Church. Rather, they hope to transform the Church by revivifying its interior vitality. If parts of the Church collapse because of them, they are there beneath it all. Those priests who inject ideas into a community and then flee the responsibility of their ideas are not prophets. If they start new movements within the institution or community and then a year or two later are found somewhere else starting something else, they are not prophets. Prophetic priests are expected to suffer the consequences of what they have let loose within a community.

No prophets are prophets to the community which they abandon. Those who leave the Church are not prophets to the Church. Priests or religious who leave the priesthood or religious life are not prophets to priests or to religious. Those who jump out of the boat shake it for a moment, but those who stay in the boat keep on shaking it. Moreover, those who stay are the only ones who can continue to remind the group of their harbor and steer the boat toward it. They suffer with the Church, dying within it, so that their dreams can be transmitted to a new generation. And the next generation will canonize the prophets of an earlier age. In the next generation priest-prophets will rise from the dead and the Church will fulfill and authenticate its prophetic mission, ultimately the mission of Jesus himself.

Chapter Four
Theology of Vocation in Jeremiah

This chapter could be titled, "The Search for Vocation." Not only did later great religious leaders search the book of Jeremiah for the meaning or explanation of their own vocation, but we also find Jeremiah himself constantly searching through his own long ministry for the meaning of his vocation. When he was finally able to write down *how* God had called him to be a prophet, he was already near the end of his life. The story of his call was the last thing he wrote, but it was placed as an introduction to his prophecy heading the first chapter.

This search of Jeremiah for vocation gives us an opportunity to search for the meaning of our own vocation. St. Paul, we know, looked to Jeremiah as he himself was seeking his own identity and striving to convince others within the Church that he had truly been called by God. He quotes from Jeremiah in that important passage of his Epistle to the Galatians: "But the time came when he who had set me apart before I was born [these words a quote from Jeremiah] and called me by his favor [this phrase comes from the Suffering Servant of Isaiah, written under the influence of Jeremiah], chose to reveal his Son to me, that I might spread among the Gentiles the good tidings concerning him" (Gal 1:15-16).

"To be a prophet to the Gentiles"—that was the hope of vocation with which Jeremiah died, the ideal which surfaced only when it was too late for him to act upon it. St. Paul, seeking to find peace in his own vocation, looked not only to Jeremiah, but also to the Suffering Servant of Isaiah. In the second song of the Suffering Servant, chapter 49 of Isaiah, we hear this mysterious, agonizing, extraordinary person saying (again under the influence of Jeremiah): "The Lord called me from birth, from my mother's womb, he gave me my name."

There are other allusions to Jeremiah. Luke, for instance, speaks of John the Baptist being sanctified from his mother's womb (Lk 1). Jesus, in chapter 4 of Luke, begins his own public ministry drawing from a reference to the Suffering Servant, this time in chapter 61 of Isaiah. All in all, we find that some of the most extraordinarily active, apostolic-minded persons of the Bible —Isaiah's Suffering Servant, John the Baptist, St. Paul, and Jesus himself—all appeal to that soul-searching attempt of the Prophet of Anathoth to appreciate the meaning of the call of God.

The theology of Jeremiah on vocation became the classical biblical model. His theology, like his style, cannot be detached from the character of the man. What he wrote exploded from his heart, sometimes in staccato phrases, other times in poems and sermons, seemingly without structure or order. As Albert Gelin observed, "The theology of Jeremiah is less a system than a ferment." Jeremiah's theology of vocation, therefore, emerges from a life fermenting with anguish, confusion and constant seeking.

The search of Jeremiah for his vocation began, as he himself points out, in the thirteenth year of King Josiah, therefore in 627 or 626. This date provides the occasion, but hardly the explanation, of how he began his prophetic ministry. Jeremiah, we read in his book, belonged to a prominent priestly family. At least it was prominent once upon a time when his forefathers, men like Eli, possessed the Ark of the Covenant and ministered before the Lord at the famous and ancient shrine of Shiloh (1 S 1). The family showed up again, prominent and respectful, when two other priests, Abiathar and his son Ahimelech, were among the high priests designated by King David (1 S 22:20-23; 2 S 8:17). The family, however, fell into disrepute when Solomon banished Abiathar to his village of Anathoth (1 K 2:26).

Out of the shadows of Anathoth came Jeremiah. Jeremiah emerged with prospects of an extraordinary apostolic opportunity. The Assyrian empire was collapsing. Assurbanipal resigned in 633, the year King Josiah of Jerusalem was converted (2 Ch

34). Assurbanipal died in 629 or 627, and at once the empire was rent apart with civil war. It was the year King Josiah swung vigorously into the work of reform. As revolts spread within the empire, Babylon, the rival of Assyria, declared its independence in 626. That was the year of Jeremiah's call.

We ought to put quotation marks around the word "call" of Jeremiah, because Jeremiah simply responded to the apostolic opportunity. National independence for Babylon meant the resurgence of Babylonian deities and Babylonian religion. Independence of Judah meant the resurgence of a new enthusiasm for Yahweh, the God of Israel. At once Jeremiah was preaching hopefully and enthusiastically. We can still catch the rhythm of dancing joy in youthful eyes, as we read his words in 31:7:

> Shout with joy for Jacob,
> exult at the head of the nations;
> proclaim your praise and say:
> The Lord has delivered his people,
> the remnant of Israel.

A little later Jeremiah announced that the sound of mourning and the bitter weeping of Rachel mourning for her children at Ramah must stop, for

> Thus says the Lord:
> Cease your cries of mourning,
> wipe the tears from your eyes.
> The sorrow you have shown shall have
> its reward,
> says the Lord,
> they shall return from the enemy's
> land.
> There is hope for your future . . .
> (31:16-17).

The first six years of Jeremiah's preaching career (627/6-621) were years of excitement over hopes, ideals and undreamed-of possibilities. Achievement came quickly. This success, thought

Jeremiah, must certainly demonstrate the genuineness of God's call and the nature of his vocation.

PLATEAU OF FAILURES

Then came a series of reversals. In 621 the youthful and over-zealous king began to impose reformation upon the people by royal edict. Jeremiah could only be silent and restrain his bitter-ness as a group around the king seized the initiative of his preach-ing and by a heavy hand ruthlessly pushed reform. They contra-dicted Jeremiah's "new covenant," inscribed upon the heart, spontaneously expressing itself in an interior knowledge of the Lord and purity of soul (31:31-34). Jeremiah rubbed his eyes and questioned what must be happening. Later he was shocked to find that even this kind of reform stopped. The sound of a dirge emerged from Jeremiah's heart as he lamented the death of the young king on the battlefield of Megiddo (2 K 23:29-30). Now began the second period of Jeremiah's life—that long, long trek across the dreary plateau of failures.

King Josiah was succeeded by a king who became an apostate. King Jehoiakim was a puppet, first of the Egyptians and then of the Babylonians. How wily he could be! He revived the worship of pagan deities in Jersualem, even child sacrifice and the orgiastic fertility rites. He forced his own people into slave gangs to ac-complish grandiose building plans. Jeremiah almost spit the acid words out of his mouth as he shouted: "Give Jehoiakim the burial of an ass . . . dragged forth and cast out beyond the gates of Jerusalem!" (22:19).

A DIARY OF PRAYER

During the reign of Jehoiakim, Jeremiah began to trace his *via crucis* with tears and lamenting. He recorded his anguish in autobiographical accounts called "confessions." These were like challenges thrown in the face of God. According to a very repu-table scholar, Wilhelm Rudolph, they actually came from a per-sonal diary of his prayers. The confessions were never intended to be read or heard by anyone but God himself. However, after

Jeremiah died, Baruch, his secretary, found the diary and spliced these confessions here and there throughout the book or scroll of Jeremiah and inserted them where he felt they belonged in the historical sequence of Jeremiah's life. Actually, where each confession occurs, the Hebrew text is ragged. It shows signs of something added or super-imposed.

At each of these points Jeremiah is arguing with God. In the first of them, found in 12:1-5, Jeremiah begins with a strong expression of faith. In Hebrew it reads: *saddiq 'attāh yahweh*—"You are just, O Lord." Jeremiah, however, adds at once: "Still I must dispute with you." It was the strength of Jeremiah's faith that leaped beyond his ability ever to articulate it fully, that precipitated the problems and the questions of Jeremiah.

If God were "maybe just, but maybe not," then, when "the way of the wicked flourishes," as Jeremiah complained in this first "confession," his answer was ready at hand in the weakness of his faith. This day would be one of God's "maybe not" days. Jeremiah's staunch, loyal, and consistent faith could never tolerate a "maybe—maybe not" God. "You are just now and always, O Lord!" Jeremiah was really saying: "You are truly God. Therefore, why doesn't the way of the good flourish?" Or, to reflect the prophet's mind still more precisely, "Why doesn't my way flourish, undertaken as I best understand your will and desire?"

In this confession Jeremiah wrote perhaps one of the most perceptive lines of the entire Bible: "You, Yahweh, know me and see me. You explore my heart within you." The Hebrew word implies, "You explore, walking with my footsteps. As I plunge into the darkness of my heart, you, God, are there with me." Jeremiah must search into darkness to be where God is to be found. God's answer to Jeremiah, written indeed by Jeremiah after long, silent prayer, says literally in the Hebrew: "If you have run with legs (that is, with other human beings) and have fallen exhausted, how are you going to get along galloping against horses? If in the land of peace, you seek to find your confidence, how are you going to fare in the jungle of the Jordan?" (Jr 12:5 CS).

We can think and ponder and pray long over that verse of

Jeremiah. Basically, what it says is: "Jeremiah, things will get worse before they will get better. You are going to gallop against horses, no longer run against men. You are going to cut your way through a jungle of the Jordan, no longer walk peacefully where you can see the next step ahead of you." When Jeremiah wrote these words as God's response, he was equivalently saying, "God, I am willing to let the future bring what it may."

In another confession (15:10-21), God responds to him with the words, "If you bring forth the precious without the vile, you shall be my mouthpiece." These extraordinary lines admit that some of the inspired words of Jeremiah contain an alloy of vile stuff mixed with the precious. It points out what is so obviously true and yet so obviously overlooked by so many apostolic workers. Not only must the apostolic worker, even the prophet Jeremiah, undergo further and further purification, releasing the vile so that the precious may emerge ever more purely an expression of God's will, but even the idea of one's call, the idea of one's vocation, must be purified still more. No trial sears the soul more painfully than that which purifies one's hopes! That can come about only as the apostolic worker walks into the further depth of the darkness of faith, led only by the conviction that God must be there.

Finally, at the end of his life Jeremiah writes the story of the meaning of his vocation. It begins with that very familiar line, when God is saying to Jeremiah, "Before I formed you in the womb I knew you, before you were born I dedicated you; a prophet to the nations I appointed you" (1:5). When Jeremiah realized that his plans for God were not always and necessarily God's plan for his life—and he could realize this only after repeated failures and frustrations in life—then Jeremiah could reach back to the moment before his conception and realize in the depth of his heart that his vocation was what God wanted of him even before he was conceived.

A vocation, then, according to Jeremiah, is not doing what one thinks God wants of a person. It is doing that which God has known even before one's conception. A vocation can, in fact it must, begin by responding to apostolic opportunities. Yet, such a response is only the occasion, not the deepest meaning, of a vocation. In the most profound level of the heart, a vocation is a personal union with a God who seeks everyone in peace and love. A vocation must not degenerate into personal ambition. Rather, it means losing one's self totally in God, there to find one's self again in the union of all persons with God.

How is such an interior conviction to be established? In Jeremiah's case, it demanded that his apostolic dreams crumble like paper houses. Somehow he had to sustain repeated failures and difficulties. Only then would he confess deep within his heart: My desire for God must be none other than God's desire for me. Here is the consummation of a personal union with God in purest love; here is vocation in its truest meaning.

GOD'S POETRY AND HUMAN PROSE

In so many ways Jeremiah brings out such an understanding of vocation. For instance, in 1:4-10 when God speaks, Jeremiah puts his words in poetic meter. When Jeremiah responds to God, he answers in prose. Poetry sweeps along the clouds; prose bumps along on the gravel path of earth. Poetry soars with intuition; prose drags the weight of discouragement. At the end of his life Jeremiah confessed that by repeated obedience to God he was whisked beyond his earthly vision with a dream beyond all his hopes.

Religious leaders, too, are charged with the obligation of leading people who are frustrated at times, people who find it difficult to move any longer on the plateau, people who are exhausted climbing the mountain peaks. Unless they can sustain perseverance in their own trek across the plateau, continue in the strength of God up and over the mountain, they cannot give the kind of religious leadership needed by others. Jeremiah's lifework was never to be measured by the length and breadth of his own mind. His vocation grew to greater clarity from his ability to sustain hopes that seemed beyond immediate fulfillment. Only when the smaller works collapsed could he arrive at that extraordinary truth in the anguish within his soul: "I want what God wants.

What God wants is the only thing that can ever answer the desires and possibilities of my life."

In conclusion, every vocation has an occasion, that which gets it started. Every vocation has a long search for the deeper meaning of what one started out to do. Only at the end can one write the story of what is the real meaning of a vocation. That, at least, is what Jeremiah tells us. Jeremiah adds this important warning: Do not confuse the occasion, which comes first, with the meaning of a vocation, which comes last! At the end of his life when he wrote chapter 1, Jeremiah said that his vocation was to be a prophet to the nations, a prophet to the Gentiles. Jeremiah never was a prophet to the nations. Jeremiah died with that hope which he left to the next generation, picked up by the Suffering Servant and by St. Paul. Jeremiah's vocation was to be the carrier of hopes to the next generation.

A vocation, then, is a call to sustain hopes never to be tasted in all their joy. A vocation is a call to transmit hopes, too great for the present but possible in the next generation. Secondly, such a vocation projects the image of persons willing to be purified even in the understanding and hopes of what God wants of them. Thirdly, Jeremiah points out that the greatest mystery of faith is the mystery of vocation, the mystery of one's individual relationship to God and of God to oneself. Faith is always a matter of hope beyond vision. If faith is realized only after death, then vocation can never be understood at the beginning of life, but only at the end.

Finally, vocation, according to Jeremiah, proclaims the necessity of trust in one's intuitions. A vocation begins by a response to a particular opportunity, but what sustains a vocation is that hidden inarticulate intuition where God is present, compelling one ever onward, seeking what the person cannot yet understand. Trusting one's intuition means trusting that hidden inspiration of God. Trusting intuitions, therefore, means a complete obedient surrender to God.

Jeremiah is *par excellence* the person of prayer. The surest indication that one is following the intuition of God's will is the ability to be at peace in the midst of darkness and mystery. That is the moment when God is most present, sweeping one beyond the ability to put things into words, sweeping one beyond the horizons of the intellect and allowing the heart to seek an ever-deeper mystical union. In such a seeking of mystical union, one finally arrives at the meaning of what God intended before one was conceived.

Chapter Five
The Mystery of Love in Hosea

Hosea belongs to the early years of Israel's prophetic movement, but his ideas and his spiritual attitudes possess a maturity which we ordinarily associate with the end of a long development. As we read his prophecy, we sometimes wonder whether we have perhaps slipped ahead into New Testament pages. Hosea's heart seems to beat sympathetically with the heart of Jesus and to suffuse his warmth. We would never fully accept his daring words on the love of God if Jesus had not been even more daring in transferring those words into action. Hosea's message, like Jesus' death, leaves no doubt that the most baffling mystery about God is his love. That which brings God or any one else personally close to us should be the easiest feature for us to understand; yet it always remains wrapped in the greatest mystery. Friends, and especially lovers, can never adequately explain how they feel toward one another, nor why they feel that way.

Could Beeri and his wife, the parents of Hosea, have suspected the future role of their infant son, when they gave him his name eight days after birth? It does not seem that they were more ambitious than any other new parents; *Hosea* was a common enough name in Israelite families. The last king of the northern country of Israel was called *Hosea*. The parents of this child, however, truly deserved the honor of giving their son that name which would become the most sacred in the world. They called their child by a name almost the same as that which Mary and Joseph would use in addressing their son.

We like to think that God thus rewarded Beeri and his wife for the extraordinary love and exquisite kindness with which they reared their child. Hosea owed it to his father and mother that he would one day be hailed "prophet of divine love." What they initially imparted, Hosea transformed into an integral part of his character. When later as a prophet he announced the gentle yet courageous and even agonizing nuances of divine love, he was but echoing the tones heard long ago in his parents' home.

The name *Hosea* means "one who saves." It will be recalled that the famous warrior-conqueror, hand-picked by Moses to be his successor, and chosen by God to lead the Israelites across the Jordan river and to wrestle the land of Palestine out of Canaanite control, was first called *Hosea*. In Numbers 27:16-17 we learn that Moses changed it to *Yehoshua* ("Yahweh saves"—*Joshua* in our Bibles). During the last several centuries before the birth of Jesus Christ, *Yehoshua* became a very common name for Jewish boys. Spoken again and again in all kinds of situations, *Yehoshua* was gradually clipped to a shorter form, *Yeshua*. In the Hebrew language, the accent rested on the second-last syllable, the ū sound, and there it has remained as the name passes into Greek and many other European languages. In Greek it was spelled *Jesōus* or *Jesus*.

The similarity of Hosea's name to Jesus' may have been a reward from God for his parents' and his own heroic love. There can be no doubt, however, of the intimate fellowship of thought between Hosea and Jesus. Hosea introduced a theme into biblical literature which Jesus will apply to himself and transform into sublime fulfillment. Hosea dared to call God the *spouse* of Israel, and Jesus braved ridicule in referring to himself as the *bridegroom* of his people.

A delegation once came to Jesus. These men, so proud of their piety towards God that they lacked the self-forgetfulness of genuine love, voiced a complaint. "The disciples of John fast often," they said to Jesus, "and make supplications, and likewise those of the Pharisees, whereas your disciples eat and drink." In his reply Jesus could have ripped away their pompousness and piousness with sharp satire. Instead, he spoke under the influence of the prophet Hosea. With the poignant melancholy of a love ever kind but already rejected, he asked, "Can you make the wedding guests fast as long as the bridegroom is with them? But the days will come when the bridegroom will be taken away from them. Then they will fast" (Lk 5:33-35).

During the centuries separating Hosea and Jesus, other prophets like Jeremiah, Ezekiel, and Second Isaiah (Is 40-55), further clarified this approach towards God; another biblical book, the *Song of Songs,* dramatized the love of God through a series of nuptial songs. The Christian liturgy quickly adopted this attitude of approaching God as spouse of his people. Nowhere does the love-bond between God and the Church reach a fuller expression than in prayer and especially in that supreme moment of prayer, the liturgy. The greatest act of the liturgy, the Eucharist, was re-enacted in a ceremony called *agape,* a Greek word meaning *love.*

The image of God as bridegroom constantly appears in the writings of the early Fathers and in the works of the later spiritual masters. Not only saints of southern lands like St. John of the Cross and St. Teresa of Jesus, but mystics of the Rhineland like Tauler and Ruysbroeck, structure their spiritual theology around the motif that God is spouse of the soul. To understand and appreciate this long tradition, repeatedly sanctioned by God over three thousand years, we must return to its source. There we will discover a vigorous expression and a personal intuition, fresh and appealing like new life, mysterious and attractive like a pioneer adventure, tested and mature like battle scars. The book of Hosea, like the gospels and the crucifix, bears the marks of such a love and possesses the power to infuse a similar love in the strong.

Hosea's message, like genuine love, is ever-demanding, but it is also very encouraging. Presenting his ideas within the context of marriage, Hosea tells each reader that no desire, noble and true, is ever snuffed out unfulfilled. Marriage not only satisfies the deepest desires, but it also enables us to beget new life and more love. By the very fact that God calls himself the bridegroom of each of his followers, he cannot destroy what is consecrated to him. He obliges himself to fulfill and make fruitful the love which he receives.

Many Christians renounce the right to marry by a vow of celibacy or virginity. There are others whose initial joy in marriage is overwhelmed by a prolonged separation. Death (or what can even be worse, divorce) has cut the bond. Still others proudly bear children, only to lose them through the call of war or the forced migration of people or the stroke of mortal illness. Every neighborhood holds lonely couples, aching for children yet somehow unable to beget them. All of these cases exist in Christian life, and each pounds out the hard sound of sacrifice.

To each and all of these persons Hosea declares: no desire, true and good, will remain sterile and unfulfilled. To deny this fulfillment is to substitute some lesser deity for the God whom Christians worship. This God has pledged:

> I will espouse you to me forever. . .
> I will espouse you in fidelity,
> and you shall know the Lord (2:21-22).

God will be faithful to every promise, especially to those which he placed deep within the nature of every human being. In the moment of fulfillment we shall truly *know* the Lord. To claim that God will leave good desires empty or only half fulfilled, reduces his love to something less abundant than what he expects of our generosity. God's measure of giving must exceed ours, which Jesus wants to be a "good measure, pressed down, shaken together, running over" (Lk 6:38).

A MYSTERY TO BE EXPERIENCED

This whole mystery of love can never be explained but only experienced. Hosea's explanation does not remove the mystery; but to the person who has been open and generous with God and has willingly accepted the full demands of divine love, Hosea speaks a message which spreads peace and understanding. His prophecy records what has happened to a person intensely alive in God; such secrets will be shared only to the extent that the recipient, like Hosea, lives in God. The law of communication always presumes this community bond, this sympathetic sharing, this experimental grasp of what the other is saying.

To transfer for a moment from the problem of Hosea to a

major problem of the modern world, can it not be said that excessive individualism is responsible for the poor communication between racial and national, religious and social groups, even between blood members of the same family? All this failure exists amidst unbelievable advances in the technological means of communication. When people are afraid to love and are hesitant about the outcome of love, they throw up defensive barriers to separate themselves from others. Someone like Pope John, on the contrary, who lacked most of the accepted means of communication, communicated most effectively. His rotund build and uneven gait and thumping feet hardly won respect from a sophisticated world. His ignorance of modern languages and dependence on interpreters considerably slowed down the transmission of his thought to others. Yet, he was understood and appreciated by people everywhere because he communicated in charity, an instinct deeper than style and protocol, a rallying point where all people meet one another.

Hosea also spoke through the medium of charity, though he dealt with its more mysterious aspects. In spite of this, the charitable person today nods in agreement with the prophet's words and somehow understands his message. This understanding, in turn, leads to a desire to know more and more about the prophet himself—his early home life and education, his talents and ideals, his conflicts and problems, his whole environment and personality. And because these factors are deeply rooted in and common to all human beings, such a study increases the modern reader's ability to identify with Hosea's thought.

Nevertheless, though Hosea will undoubtedly appeal to all readers, he will appeal to some more than to others. His book has a universal character about it, but it evidences also some of the prophet's unique characteristics. These may jar the more practical mind. However, it must be remembered that charity grows not only in fostering the characteristics which people share in common, but in the mutual respect they have for one another's differences. Ultimately, the unique gifts of one person complement the gifts of others and serve to create a diverse yet unified whole.

THE PROPHET

One way to introduce Hosea is to say that he is the exact reverse of the Prophet Amos. Amos grew to manhood as a shepherd. As he led his flock across wide, sandy stretches for patches of tough grass or for wells of sulphurous-tasting water, Amos became as thin, wiry and tough as his desert breed of sheep. Like desert nomads of any age, Amos was fiercely independent. Accustomed to solitary life and seldom if ever craving for human friendship, yet intensely loyal to the friends of his choice, Amos bluntly spoke his mind and cared little how other people reacted.

Never could his audience forget one occasion at the sanctuary of Bethel. The stylish women of Samaria had assembled very properly for worship, only to hear the uncouth Amos call them to their faces: "You herd of cows!" (Am 4:1). He was voicing the pent-up anger of countless poor people whose families were crushed by all manner of social injustices, in order that their overlords might pamper these luxurious cows with soft delicacies. Amos also lashed out at the men, those stalwart warriors who stretched out comfortably on ivory-embellished couches and sang their own poetry as though they were David. Here too is the voice of every man and woman shouting down the sham which confuses sentimentality for culture, and exposing the shame which mistakes animal lust for human love. But this was not the voice of Hosea.

Still other differences separated them. Amos was a southerner from the kingdom of Judah, whom God summoned to preach to the northerners of the kingdom of Israel. In this way Amos fulfilled a need felt by all people, the need for an outsider, cold and impartial, to clear away vague excuses and to hand down clear judgments on their actions. Amos, though probably a young man, spoke like a gruff, elderly person whom the entire neighborhood respects but only the children love. The world always stands in need of honest, plain-spoken people like Amos. Such people attract only the innocent, but they still manage to salvage a great deal of goodness in others. The world, for the most part, consists of men and women who are no longer innocent; and even though

they have regained their goodness, they cannot endure for long
the cauterizing agony inflicted by an Amos. Truth, ironically
expressed, sours the stomach of most people. They must also hear
the sympathetic voice of an Hosea and realize that here is a
prophet agonizing with them.

Hosea, we must admit, possessed all the ingredients which
form an Amos; he was capable of anger, bitterness and even satire,
but the genes of his character combined very differently. In
Hosea, we detect not only the perceptiveness of Amos but also
a strong admixture of sensitivity and warmth. Hosea was endowed
with a tenderness which thrived on love, with a glowing hope
which had to be encouraged, with a simplicity which could be
easily spurned and hurt, with an optimism which searched out
the least speck of goodness in others. Hosea was the kind of
person which all of us, even an Amos, would like to be, for he
activates our delicate and finest human qualities. All of us possess
his traits of character; few of us, however, in exactly the same
mixture, and even fewer still with the same courageous simplicity.
No gift is more demanding of its owner than the grace to think
kindly and to love tenderly. And though we can usually forecast
the outcome of hate, we rarely know where love will lead us.

Hosea paid the heavy cost of such a sensitized personality. He
was quite emotional. Loving greatly, he reacted at once to the
least manifestation of friendliness or hostility. He was swayed
quickly from one extreme to another. He was not the victim of
irrational impulses, nor was he a pampered child who never grew
up. He was an adult who keenly appreciated all the human in-
volvements of life situations. In chapter 2, for instance, he is the
husband betrayed by an adulterous wife. He shouts angrily to the
children:

> Protest against your mother, protest!
> [Show her that] she is not my wife,
> and I am not her husband.
> Let her remove. . .
> her adultery from between her breasts,
> Or I will strip her naked,

leaving her as on the day of her birth
(2:4-5a).

If he did not love so dearly, he never would have felt the agony
so intensely. Here is a voice, shouting protest against life's vilest
betrayal. True love, like a healthy body, battles fiercely against
corrupting disease.

Gomer, the wife to whom he has entrusted the personal treas-
ures of great love, was overheard to say:

> I will go after my lovers,
> who give me my bread and my water,
> my wool and my flax, my oil and my
> drink (2:7).

Sorrow floods upon Hosea like a massive wave of salt water.

> . . . she has not known
> that it was I who gave her
> the grain, the wine and the oil (2:10).

Gomer evidently entertains her paramours with gifts which Hosea
had generously lavished upon her. Anger stirs, and quickly Hosea's dejection explodes in outrage:

> Therefore, I will take back my grain. . .
> I will snatch away my wool. . .
> with which she covers her nakedness.
> So now I will lay bare her shame
> before the eyes of her lovers (2:11).

Hosea, however, loves too dearly. Even if he flares up in rage
at the betrayal of his affection, yet in the next instant he is again
hopeful and forgiving. What others would call groveling abject-
ness is heroic confidence in Hosea:

> Therefore, I will hedge in her way
> with thorns
> and erect a wall against her,

so that she cannot find her paths.
If she runs after her lovers,
she will not overtake them;
if she looks for them she shall not
find them.
Then she shall say,
'I will go back to my first husband,
for it was better with me then than now.'
So I will allure her;
I will lead her into the desert
and speak to her heart (2:8-9, 16).

Such, then, is the character of Hosea, swaying from one extreme to the other. Such quick transitions are not confined to any single chapter but are duplicated throughout all fourteen chapters. When love is most tenderly expressed, as in chapter 11, reversals are swiftly and dramatically introduced. Speaking of God's love for Israel, Hosea rises in idyllic hope; God is a father, fondling his child as he carries it in his arms. But suddenly these same hopes crash in anger; the sword will cut a bloody swath through the cities belonging to this child, extending to desert solitudes. Tears, it seems, almost overwhelm God, and he cries in agony:

How can I give you up, O Ephraim,
or deliver you up, O Israel? (11:8)

Finally, a triumphant line rings out. Human beings declare: "So much, no more. I shall forgive no longer!" But God's love and forgiveness reach to the sublimest of mysteries: "I am God and not man" (11:9).

Hosea baffles us in his quick changes of mood, in his rapid swing from tender love to violent hate, from listless depression to aggressive anger, from a final verdict of punishment to the hope of a new beginning. There is no easy answer for the way Hosea plummets into one area of the human heart, soars out of it and then falls again into another. A saint, he steps into the incomprehensible sweeps of divine love. The fact of Hosea's mysticism must always be kept in mind in any evaluation of his character and preaching.

Though at a loss for detailed reasons, we can make out some kind of consistency in Hosea. He is always strong in his love. He faces all persons in such a way that they know beyond a doubt how greatly he loves them. Hosea has an instinct for challenging others to respond to him either by love or hate. Love has a way of bringing out the true character of individuals. It can be only eagerly accepted or stubbornly refused. Unless God had aided Hosea, he could not have maintained his heroic forgiving love over such a long stretch of years. Yet, though spirited by a divine power, he was not divine. As a human being, he had his faults. He groaned under the damaging effects of sin. He had to battle against evil tendencies; he was never able to direct activities from the serene heights of undisturbed holiness.

STRENGTH IN WEAKNESS

Hosea's occasional lack of balance, his frail emotionalism, his distorted tenderness—all of these deviations show up in moments of stress; the prophet reacts with strong love; the victory of righteousness is won only after prolonged struggle. With St. Paul he would also frankly remind us: "I do not accomplish the good which I wish to do but the evil which I do not wish, that I perform. . . . I see another law in my members, warring against the law of my mind" (Rm 7:20, 23). Nevertheless, while admitting Hosea's emotional problems—stemming from his excessive sensitivity—we need not reverse our judgment on his true greatness.

We, on the other hand, do not receive a *carte blanche* from the book of Hosea to act like *prima donnas* pouting over small offenses, demanding rigid protocol, always suspicious of breaches in etiquette, any more than Amos justifies us in coldly spurning people or indiscriminately lashing out at them with a sharp tongue. In both cases God made use of human beings with the widest variety of character. As each struggled against his own weakness and against the hostility of his environment, each received the help of God's spirit. Because of God's presence, each prophet manifested an extraordinary endurance and lifted himself as well as his fellows to a super-human level of existence.

Another weakness appears in the prophecy of Hosea: the disorderly condition of his book. The lines follow no discernible pattern. Whoever was responsible for editing the book, Hosea or a disciple, seems to have quickly dispatched the work by heaping everything together. We can spot only two breaks or divisions in all fourteen chapters. The Yahweh-Spouse theme is confined to the first three chapters; chapter 14:2-9 marks the messianic conclusion. Everything else lies in between. As though to warn the reader that this book is not to be read quickly or easily, a later editor added a final word, advising prayer and faith:

> Let him who is wise understand
> these things;
> let him who is prudent know them.
> Straight are the paths of the Lord,
> in them the just walk
> but sinners stumble in them (14:10).

What other kind of book, though, could come from the highly sensitive character of Hosea? A man whose ideas swing from one end of the horizon to the other should not be expected to think along straight lines nor follow a strictly logical sequence. All biblical writers, in fact, prefer a circuitous approach; they attack the issue in one way, then in another. They are free of our more philosophical, more theoretical way of argument, but by that fact they stayed closer to reality and remained more conscious of human complexities. No prophet allowed such uninhibited flow of thought as Hosea; his words, like himself, rush from one emotion to another.

Hosea can place some of the blame for the disorderly condition of his book on the chaotic state of his country's politics. We learn from the superscription over his book that he began to prophesy "in the days of Jeroboam . . . king of Israel" (1:1). During the long reign of this king (783-743 B.C.), the standard of living for the well-to-do rose to a peak of ivory luxury. Israel's boundaries spread out to embrace an area almost as extensive as David's domain. The social condition, however, was at the point of explosion.

Tirzah, one of the principal cities, was sharply divided between the very poor and the very rich. On one side of a thoroughfare, according to recent excavations, lay extensive holdings and palatial residences; just across the street were very small homes heaped one upon another. Hosea called this condition a "hearth cake unturned" (7:8). This image comes from the Palestinians' practice of baking thin, round patties of unleavened bread on open stones which had been heated by the sun. When the bread is left unturned, raw dough appears on one side; the other side turns black and throws off smoke like charcoal.

Israel was such a country of sharp differences. A few grew too rich and the rest stayed too poor. Homes and furniture were either decorated with inlaid ivory, or else were put together from unfinished wood. Religious ceremonies were elaborate and costly; the poor were forced to stay away. Politics degenerated into quick, selfish decisions, first in one direction, then a fast reversal in another. It was a nation overfed, or undernourished; ornate or destitute; reeking with sacrificial smoke or coldly disdainful of religion's solemn mockery—"a hearth cake unturned."

Dark clouds were massing, a hurricane was being born. After Jeroboam II died, Assyria again asserted her rights of overlord; this demand for tribute and hostages bled the country of wealth and strength. The army revolted time and again, sweeping to power first an aggressive anti-Assyrian group, then a pacifist pro-Assyrian party. The poor joined each revolt, for they had nothing to lose. The wealthy proceeded to kill off their rivals, especially the remnants of the former royal family.

In 732 B.C. the Assyrian army invaded the country. After allowing the soldiers to satisfy their lust for loot and pleasure, the Assyrian monarch sent the inhabitants of the northern section into exile. Between 724 and 721 B.C. Assyria suppressed another revolt, and this time she made sure that it would be the last. Nothing was left standing; the people, almost to the last person, were deported. Hosea lived through these years of excessive luxury, senseless revolt, and final ruin—a hearth cake never turned. Always a man of exceptional sensitivity, he could not help but speak in a way reflecting the disorder and panic of his age.

This disordered state of Hosea's prophecy provides a clue to modern art and music, literature and philosophy; these, in turn, enable us to understand Hosea a little better. Contemporary culture is often an explosion of line and sound, hideous at times in its realistic portrayal of sex and hate, depressive in its use of heavy black lines. What might be unintelligible to an observer of another age makes a great deal of sense when seen against the background of two world wars, the forced migration and even the massacre of entire nations, the use of police dogs against racial minorities, the threat of nuclear holocaust, the disintegration of trust among nations, and the massacre of world leaders. The most violent hate, however, usually produces the reaction of the greatest love; society rises up to cure itself. This ferment indicates that God is still present within his world. Hosea proclaimed that divine indwelling to his contemporaries.

YAHWEH—SPOUSE OF ISRAEL

In the three opening chapters of his prophecy, Hosea develops his extraordinary and unique theme of Yahweh-Spouse. To appreciate this exceptional intuition given to him by God, we must observe the slow, agonizing process by which it emerged in the consciousness of the prophet. We go back to Hosea the young man, loved by his friends for being idealistic, affectionate, enthusiastic, generous. Such a person, they knew, promised to be a kind, loving husband who would delight in his children and make his family his kingdom. Everyone remarked how fortunate would be the wife of his choice. Hosea asked a girl named Gomer to share his life and thus to fulfill its hopes. He, in turn, promised to love her dearly. Hosea treasured this promise. Although we do not know how wealthy he may have been, there is no indication that he was poor. His was the joy of bringing many gifts home to his wife.

Then Hosea noticed that Gomer began to act in a strange

way. He could not believe what was happening; for the first time in his life he felt suspicious of another. Was Gomer betraying his love? Once it became certain, the woman made no attempt to conceal her adultery. She deserted Hosea. As the outraged husband looked back on the day of his marriage, he felt that God had then ordered him: "Go, take a harlot wife and harlot's children" (1:2).

Somehow or other, Hosea recognized a demand to take the woman back. He was convinced that this too came from God.

> Again the Lord said to me:
> Give your love to a woman,
> beloved of a paramour, an
> adulteress (3:1).

"Again!" What agony was spelled out in that word! The other men in town may have once pitied Hosea for his broken marriage; but when he claimed his wife from the arms of a paramour and was willing to take her back not once but again and again, they scoffed: "That fool!" and added their own expletives.

At other times Gomer came back of her own accord. She no longer had any support from Hosea who had stopped his gifts. With nothing to flatter her paramours, she lost their interest. Gomer, like any woman, could not compete in the gamble of sexual promiscuity. Her lovers could go elsewhere and always find other women, younger and more attractive, but where could she go? Her happiness depended upon marital fidelity. Fortunately for Gomer, Hosea was not only staunchly loyal to his marriage vows but also humbly forgiving toward his wife. She knew her man, and so she reflected, "I will go back to my first husband, for it was better for me then than now" (2:9).

When the second child was born, Hosea named the daughter *Lo-ruhama*, which means "without mercy" or "without tenderness." How he would have loved to gather the child into his arms and press this part of his own flesh against himself. But did the child really belong to him? He could not be sure. When a son was born, he openly declared his name to be *Lo-ammi*, which means "not my people." In chapter 11 Hosea pictures God as a father, holding a child in his arms and drawing the little one "with bands of love." Yet the child was continually wandering off as if someone else were the father. This scene could easily have emerged from the tortured moments in Hosea's own life.

Hosea writhed in agony, victimized not only by a woman's infidelity but also by his own sensitive nature. During this dark night he was able to look far deeper into the heavens than had ever been possible during the distracting glare of the daylight. Loneliness turned his prayer into the challenge of another Job:

> I cry to you, but you do not
> answer me;
> you stand off and look at me,
> Then you turn upon me without mercy
> and with your strong hand you
> buffet me.
> Of all my steps I should give him an
> account;
> like a prince I should present myself
> before him.
> This is my final plea; let the Almighty
> answer me! (Jb 30:20-21; 31:37).

Does God give Hosea the passion to love that he might torture it with another's crude unworthiness? Does God impart high ideals for the sole reason that he enjoys their violent disintegration? Is this Providence, only to make sure that people suffer from the excess of their goodness? Hosea, seemingly deserted by God, hurled questions close to blasphemy against the heavens. Each time he sharpened the intensity of his words. God had left him alone to search the darkness and to stumble against its hazards.

God finally gave an answer. It probably did not happen by direct revelation. Perhaps—we can never be absolutely certain in matters of great psychic and mystic depths like this—as Hosea was questioning God, he saw himself directly confronting God. Sharp differences showed up, but these differences resulted from the close union of one with the other. God's light gradually trans-figured Hosea's darkness. Through the struggle of his love, Hosea experienced sympathetically something of God's thoughts and love. Love, human and divine, fidelity accepted and betrayed, sympathy turned into anger and ending in compassion, a power human in experience and divine in endurance—all of these min-gled in the dark night of life in God. Then it was that the answer broke through to consciousness and Hosea could never forget it. It was as simple and as mysterious as is God: *"Thus the Lord loves the people Israel"* (3:1).

This answer necessarily came at the end of a prolonged ordeal. The strongest faith always exists on the brink of the deepest cavern of unbelief. Faith is not a lesson to be learned from books; for nothing human, not even the most sublime expression of human words, can capture its contents. Faith does not find its security in anything human, but in God. Hosea must experience the agony of a love more than human before he can faintly grasp the meaning of God's love. This love was thoroughly divine, yet known only through its total involvement in human existence. It expressed itself in great redemptive acts like the exodus out of Egypt and the conquest of Palestine; as human, therefore, as mass migration and military conquest.

This mystery of divine love eluded all human explanation. Hosea had searched its meaning in the experience of the dark night. He could now become God's spokesman, never removing the mystery with his human language, but somehow or other always able to allow the echo of the divine to sound within the tone of his voice and to be heard between the words of his sentence. Hosea's message would communicate to the degree that others like him had undergone the same agony of love. This com-munication meant a power to help others find a way out of frus-trations and agonies by recognizing the divine meaning hidden beneath them. Hosea was leading others to the most intense form of life in God, thereby becoming a human instrument in the com-munication of divine life.

Chapter Six
Christian Tension: Prophetic Challenge Today

Man and woman, who are told to work out their divine salvation by living humanly, are constantly required to abandon the tried and proven that they have worked to achieve and plunge into the unknown: this is the tension created in human life when God made the human family. And this tension between human wisdom and divine faith is not only inevitable, it is even desirable.

This mixture of human with divine, of material and spiritual, of finite with infinite was bound to produce a brewing concoction of bubbling and simmering, of pull and pressure, of small and large explosions. God formed clay into his own divine image. The Scriptures speak of God as a potter, his feet turning the wheel and revolving the board on which lay a mass of clay. His hands deftly made every indentation and curve into what was to be the body of man and woman. After the model had been carefully shaped, God made it live by breathing his own divine spirit into it. Man and woman thus formed to the image and likeness of God and pulsing with divine life were told to think and act divinely. When they tried to be like God, however, they sinned.

God's most precious gifts to humans have always occasioned their most humiliating failures. As children of God, the first man and woman conversed with their Maker in the cool of day. According to the exquisite poetical style of Genesis, they heard the Lord speaking in the evening breeze. So harmoniously did their minds and hearts beat in unison with God's that they intuited the secret thoughts of God. They listened in on divine soliloquies; Adam heard God saying deep within the intimacy of his divine life: "It is not good for man to be alone; I will make him a helper like himself" (Gn 2:18). Yet the wife who made possible the joys of marriage, children and family life, also brought man his most tormenting problems and his most embarrassing sins.

When humans endeavored to lift themselves above every earthly threat and sought a safe way of life close to the divine in their tower of Babel, they were cursed and punished. Their worst sins can be traced to a proud self-assertion and a cruel, reckless drive for their own betterment. But men and women can live only by energizing the powers and exploiting the potentialities put into their keep by Almighty God. Their faults arise from their potentiality for genuine goodness, but greatness can never be achieved without risking failure.

THE RISK OF GREATNESS

We are told to live for God and with God, but before we can fulfill this injunction, we must begin to *live*. We can never think about God unless we have the courage simply to think. Yet, the more energetically we live and the more creatively we think, so much the more openly do human weaknesses manifest their ugly selves. We cannot think about God without running the risk of distorting his image with wrong ideas. Which one of us dares judge the conscience of a Buddha, a Mohammed, a Luther or a Calvin for the risk they took? No one can act for God unless he or she is willing to risk the danger of crusading for a cause which they wrongly judge divine.

It seldom happens that we are completely right or completely wrong. Our most heroic decisions for God are not reached all at once with the brilliant clarity of a desert sunrise. Decisions slowly mature as we struggle against opposing ideas, slough off unacceptable aspects, and grow with the help of friends and counselors. Even at the end of this long process, wise people admit that they still have more to learn. They must cast off ingredients of hidden error and submerged prejudice; they must remain open to new insights and opportunities.

I would apply the term *wisdom* to this continuing human endeavor to obey the divine command of mastering and subduing the created universe. Wisdom applies best of all to those who have reached a high and clear plateau of earthly existence. They have expended years persistently climbing, pulling and straining. Sooner or later the hills level off and they gain their vocation or place in life. From this plateau they can look down upon the rest of the world; here they can exert the fullest and most competent effort at the work assigned to them by God. They expect peace and serenity, for they can now exercise their talents most serenely. From this height of wisdom, they hope to be most productive of good, filling in, as St. Paul remarked, whatever is wanting to the body of the Lord, his Church (Col 1:25).

It is on this plateau of wisdom, however, that they begin to feel the dull, gnawing pain of monotony and dissatisfaction, of loneliness and misdirection. When matters have settled and reached maturity, they are already old and in need of rejuvenation. What one person acclaims as a signal achievement, others are already dubbing as old-fashioned. A culture at its height is always closest to its decay. When the Catholic educational system, for example, seems at its best and can evoke long experience, some educators call for reassessment and, perhaps, redirection. School administrators are told to form something new and different, but they are not told exactly what. It is at this moment that they must act in faith. They must step forward into the unknown, convinced that God wants it. This step off the plateau seems to be a plunge into mystery. It is this struggle between the old and the new, between the tried and proven and the exciting and unknown that constitutes the tension between wisdom and faith.

The struggle between the old and the new is as old as the human race; God put it there when he created man and woman to his divine likeness and told them to work out their divine salvation by living humanly. Sometimes the Bible expresses this struggle pithily and satirically. The preacher Ecclesiastes probably chuckled to himself when he advised the older men in his own age bracket: "Do not say, 'How is it that former times were better than these?'" (Ec 7:10). Ecclesiastes is responsible for many famous proverbs and apothegms, but, perhaps his best known and most quoted saying is his opening line: "Vanity of vanities! All things are vanity" (1:2). As he repeats this refrain throughout his book, he usually balances it off with, ". . . and a chase after wind." This patron saint of agnostics and agitators, of the impatient and the pioneering, investigates every possible avenue of human activity. He employs the phraseology of the Ugaritic culture which flourished over a thousand years before his birth; he shows the influence of Stoic philosophy, whose founder, Zeno, was born alongside his own country. He concludes every search, whether it be after wisdom, wealth, esteem, youth, marriage, children or pleasure, with the haunting melody: "This also is vanity and a chase after wind."

The Scriptures provide company in our misery as well as direction in our struggle between wisdom and faith, despite Ecclesiastes' warning: "In much wisdom there is much sorrow, and he who stores up knowledge stores up grief" (1:18). The Bible, in fact, will make it clear that there can be victory only through struggle. God first announced salvation in a context of war; he said to the serpent who tempted Eve: "I will put enmity between you and the woman, between your seed and her seed; he shall crush your head, and you shall lie in wait for his heel" (Gn 3:15). Goodness will triumph, but only if it struggles and braves wounds and minor defeats. Toward the end of the long story of salvation, Jesus announced: "I have come to cast fire upon the earth . . . I have a baptism to be baptized with; and how distressed I am until it is accomplished. Do you think that I came to give peace upon the earth? No, I tell you, but division" (Lk 12:49-51).

From the Bible we learn that faith does not emerge from a refusal to think. On the contrary, it comes from a courageous and persistent search for truth. We must think before we can become dissatisfied with poor reasons and inadequate knowledge. Only by plumbing the depth of human wisdom can we fully experience its weakness and darkness. As we think beyond that point, we step forward into the unknown of faith, convinced that God wants this progress and will remain at our side. This step of faith eventually leads to greater wisdom and more secure positions. Then once again as we reassess our knowledge, we sense a new tension or pull, a fresh compulsion to step forward again.

We are not relativists who deny absolute truth, but we admit that each certainty is never fully grasped nor completely and perpetually organized. We cannot over-rationalize and lose the keen awareness of faith.

When we turn to Scripture, we do not find any single solution. The work of salvation is as complicated and tense in the biblical world as it is today in the world of the Church or in the scholarly world. There is, for instance, an anti-intellectual movement repeatedly manifesting itself in the Bible. We might call it the "desert spirituality" of the Scriptures. Insofar as it is anti-intellectual, it does not correspond to the spirituality represented either by the ancient desert Fathers nor of those who follow such a monastic tradition today. However, it does resemble the latter spiritualities in the sense that it took a critical stance against certain contemporary cultural trends.

This desert spirituality appeared very early in sacred history and has deeply colored an important biblical stream of thought, the Yahwist tradition. The Yahwist tradition is represented in key chapters of Genesis (for example, chapters 2-4). It may annoy many of us to be reminded that chapter 4 of Genesis attributes the creation of music, especially of the harp and the flute, to the wicked offspring of Cain. This same evil line was the first to produce artistic works of bronze and iron. Cain's descendants established the first cities, according to the Yahwist tradition, and these became the first centers of learning and refinement. The Yahwist also condemned the great Mesopotamian endeavor where writing first appeared and where trade and military alliances joined people together in strong, mutually beneficial agreements. In the account of the Tower of Babel the Yahwist calls people back to the simplicity of Abel who "was a keeper of flocks," roaming the open wilderness like Palestinian shepherds do today (Gn 4:2).

The Yahwist, however, was not totally consistent. He actually looted and robbed the ancient centers of culture. He drew upon the *Enuma Elish* and the *Gilgamesh*—or upon a common source shared with these epic legends—in order to prepare his long ballad of human life as it was from the beginning and as it continued into his own day. He was well acquainted with the creation and flood stories of the Sumerians, the legal procedure of the Amorr-hites, the temple designs at Mari, the Canaanite liturgy at Megid-do. He wove all these cultural riches of the ages into his own account, only to condemn them. This problem of faith led him to a new depth of appreciation of God. It was occasioned by many generations of strenuous intellectual effort. If men had not reasoned and experimented, judged and legislated, created poetry and composed music, the Yahwist would not have felt the restless seeking for something, or rather *someone*—vaster, richer and still more lovable.

We can explain the background of the Yahwist tradition in this way. The music and liturgy, the folklore and poetry, the intellectual questioning and legal arrangements which the Su-merians created around 3000 B.C., and which the Amorrhites inherited and systematized around 2000 B.C., were passed on to Abraham and his children. This deeply imbedded inheritance stayed within the bloodstream of the Israelites during their years of bondage in Egypt. At the time of the Exodus, Moses integrated it into his own religious organization. It was revived again, this time in a thoroughly Israelite mode, during the kingships of David and Solomon. It is praised in Psalms 45 and 72. When the Yahwist author, however, witnessed the glorious display of cul-ture and religion under Solomon, he felt as though he were look-ing at a corpse, handsomely laid out in a coffin. He knew that underneath the powder, satin and silk, the decaying process had begun.

All this previous intellectual endeavor was necessary for the Yahwist to appear. The ancient semitic quest for wisdom had to be integrated thoroughly with the Mosaic religion and to be pushed to its fullest and most perfect expression. If the Israelites hoped to build a temple, to organize a liturgy, to compile sacred music, to regulate community life and to recall ancient days, indi-vidual scholars and artists as well as national and religious leaders were conscience-bound to seek the most harmonious and richest expression of social and religious life. Yet, when Israelite wisdom finally reached a world-renowned status, it was near collapse and was provoking many problems of faith. The problem of faith emerged from the prevalent belief that wealth reflected divine good pleasure, that liturgy produced divine contentment and that the quest for God was identified with the possession of what God had promised, a land of pleasure flowing with milk and honey.

SCHOOL FOR NOBILITY

Before proceeding into the New Testament, we must take cognizance of another Old Testament attitude. It will be sufficient to cite the spirit of Yeshua ben Sira, whose wisdom was collected around the year 190 B.C. into a book called *Sirach* or *Ecclesiasticus*. Yeshua ben Sira conducted a school where aristocratic youths were groomed for positions of responsibility in civil and religious circles (Si 51:23). The old man was probably, though unconsciously, drawing his own portrait when he composed this description of the wise man:

> The scribe's profession increases
> his wisdom;
> whoever is free from toil can
> become a wise man.
> How can he become learned who
> guides the plow,
> who thrills in wielding the
> goad like a lance . . .
> and whose every concern is for
> cattle? (Si 38:24-25)

After these and still other deprecating remarks about manual laborers, so diametrically opposed to the spirit of the Yahwist tradition, Yeshua ben Sira continues:

> How different the man who devotes himself
> to the study of the law of the Most High!
> He explores the wisdom of the men of old
> and occupies himself with the prophecies;
> He treasures the discourses of famous men,

and goes to the heart of involved sayings;
He studies obscure parables,
and is busied with the hidden meanings
of the sages.
He is in attendance on the great,
and has entrance to the ruler.
He travels among the peoples of foreign lands
to learn what is good and evil among men.
His care is to seek the Lord, his Maker,
to petition the Most High . . .
Many will praise his understanding;
his fame can never be effaced . . .
Peoples will speak of his wisdom,
and in assembly sing his praises.
While he lives he is one of a thousand,
and when he dies his renown will not cease.
(Si 39:1-11).

Yeshua ben Sira wanted his charges always to assume the correct poise and ever to say the right word. He even instructs them on the proper etiquette at formal banquets:

If you are chosen to preside at dinner,
be not puffed up,
but with the guests be as one of themselves;
Take care of them first before you sit down;
when you have fulfilled your duty
then take your place,
To share in their joy
and win place for your hospitality.
Being older, you may talk; that is only your
right,
but temper your wisdom, not to disturb
the singing . . .
Like a seal of carnelian in a setting of gold
is a concert when wine is served.

Like a gold mounting with an emerald seal
is string music with delicious wine.
Young man, speak only when necessary
when they have asked you more than once . . .
Like the lightning that flashes before a storm
is the esteem that shines on modesty.
When it is time to leave, tarry not;
be off for home! (Si 32:1-11).

These few excerpts run the danger of misrepresenting Yeshua ben
Sira as being stiff, pompous and distant. One must read all fifty-
one chapters of his book to appreciate his warmth and to smile
at his humor. There is no doubt, however, that he and the Yahwist
author—had they lived at the same time—would not have been
compatible. Each would have been a thorn in the other's side.

Yeshua ben Sira composed almost rapturous passages on the
wonder and goodness of God. The breath of God is felt throughout the book. But his greatest insistence is upon correct external
behavior and a broad human wisdom. Right here he prepared
for the almost violent conflict between wisdom and faith in the
days of Jesus and St. Paul. Even though we must not put all the
blame of this New Testament crisis upon Yeshua ben Sira, nonetheless, he is thoroughly representative of a school or movement
which eventually led to the "legal" holiness of external behavior.

It is very interesting to note the difference between the Books
of Sirach and Genesis. In Genesis, God first calls Abraham and
blesses him with the divine presence; with God's inspiration and
help, Abraham is then capable of heroic faith. Yeshua ben Sira
reverses the process. He first enumerates the great works of
Abraham:

Abraham, father of many peoples,
kept his glory without stain:
He observed the precepts of the Most High,
and entered into an agreement with him;
. . . and when tested he was found loyal.

> *For this reason,* God promised him with an oath
> that in his descendants the nations would
> be blessed (Si 44:19-21).

The book of Sirach seems to say that by good works Abraham merited his call: "For this reason, God promised him. . ."

Yeshua ben Sira brings us into contact with a movement or attitude which will not only become progressively dominant in Israel, but which will also harden in its demands. Law, wisdom and riches—all created by God and given to man and woman—can be over-rationalized into a self-sufficient way of life. All the while, however, proponents of the doctrine are crusading in the name of God and religion. We are well acquainted with the opposition and the hostility met with by Jesus when he strove to induce people to take the step of faith beyond human security into the frontier of faith. We know, too, how vigorously St. Paul continued this same battle in the early church. Over and over St. Paul preached that people are justified by faith. His doctrine is summarized in the epistle to the Ephesians: "By grace you have been saved through faith; and that not from yourselves, for it is the gift of God; not as the outcome of works, lest anyone may boast" (Ep 2:8-9).

St. Paul, it must be noted, is not condemning human activity. No apostle was more active than Paul in harnessing every human talent to the cause of the Christian apostolate: knowledge of the law; ability to argue like the rabbis; the treasury of pagan classics; appreciation of hymns and creeds; extraordinary knowledge of the scriptures and oral traditions. He bravely faced every hazard: robbers, shipwreck, persecution, prolonged imprisonment, legal confrontation (2 Cor 11:16-33). In fact, it was only through his full command and total exploitation of human wisdom that he realized that the power and source of life were still deeper and still more transcendent (2 Cor 12:1-13). The greatness of his wisdom produced the tension of his faith. This fact becomes evident in an extraordinary passage in the second epistle to the Corinthians. Only through full energetic involvement in the Christian apostolate could he have written:

We carry this treasure in vessels of clay,
to show that the abundance of the power is
God's and not ours. In all things we suffer
tribulation, but we are not distressed; we
are sore pressed, but we are not destitute;
we endure persecution, but we are not for-
saken; we are cast down, but we do not
perish; always bearing about in our body
the dying of Jesus, so that the life also
of Jesus may be made manifest in our body.
For we the living are constantly being
handed over to death for Jesus' sake, that
the life also of Jesus may be made manifest
in our mortal flesh (2 Cor 4:7-11).

SUMMARY

Man and woman, formed from the earth, are obliged to live with and on the earth. This earthly creature, however, is spirited by a divine breath of life. As they work with their hands, picture with their imagination, think with their intellect and form decisions with their will, they are being impelled by a divine power. Even when they perform their humanly best, this divine source of vitality will always leave them dissatisfied. Humans have no other way to live for God and to think about God, except it be with their earthly substance and human intellect. Yet, they are driven to exceed all earthly substance and human possibilities. Tension or struggle is inevitable.

The impulse to step beyond the human is the moment of "faith." Faith is a recognition that God demands more than man and woman are capable of performing by themselves. Faith is the commitment of oneself to the divine will; it inspires the confidence that will sustain, guide and perfect a person's step into the unknown. Faith does not result from abdicating intellectual activity, but, on the contrary, faith is strongest when people have pushed their mind to its limits. The more a person strains for the fullest possible intellectual endeavor, so much more ecstatically will he or she gasp in wonder before the still greater might and wisdom of God.

The "anti-intellectual" attitudes sometimes assumed in the Bible do not condemn wisdom; what they take offense at is human wisdom, satisfied and content with itself. God curses man and woman for feeling that their strenuous efforts have already modeled them perfectly into the divine image. Human beings at their best, must stir with a discontent which is engendering new hopes and further ideas. Tension between wisdom and faith is not only inevitable but desirable. The most important factor in developing this tension and bracing this faith is vigorous, courageous intellectual activity. We confront the "beyond" of God's love and wisdom only by stretching our human love and wisdom to their limits. We recognize how much further beyond is God only by straining towards the furthest point of human endurance.

Chapter Seven
Church Law Today: Prophetic Implications

The Church in interpreting Scripture is never its master but only its servant. The Church dare not read ideas into the Bible; her whole effort must be dedicated to drawing out the rich inner meaning which is always in the word of God but which is not always appreciated. On the other hand, the Bible cannot get along without the Church. The Bible will never live unless Christians think and proclaim the biblical message. "There are indeed many members and parts of the Church, yet one body. And the eye cannot say to the hand, 'I do not need your help'; and the head cannot say to the feet, 'I have no need of you' " (1 Cor 12:20-21). Neither the Bible nor the Church can say to the other, "I do not need your help."

The Bible needs to be thought about as well as spoken in order to be appreciated and understood; it must be re-lived and re-explained before the full wave of its life and inspiration sweeps into the minds and wills of people. This reliving, however, does not create new doctrines. It carries the past forward into the present. Biblical interpretation presumes a loyal dedication to the past and a close continuity with it, so that at the heart of present-day life lies the vitalizing force of the ancient Scriptures. Biblical history, as is the case with all history, never repeats itself, at least in the minutiae of details; no person and no age are ever a perfect reproduction of other persons and earlier ages.

If the Church today is to be worthy of being called Christian, it must possess the word of God at the heart of all its activity. Its law, consequently, must be the law of Scripture. Canon law, in fact, should be none other than biblical law re-lived today and understandable in terms of today's world. Canon law, like the

Church, is the servant of the Scriptures; it puts no words, not even a jot or tittle, into Scripture, but fully draws out the meaning of Scripture in terms of modern existence (cf. Mt 5:17-19).

Contemporary biblical studies have contributed a vitalizing, reforming force to Church life. What can these same investigations offer the canonist? Archeology has focused new light upon the biblical concept of law and covenant, upon legal development and juridic enforcement in Israel. Bible students could present these new insights to the canonist, who can then apply and integrate them into modern life. From this canonical implementation of ancient biblical procedure, scripture scholars, in turn, obtain new insights and more profound appreciation of their own discipline. God's word, like all words, must be re-thought, re-spoken and re-lived, before it releases its hidden riches and vitalizing power.

GOD PERSONALLY PRESENT: ABRAHAM'S LIFE

God's initial action upon entering the lives of his chosen people did not impose a series of laws. Abraham was not handed a marriage code which forbade polygamy and divorce. Neither, for that matter, were the early Christians presented clear directives about outlawing slavery. In each case, law slowly appeared and gradually developed within the lives of the people. Nowhere does the Bible elaborate upon Abraham's first meeting with God. Writing sixteen centuries later, Jeshua ben Sira liked to think that Abraham from his early years already knew and obeyed the law. He developed his thought about Abraham in this way:

> He observed the precepts of the Most High . . .
> For this reason, God promised him with an
> oath that in his descendants the
> nations would be blessed (Si 44:19ff).

The aged Ben Sira, to our surprise, reversed the order of events as given in Genesis. Genesis placed first the call by God; then, in the strength of the divine presence, Abraham gradually grew up into a stronger and more enlightened moral sense.

In the fragment of the apocryphal *Book of Jubilees,* found among the Dead Sea Scrolls, we are informed that Abraham, while yet a very young boy, turned away from the pagan errors of his family and began to worship the one true God. He thus anticipated Moses in obeying the levitical regulations. These late traditions place so much importance upon the works of the law, as even to claim that Abraham was awarded the covenant because of his obedience to the *Torah.* God was no longer seen as taking the initiative of drawing the patriarch into a close, personal, friendly bond with himself. Postexilic traditions focused attention almost exclusively upon human works rather than upon the faith response of following God's prior action in the promises he gave to all people. This aberration infected early Christianity and was strenuously combated by St. Paul.

Although Genesis grants us only quick, obscure glimpses into the soul of Abraham, still it recognizes that the momentum of Abraham's life was always as St. Paul later described to Christians: "from faith to faith" (Rm 1:17). Biblical faith, especially in Abraham's case, did not center around precise doctrines and detailed laws. It consisted, instead, in a strong attachment to God. Faith was Abraham's response to the impact of God's personal presence. The Bible stresses how God was breathing great hopes into the soul of the patriarch; these hopes, however, did not rest upon the striking prowess of Abraham's works, nor upon any overwhelming, supernatural wonders, but solely upon a tenacious, confident love which the Lord inspired.

In Genesis 12:1, Abraham and Sarah, childless through many years of married life, leave for an unknown country, drawn and motivated by a promise that their name and offspring will be great. Promise rather than fulfillment, faith instead of works, constitute the theme threading its way through the chapters of Genesis and linking its chapters together. God repeats the promise in 13:14-17 and a third time in 15:1. There is a first allusion to a covenant in 15:18 and to circumcision in 17:10. A few verses later in 17:15 the promise is reiterated a fourth time. Only in chapter 22 does Abraham "prove"—or, to speak more accurately, "partially reveal" by works—the heroic fibre of his faith. He actu-

ally proceeds to sacrifice Isaac, his only son by Sarah, in obedience
to what he considered God's command. Once more God repeats
the promise, this time with an oath. Throughout his life, Abraham
remained a person of faith, "hoping against hope" (Rm 4:18).

Abraham's faith is hardly distinguishable from his charity. He
did not live from any elaborate doctrinal synthesis. There is very
little formal doctrine and even less dogmatic development during
the patriarchal period. These people believed in one God, but they
were not ashamed to worship their God at the Canaanite sanctuaries. As in the case of Judah (Gn 38), they married and inter-
mingled freely with the local inhabitants, even to the point of imi-
tating their sensuous immorality.

Abraham's starting point in understanding God was the knowledge and appreciation of the deity which he learned from his
neighbors. Abraham not only addressed God with the Canaanite
word, El, but he usually felt that his El would make the same
demands as the Canaanite deities. Abraham was a monotheist only
in a very rudimentary sort of way. God gradually transformed
the patriarch's somewhat crude, always imperfect appreciation of
himself, not by putting a completely new idea in its place, but by
living in a personal way within the soul of Abraham. God did not
want to be just an idea open for study and investigation but,
rather, a person anxious for love and response.

A good example of this slow process of transfiguration is found
in chapter 22 of Genesis which relates the binding and sacrifice
of Isaac, known to Jews as the Akedah. Although this event has
acquired a prominent place in the Rosh Hashanah or New Year
ceremony of orthodox Jewry, many Jews now, as in the past, have
encountered great difficulty in reconciling it with any appreciation of a compassionate God. The Bible, outside of Genesis, maintains complete silence. The Talmud explains that Jeremiah (19:5)
and Micah (6:7), in leveling condemnation upon child-sacrifice,
actually had this incident in mind! Most reformed congregations
in America have suppressed the Akedah prayer, which asks God
to "consider the binding of his son Isaac upon the altar when he
suppressed his love in order to do thy will with a whole heart."

Even the author of our present text in Genesis 22 felt obliged to warn the reader that God is only putting Abraham to the test. By contrast, however, Abraham himself in deadly earnest is intent on executing his son. This heroic pull in opposite directions is one of the many literary devices by which the author has prepared a tense, powerful drama. The tension is transferred to our mind in still another way. Granted the assurance from the start that God will interfere in some way, we are still obliged to ask what kind of God did Abraham think himself to worship. Abraham was convinced that his God, like the Canaanite deities, pleasurably accepted the slaughter and cremation of the first-born male child.

Rather than think God deliberately cultured such false ideas in Abraham by ordering him to proceed with the killing of Isaac, would it not be more normal to think that Abraham, here as elsewhere, absorbed Canaanite ideas and followed their practices? What we describe with theological sophistication as the permissive will of God, the Bible attributes immediately to God. For other, somewhat similar examples, see Exodus 4:21, Joshua 11:20, and 1 Samuel 2:25. The Bible employs such phrases as, "The Lord ordered," or "The Lord did such and such," when, as a matter of fact, many secondary causes were at work in the events. Abraham's conclusion, based on an imperfect and even erroneous notion of God, that God should want the ritual destruction of his only child by Sarah, is described as a divine command.

Can we apply this same method to solving the finale of the story? Does the sacred author draw up an ordinary occurrence and present it as a divine intervention? He relates that the angel of the Lord intervened and stayed the arm of Abraham, as he was about to slaughter Isaac. In various parts of the Bible, the phrase, "angel of the Lord," signifies some kind of divine guidance or help. The author of Genesis 22, therefore, wants to assure us that *in some way* God changed Abraham's attitude and intention.

The important biblical contribution regarding the development of law in this account lay in this fact: law emerged after and out of long, interior contemplation on God's personal love and exalted ideals. Laws were not made to force people into holiness or pre-requisites for conversion. Instead, they grew out of an intuition by faith about the person and goodness of God.

The Old Testament was inspired by God to lead the Israelites to the same holiness and the same heaven to which we aspire (2 Tm 3:16-17). It can provide us with "true divine pedagogy" (DV, no. 15), instructing us about the gradual revelation of Jesus in our midst. All of us, in one way or another, are back in Old Testament times. Very few of us adequately appreciate, much less carefully follow Jesus' heroic example of forgiveness, patience, zeal and prayer. In fact, we do not measure up to the Old Testament saints and to their record of God's redemptive and transforming presence among the Israelites. The Old Testament then presents us with exalted models for leadership and instruction today.

We turn to the Old Testament for guidance for still another reason. Because the Old Testament was formed over a much longer period of time than the New Testament and because it manifests a longer and more profound interaction between religion and world culture, it offers many more opportunities for re-thinking and re-vamping our own religious work among non-Christian or under-privileged areas. It can show us how an older style of evangelization must be adapted to the new anti-colonialism and the renewed self-respect of the third world countries. While maintaining the ideal of the Sermon on the Mount (Mt 5-7) whether it be for pacifism, communal sharing of goods, absolute honesty or sexual dignity, we still might reconsider the qualifications for baptism and full communion with the Church. The third world as well as minorities in the first and second world might require us to re-evaluate our scale of moral values. While sin remains sin, the devastating effects of specific sins will vary from age to age and place to place. We cannot baptize into our community a person whose evil ways will destroy our Christian family and ideals, but we have always tolerated many sins in those we baptize, sins of intolerance and prejudice, sins of social injustice. In many developing countries these latter sins may be far more destructive of wholesome society than other offenses against sexuality, which have been emphasized in European and American cultures. While the question remains extremely delicate and difficult, it must be faced with open theological discussion.

Are not our modern pagans in Abraham's pre-conversion situation? If we imitate God—and this is demanded of us—then we might even admit these unfortunate people to baptism and holy communion. As God's personal love burns ever more deeply within them transforming their entire being, they will begin to understand the meaning and the force of many Christian laws.

COVENANTAL LAW: EXPRESSION OF GRATITUDE

By observing God's dealings with Abraham, we discover why it is necessary constantly to restate the relationship of law both to the initial conversion of the unbeliever as well as his consequent moral reform. We must repeatedly return to the Bible in all matters in order to evaluate earlier decisions and to revitalize routine actions. The story of Abraham prompts us to return to the Bible in truthful recognition that our actions are anything but adequate as a total love response.

Our past acts show up our need for reformation and reassessment before performing subsequent acts. However, without having had the courage to act in the past we would have remained mere theorists, possessing minds always filled with excellent ideas and unlimited advice, but never willing to put the theory to the test in the arena of life. Only persons who have acted and to a greater or less extent failed feel the necessity of turning to God and the Scriptures for help. The Bible never disappoints them. Through the Scriptures God breathes new ideas into such a person and sustains him or her in devoted activity.

We can look at the Christian approach towards law from another covenantal perspective. The covenant completed what the deliverance from Egypt initiated; it led Israel into the future, profoundly grateful to God. This onward march through history reached its fullness when God's great redemptive act of love in Christ Jesus was carried out on the feast of the Pasch. Later it was to be remembered liturgically as the new covenant. Since Christian law intends to direct the community towards the peaceful and complete fulfillment of Christ's redemptive work, it can be most advantageously studied in the life situation of the covenant.

Contemporary studies are relocating the Mosaic Covenant back into the earth of Old Testament times. Within this framework, they are recognizing the pattern and rhythm of this ancient culture. The Israelites did not slavishly copy the ways of their neighbors. Whatever the children of Abraham adopted, they integrated into their own religious system. At the heart of the Mosaic religion lay an understanding of a personal God, too unique and too vital not to transform whatever it accepted from outsiders.

The earliest form of the covenant, as a matter of fact, reflects the strong bonds of family ties in the ancient Near East. Several hundred years after Moses the Israelites described the covenant in more technical formulas similar to the international treaties found among the Hittite people north of Palestine. One of the earliest witnesses of the covenant is the book of Exodus. It describes the covenant in terms of ritual rather than of contract or treaty. The ritual, moreover, resembled a style of family life and kinship. Israel is not so much the vassal of Yahweh as his family. And so the laws are not formulated in the words of international contracts but express the tone and conditions of the family.

We are familiar with the image of God as Father of his people as found in Exodus. So strongly was he devoted to them that he considered them members of his family, sharing his own life. We might interject a question here: can we make the same claim today for Church law, whether it be the Code, diocesan statutes, constitutions for religious orders or for parish regulations? Are these cast in a context of God's fatherly love? Do these same laws presume the relationship found in a close family bond?

After the death of Moses, the Sinaitic law went through its ups and downs. Preserved in both the northern kingdom of Israel and the southern kingdom of Judah, the law reached one of its finest forms in the north. The north was viewed with stern eyes by the self-styled "orthodox" priests of Jerusalem. These priests, the successors of Zadok, claimed exclusive control over sacred matters, and were more and more convinced that the northern levites were rebels and heretics. In addition, the northern levites suffered from internal conditions in the kingdom of Israel. The Canaanite fertility cults had infiltrated more successfully there than in the south and had degraded the moral stamina of the people. However, before the collapse of the north in 721 B.C., the northern laws, exhortations and traditions were carried south and were enthusiastically received by the honorable King Hezekiah (716-687 B.C.). Then came a long, dark period of eclipse during the apostasy of Kings Manasseh and Amon (687-640 B.C.).

The re-discovery of these laws during the reign of good King Josiah (640-609 B.C.) churned up a wave of excitement which swept through all Palestine. "I have found the book of the law in the house of the Lord," cried Hilkiah, the high priest. Upon hearing its contents, Josiah tore his garments in sorrow and dismay over years of disobedience. Priests and scribes, prophets and elders were all consulted; the law, moreover, was solemnly read to the assembled congregation. Religious reformers demolished every sanctuary but Jerusalem's, beat idols into dust, disinterred and removed the bones of deceased idolators. The reform of Josiah completed a process long years in the making. The name *Deuteronomic* (= second [reading of the] law) is attached to this religious revolution, because it was based on a new codification and re-interpretation of the ancient Mosaic Law. When Josiah was tragically and violently killed in 609, at the age of forty, the Deuteronomic reform suddenly and completely collapsed.

These trials of suspicion and frequently of open persecution forced the northern levites to reconsider their traditions and laws. The entire history of the deuteronomic law was that of their leaders' persistent effort to clarify the law as well as exerting effective leadership. The northern levites, therefore, developed an interpretation of law strongly influenced not only by prophets like Hosea and later Jeremiah, but also by the legal practices of the ancient Hittites. Deuteronomy, therefore, deserves special consideration. Not only is it a part of the Bible, but it also strongly colored the thinking of Jesus and the early apostolic Church.

Deuteronomy reorganized the terms of the Mosaic covenant under the form of a Hittite Suzerainty treaty. This specific type of treaty had six major sections:

1) *Introduction of the speaker or identification of the Great King.* This style preserved the biblical intuition of Yahweh as a

strongly personal God, interested in his people and sharing with them his thoughts and hopes. The covenant renewal at the northern sanctuary of Shechem began in this way: "Thus says the Lord, the God of Israel." See Joshua 24:2a; Deuteronomy 1:1; 5:1-5.

2) *Historical Prologue.* This section usually related in a free-moving style the military conquests and other types of assistance by which the Great King came to the aid of the vassal. These benevolent acts are intended to inspire the vassal with gratitude. Biblical religion rests four square upon Yahweh's great historical acts of salvation, and especially the greatest of them, the exodus out of Egypt. See Joshua 24:2b-13; Deuteronomy 1:3-4.

3) *Stipulation or obligation of the vassal.* In view of the Great King's many kind and protective acts, the vassal responded with grateful obedience. This is the section where laws were inserted into the document. See Joshua 24:14; Deuteronomy 1:5, 5:7 ff.

4) *Preservation of the document.* The Suzerainty treaty at this point prescribes that the document be deposited in the sanctuary of the vassal and be publicly read at regular intervals. The book of Deuteronomy, with its persistent homiletic style of commenting upon the law, probably originated at these public readings during the great feasts. See Joshua 24:25-26 and Deuteronomy 31:9-13, 24-26.

5) *Invocations of the deities of the signatories as witnesses of the covenant.* This feature of the Suzerainty treaty is missing in the Israelite documents, for no one is higher than Yahweh to vouch for and protect the conditions of his covenant. In Joshua 24:22-23, however, we hear the leader saying dramatically to the people: "You are your own witnesses . . . Now, therefore, put away strange gods." See also Joshua 24:27; Isaiah 1:2; Hosea 2:21-22; Micah 6:2.

6) *Series of curses and blessings.* Fidelity and disobedience are both treated seriously. Life simply will not go on the same, now that the covenant has been ratified. Life radically changes for the better or for worse, depending upon the people's loyalty to the Suzerain. See Deuteronomy 28; Joshua 8:34.

In many cases, we must admit, the Suzerainty treaty was probably a deceptive way of maintaining order and discipline. The Mosaic covenant may have been one of the few instances when the Suzerainty treaty achieved its ideal. The Lord could rightly claim the loyal affection of his people. Their freedom and their land, their bond of union with one another and with him, all flowed from his great redemptive acts. He had brought them out of Egypt, cared for them in the desert, delivered over the Promised Land to their tenure, and consecrated David as their king and protector.

Israel, according to Ezekiel, lay an abandoned child, unwanted by its foreign parents, until, as God himself expressed it, "I passed by and saw you weltering in your blood. I said to you: live . . . and grow like a plant in the field. You grew and developed . . . Again I passed by you . . . I swore an oath to you and entered into a covenant with you; you became mine . . ." (Ezk 16). Israel's repeated failure, which Ezekiel sharply delineates, reduced her to greater dependence upon God. And the Lord just as often forgave her: "For I will re-establish my covenant with you, that you may know that I am the Lord, that you may remember and be covered with confusion, and that you may be utterly silenced for shame when I pardon you for all you have done" (Ezk 16:62-63). Israel's laws, like her entire life, lay within the context of covenant-gratitude.

Obedience became the most obvious way of expressing love for the person of the Lord. These two ideas—obedience and love— are closely linked in a Deuteronomic passage which Jesus canonized as the greatest commandment:

> Hear, O Israel! The Lord is our God, the
> Lord alone. Therefore, you shall love the
> Lord, your God, with all your heart, and with
> all your soul, and with all your strength.
> Take to heart these words which I enjoin on
> you today. Drill them into your children.
> Speak of them at home and abroad, whether you
> are busy or at rest. Bind them at your wrist
> as a sign and let them be as a pendant on your

forehead. Write them on the doorposts of your
houses and on your gates (Dt 6:4-9; Mt 22:38).

Men and women were Israelites, not to keep laws, but rather to
be drawn within the family bond of the Lord where laws helped
in the expression of love and the maintenance of peace.

Love became their life. Another deuteronomic passage subtly
passes from life to love and laws.

> Now, Israel, hear the statutes and decrees
> which I am teaching you to observe, that you
> may live, and may enter in and take possession
> of the land which the Lord, the God of your
> fathers, is giving you. In your observance
> of the commandments of the Lord, your God
> . . . you shall not add to what I command
> you nor subtract from it . . . You
> who clung to the Lord, your God, are all
> alive today . . . Observe them carefully,
> for thus you will give evidence of your wis-
> dom and intelligence to the nations, who will
> hear of all these statutes, and say, 'This
> great nation is truly a wise and intelligent
> people.' For what nation is there that has
> gods as close to it as the Lord, our God, is
> to us whenever we call upon him? Or what great
> nation has statutes and decrees that are as
> just as this whole Law which I am setting
> before you today? (Dt 4:1-2, 4, 6-8)

This inter-dependence of love, law and life appealed to Jesus.
He quoted another passage of Deuteronomy during a moment of
tense anxiety and thereby settled the issue of the first temptation.

> Remember how for forty years now the Lord, your
> God, has directed all your journeying in the
> desert, so as to test you by affliction and
> find out whether or not it was your intention

to keep his commandments. He therefore let you
be afflicted with hunger, and then fed you
with manna, a food unknown to you and your
fathers, in order to show that not by bread
alone does man live, but by every word that
comes forth from the mouth of the Lord. The
clothing did not fall from you in tatters, nor
did your feet swell these forty years.
So you must realize that the Lord, your
God, disciplines you even as a man
disciplines his son (Dt 8:2-5).

CONCLUSION

These new insights into the Mosaic Covenant provide the
setting for legal discussion among believers. It asks canonists to
place the law within the framework of God's redemptive acts in
Christ Jesus. If the deuteronomic reform based its re-codification
of law upon the Suzerainty treaty, that is, upon the explicit identification of the "Great King" and the detailed presentation of his
redemptive acts, then the modern reform of the Code already has
an excellent norm for any future revisions.

What is more important than surface formulation of the Code
is the spirit of obedience. Laws should help the believer to express
as spontaneously and freely as possible his gratitude to God for
redeeming him through the death and the resurrection of Jesus.
Still another application of the deuteronomic spirit lies in that very
word *spirit*. Laws must tend towards interiorization. This norm
was primary in the thinking of one of the great initiators of
the deuteronomic reform, Jeremiah. The prophet, so sensitive to
love and affection, projected the spirit of Deuteronomy into the
messianic age with these words:

The days are coming, says the Lord, when I
will make a new covenant with the house of
Israel and the house of Judah. It will not
be like the covenant I made with their
fathers the day I took them by the hand to

lead them forth from the land of Egypt; for
they broke my covenant, and I had to show
myself their master, says the Lord. But
this is the covenant which I will make with
the house of Israel after those days, says
the Lord. I will place my law within them,
and write it upon their hearts; I will be
their God, and they shall be my people. No
longer will they have need to teach their
friends and kinsmen how to know the Lord.
All, from least to greatest, shall know me,
says the Lord, for I will forgive their evil-
doing and remember their sin no more.
(Jr 31:31-34).

Jeremiah is not rejecting the Mosaic covenant. He rejects the
ungrateful way with which the people received and kept it. The
Messianic age would restore God's great ideal. If we follow Jeremiah's advice, we will understand that laws do not form the
spirit but flow from the spirit. Law provides an atmosphere of
spontaneity and freedom, for nothing is so proper to human life
as the liberty to serve God. Religion must never be described in
terms of obedience to laws. Obedience, instead, ought to be formulated in terms of love. Religion is the life of love between God
and his people. Laws express this way of life and allow it maxi-
mum initiative.

The Old Testament law, St. Paul once wrote, is "our tutor in
Christ that we might be justified by faith" (Gal 3:24). Simply
because Christ has come, we are not allowed to put aside our
tutor. If we were all fully grown to the stature of Jesus, then not
only biblical laws but all laws, including those of the Code, could
be put in a museum of antiquities. So long as any one of us is
still growing in the grace of Christ and is coming to new awareness of person and love, the biblical law can be of service.

Old Testament study admits at once that laws are not to be
applied literally to an infinite degree. Many Mosaic prescriptions
(for example, the "casuistic") have passed into disuse. Two areas

of legal procedure in biblical times have been considered in this chapter. From Abraham's case we find help for the evangelization of the pre-Christian or the conversion of the morally and subjectively ignorant of our own times. From the deuteronomic reform we learn the necessity of putting all laws in a setting of gratitude for God's redemptive acts. Gratitude rejects the minimal application of law and seeks its freest and fullest expression.

— I will give to drink without cost from the spring of life-giving water — Revelation 21:6

Chapter Eight

Scriptural and Liturgical Depths in Christian Living

In the Church at prayer lies the source of a genuine under-standing of the faith. In the liturgy lies the power for transform-ing dogma into a spiritual force in modern society. At no other moment does the Church live so intensely and therefore proclaim so effectively her life in Christ Jesus than during liturgical wor-ship. Those who come together for prayer, St. Paul wrote, are not wrapped in silence, but they "proclaim the death of the Lord until he comes" (1 Cor 11:26). The Apostle here employed the same Greek word, *kataggello*, which he had used earlier for apo-stolic preaching (see 1 Cor 9:14).

St. Paul's statement is important, not only for the key word, *preaching* or *proclaiming the death of the Lord,* but also for the other expression, *until he comes.* That phrase reveals the com-pelling power of the liturgy to teach and apply the mystery of Christ in a most practical way. The liturgical proclamation of the word announces the presence of the Lord Jesus who is renewing at that moment his great redemptive act. But the liturgy does more. It alerts the worshippers to the coming of the glorified, risen Lord in each event of their day. Christians are thoroughly God-conscious people, awaiting him until he comes. For this reason they greet one another with "Maranatha! Come, Lord!" (1 Cor 16:22; Rv 22:20).

St. Paul, it seems, is attributing to the liturgy the power to form intelligent, apostolic Christians. The liturgy is an educa-tional force which can give direction for intelligent scripture study and impart attitudes for enthusiastic Christian living. But first it is necessary to look to the ancient Bible before viewing our present liturgical worship. We will then be in a position to consider the scriptures as liturgical documents of Old and New Testament times. From this biblical-liturgical depth, we can proceed from a study of ancient biblical worship to our present liturgy. Finally, from liturgical, ceremonial actions we can move to the area of Christian living itself.

In the beginning, one can raise the question: why is the present Christian liturgy so important for Bible study? Why is the liturgy more effective than any other means of instruction, "more efficacious than even the most weighty documents of ecclesiastical teaching"? (from Pope Pius XI's encyclical on Christ the King). The Holy Spirit put the directives of this encyclical into action by directing John XXIII to give the schema on the liturgy priority over all other agenda at the Second Vatican Council. With God, this switch to the liturgy was no last minute decision. With great care he was making sure that the liturgy provided the context for considering everything else about the Church, Scripture included. The Christian must approach doctrine and life in the Bible in the same way as the Church—through the liturgy.

But there is another strong argument why the liturgy is important for Bible study. It is found in the traditional formula, almost as sacred as any word of Scripture: *Legem credendi lex statuat supplicandi—Let the rule for prayer determine the rule for belief.* Explained in one way, certainly valid and acceptable, that statement invites us to investigate how the Church prays if we would know what the Church believes. Another, and perhaps a truer, way of measuring the full import of that classic formula is to remember that when we pray with the Church, we are personally absorbed into the most intense moment of the Church's life. From the experience of that moment we can affirm with St. John, "What *we have seen and heard* we proclaim in turn to you" (1 Jn 1:3).

According to St. John, a Christian is not so much a scholar as a witness proclaiming what he or she has experienced: the Lord Jesus lives. In the liturgy the Christian beholds the *parousía* or *epiphaneía* of the gloriously risen Christ. Dogma comes to life and the Christians cannot but speak with boldness of what they have seen and heard (see Ac 4:13, 20). Religion without liturgy is the passion without the resurrection, a dead body laid out to be examined, rather than a living person to be worshipped. Without liturgy Christians stand condemned by the desperate words of St. Paul, "If Christ has not been raised [from the dead], our preaching [proclamation, *kērygma*] is void of content and your faith is empty too" (1 Cor 15:14).

In order to have liturgical worship and scriptural investigation draw the fullest meaning from each other, they must maintain close ties for yet another reason. By studying sacred doctrine in the context of liturgical worship, the Christian anticipates the direction and the contribution of modern biblical scholarship. It is incorrect to assume that prayer dispenses with such scholarship. If in the past Scripture had been taught and read with a keen sense of its constant liturgical use in Israel and in the apostolic Church, then the discoveries of the contemporary scriptural movement would not have taken Catholic theologians, religion teachers or Bible readers by surprise.

With such an approach, each of these groups would have realized all along that the Scriptures emerged from the people of God at prayer rather than from the scholar at study. They would have been aware that very many, if not most, biblical passages present not an eye-witness record of the past, but instead, a liturgical acclamation of praise, a credal confession of faith, or a humble prayer for forgiveness. The Bible would have been interpreted as a proclamation of the redemptive acts of God, not so much as these were experienced for the first time, but as they were relived continuously by later generations in Israel and in the apostolic Church. Only a small part of this reliving of God's acts of salvation resulted from study. One of the most important contributions came from prayer. For depth of understanding, then, we must approach God's word in the liturgical spirit with which it was composed.

SCRIPTURAL DEVELOPMENT THROUGH LITURGY

If one of the correct approaches towards the Bible is through liturgical prayer, then we must begin our study of the Old Testament against the background of Israel's worship and our investigation of the New Testament against the setting of the apostolic liturgy. In ancient times the sacred traditions were transmitted quite differently than they are today. During most of the Old Testament and New Testament times, there was a continuous process of adaptation and modification by the ancients. For us today, the Bible is a sacred book, fixed and unchangeable. Out of reverence we never dare add a new word, much less a new sentence to the Scriptures; our reflections and applications are confined to introductions, footnotes and commentaries. It was not so in biblical days. The Israelite priests and prophets introduced their reflections into the very fabric of the sacred account.

Songs and confessions of later ages were inserted into the earlier traditions, like tribal blessings into the Jacob story (Gn 49) or again in the Mosaic tradition (Dt 33). Prophecies of Micah and Jeremiah, once directed against the northern kingdom of Israel, were later re-directed against the southern kingdom of Judah. In the post-exilic age, a hymn of thanksgiving was appended to the famous book of Emmanuel (Is 7-12). A careful study of the style and purpose of these various changes points to the sanctuary as the spot where this growth took place.

Priests and levites were the responsible agents for the changes, and their intention was most clearly revealed in a passage of Deuteronomy. Long after the Mosaic age, a levite repeated these words to the people gathered for sanctuary worship:

> Hear, O Israel, the statutes and decrees
> which I proclaim in *your* hearing *this day,*
> that you may learn them and take care to
> observe them. The Lord, *our* God, made a
> covenant *with us* at Horeb [i.e., Sinai];
> not with our fathers did he make this cove-
> nant, but *with us, all of us* who are *alive*
> *here this day.* He spoke with *you* face to
> face on the mountain . . . (Dt 5:14).

The levitical preacher did not want the words of Israel's law-giver simply admired as library curiosities. They were to be ex-perienced as vital forces. In this actualization of the ancient Mosaic heritage, later generations were being called out of a spiritual Egypt of sin to wander through a spiritual Sinai desert of sorrow where they too would meet God "face to face." And in that meeting they would arrive at the spiritual promised land of divine peace. What our biblical text books called "typology" was constantly at work as part of the fabric of the lives of people in biblical days. Today we add footnotes to the pages of Exodus which inform the reader that Moses, the manna, and the exodus are types of Christ, the Eucharist, and the journey to heaven. The Deuteronomist put his footnotes right into the sacred text out of the context of a lived experience. As is quite clear from the style of Deuteronomy, that life situation or occasion was liturgical worship.

Psalm 95 is an invitational hymn, sung during a liturgical pro-cession in the temple courtyard. The assembly praised God for creating and redeeming Israel. When the procession arrived at the sanctuary, a priest then delivered this solemn oracle or warning:

> Oh, that today you would hear his [God's]
> voice:
> 'Harden not your hearts as at Meribah
> . . .
> Forty years I loathed that generation . . .
> Therefore I swore in my anger:
> They shall not enter into my rest'
> (Ps 95:7-11).

Even though the congregation was already living in the prom-ised land and was actually worshipping at one of its sanctuaries, still, *today* they were spiritually back in the desert, hardening their hearts as the Israelites did against Moses at Meribah. Cen-turies after the Psalmist lived, the epistle to the Hebrews quoted this same text, and in the spirit of the Old Testament poet, actual-ized it for the Christian worshipper:

> Encourage one another daily while it is
> still 'today,' so that no one grows hardened
> by the deceit of sin. We have become part-
> ners of Christ . . . Therefore a sabbath
> rest still remains for [us] the people of
> God (Heb 3:13-14; 4:9).

This re-reading or actualization was made possible for the apostles and their first disciples through the mystery of Pentecost. Jesus had already announced this new insight into the Old Testament Scriptures and even into his own words.

> The holy Spirit . . . will bring to your
> minds whatever I have said to you. When
> he, the Spirit of truth, has come, he will
> teach you all the truth . . . He will glo-
> rify me, because he will receive of what
> is mine and declare it to you (Jn 14:26; 16:13 ff).

The apostles would have contented themselves with what they had seen, heard and understood before Pentecost. After the descent of the Holy Spirit, they proclaimed with boldness (a favorite word of Acts) the glory or wondrous presence of the risen savior. The events and words of Jesus of Nazareth were transfigured, as was Jesus himself, and became living realities, known precisely because they were relived in the apostolic Church. Every sorrow endured by the apostles became an occasion for the revelation of the messianic Christ (2 Th 1:4-10), so that the early Christians could say with St. Paul that they too were "always bearing about in our [their] body the dying of Jesus, so that the life of Jesus may be made manifest in our [their] body" (2 Cor 4:10).

In much the same way today, the liturgy presents the mysteries of the life of Jesus. The liturgy is like another Pentecost, transfiguring before our eyes the words, the deeds and above all the person of Jesus. This fact will explain the arrangement of the liturgical year which does not place the account of Jesus' ministry and teaching in the period after Epiphany but in the weeks after Pentecost. If the liturgy followed the chronology and the geography of Christ's life, these events would be spread between Epiphany and Holy Week. What we find, instead, is the re-living of our Lord's life in the Sundays after Pentecost. In the power of the Spirit, the life of Christ is our life today, and as we live that life in liturgical worship, we come to "know Christ and the power of his resurrection and the fellowship of his suffering" (Ph 3:10).

If this biblical, liturgical depth of union with Christ had remained the framework of religion programs, we never would have become obsessed with names, dates and places in courses entitled "Life of Christ." The life of Christ would have remained what it is in the Bible and in the liturgy, life *in* Christ through liturgical renewal. Advent would proclaim the birth within us of a new, more vigorous life. This life can only be that of the risen Christ; no other Jesus exists! The Triumphant Lord comes, destroying sin in what the Bible and the liturgy call a burst of "glory." Christ comes wondrously fulfilling all promises, majestically judging the world. "Glory" is here understood in the biblical meaning of the theophany of God in a great redemptive undertaking; "justice" means that God is just in living up to his goodness and in accomplishing his promises.

If religion courses possess the scriptural-liturgical depth, then special attention is directed constantly to the apostolic Church. We can see this in examining the eucharistic account in Acts and in First Corinthians. Comparing the two, we notice the important difference of mood and attitude. Acts puts the breaking of the bread ceremony in a setting of "gladness and simplicity of heart" (2:46). St. Paul stresses the sacrificial motif and states explicitly that the Eucharist "proclaims the death of the Lord" (1 Cor 11:26). This motif had always been present in the eucharistic service since its institution by Jesus at the sacrificial meal of the Last Supper. But the mystical body of Christ, the Church, had first to suffer before she would fully understand the sacrificial meaning of her eucharistic body. We ourselves will never really know the meaning of the sacrifice of the mass until we obediently share Christ's sufferings in our lives.

Other possible areas of investigation are the biblical-liturgical concepts of blood, sacrifice and redemption. Such studies can impart new and different dimensions to our knowledge of the mass. They take our interest off such notions as death, destruction, substitution and ransom, and stress, instead, the more genuinely biblical concepts of life, union and the redemptive acts of God. Another practical aspect of how such a biblical-liturgical approach imparts greater depth to the life of the Church deals not so much with Christian liturgy itself, but rather with Christian living.

GREATER DEPTH IN CHRISTIAN LIVING

Depth always produces peace and unity. The shallow waters of lakes are those which writhe with the most furious upheavals. In like manner, biblical liturgy not only bestows a depth of understanding, but through this depth can unite a person peacefully with all other members of the human family. We can be grateful for the wisdom of good Pope John. He chose the liturgy to head the Council's agenda because his primary interest in calling it in the first place was to achieve Christian unity. As we think about the smaller Vatican Council of the local community and its desired goal of unity, we, too, must turn to the liturgy for guidance and inspiration. The liturgy will lead to unity between Catholics themselves and between Catholics and their separated brethren.

When religion is taught against a background of the liturgy, then a demand is necessarily made upon the learners to do more than study the mysteries of the life of Jesus; they must pray and live each one of them personally. Study can be impersonal and objective, but not prayer. Prayer rises up from that deep point of personal existence where each one is distinct from everyone else. Liturgical prayer maintains that strong, personal aspect of all prayer, but it never succumbs to narrow subjectivism. In the liturgy, each one of necessity prays the prayer of everyone.

There is a complaint voiced very often against the liturgical use of the psalms as prayer. A person grumbles, "These prayers are not mine; they do not express my thoughts and my reactions."

This is a serious charge against the liturgy, for the psalms constitute the bulk of liturgical prayer. The complaint goes something
like this: "I am feeling happy and joyful. When I attend the
liturgy, I must say to God, 'Put an end to my afflictions and my
sufferings, and take away all my sins' (Ps 25:18). On another day,
I have a headache, the school team has just lost the basketball
game, and there are exams just ahead. The liturgy tells me to
pray: 'Shout joyfully, all you on earth, sing praise to the glory
of his name'" (Ps 66:1-2).

This species of complaint against the liturgy, like grumbling
about exams, proves that the psalms, like exams, are necessary at
times. The psalms pull a person out of this psychological intro-
version and thrust him into the Church at large. Americans need
to be reminded that there are other people in other lands at the
edge of despair; healthy people must remember there are those
who are lonely, hungry and dying. At the same time no persecution can be so black and no famine so oppressive as to remove joy
and peace. In fact, in the very moment of sorrow, obediently and
lovingly endured, there is a victory like that of the dying Jesus—a
victory which possesses within itself the power of the resurrection. The liturgy brings all persons together, so that what one
person lacks the other person supplies "for the building up of the
body of Christ, until we all attain to the unity of the faith and
of the deep knowledge of the Son of God" (Ep 4:13).

The liturgy thus keeps the worshipper alive to everyone else
in the Church, even to the point of free men voicing the suppressed anguish of the persecuted and of prisoners singing the
praise of the joyful. The implications following upon such a
liturgical piety are numerous. Visiting the sick and the imprisoned, aiding shut-ins, volunteering services in hospitals, and other
such works of mercy would not be activities to absorb spare time;
they would be necessary expressions of ordinary Christian life.
In the liturgy, more than at any other moment, all participants are
united in one prayer and one life; divisions break down and walls
collapse (see Ep 2:14). Liturgy is not so much imparting knowledge as it is forming attitudes. Knowledge easily evaporates; attitudes stay for life.

The close interdependence between liturgy and life shows up in a familiar Eucharistic text of St. Paul. He wrote to the Corinthians: "He who eats and drinks without distinguishing the body, eats and drinks judgment to himself" (1 Cor 11:29). The simplest explanation, in my opinion, is not the correct one. "Not distinguishing the body" does not imply that the Corinthians rejected the real presence. In a theoretical way they distinguished or recognized the body of the Lord in the bread which they ate. But in a real way they denied it by bickering and jealousy. They had so mangled the body of Christ—his body which was the church of Corinth—that the Corinthians no longer recognized the only Christ who exists, the risen Christ who is one with all his members. In the Eucharist they received what they called Christ, but they no longer recognized or distinguished the true Christ. In some way, the Corinthians were unbelievers, trafficking with something most sacred. In this one example it is clear that dogma demands liturgy, and liturgy demands full Christian life before Christians come to a clear grasp of their faith.

LITURGY AND ECUMENISM

The liturgy—even the ancient biblical liturgy—had an ecumenical tone. In the Bible we learn that Solomon commissioned Canaanite architects to construct the temple, and they drew its general pattern of courtyard, tabernacle and Holy of Holies according to Canaanite style. Even such details as the cherubim and the horns of the altar were a customary part of non-Israelite liturgy. The texts of religious songs and the melodies for singing them were copied—we might say, plundered—from the Philistines and especially from the Canaanites. Even the agricultural feast days of local inhabitants were absorbed into the Israelite religious calendar. The spirit of God directed these decisions.

On the other hand, the ecumenical spirit of the Scriptures may seem to be cancelled out by other biblical phenomena. Before our eyes come those texts of Deuteronomy, authorizing the *herem* wars against the Canaanites in which everyone and everything of non-Israelite taint were fanatically annihilated (Dt 7:1-5, 16-26).

We also recall the deuteronomic reform of King Josiah which leveled to the ground all the sanctuaries outside of Jerusalem and strenuously swept the Israelite liturgy clean of outside contamination. Church life in those days, like Church life today, was not a simple matter of everyone nodding in agreement. There were then, as now, fanatics on both sides.

A union of Israelites and Canaanite religion may seem as incompatible as vinegar and ice cream. Egyptian, Canaanite and Mesopotamian religions were thoroughly naturalistic; biblical religion centered on the great historical acts of God. The non-Israelite religious calendar followed the cycle of nature: dry season and rainy season; virginity, procreation and old age/death. Reacting strongly against these naturalistic cults, Mosaic religion moved around the cycle of God's great redemptive acts in history, such as the exodus out of Egypt and the covenant. The Israelites continuously re-lived these mysteries of salvation.

In general, however, biblical tradition followed a middle path of unity in the whole process of accepting prayer and ritual from outsiders. The Israelites carefully maintained their own distinct religion. Never did it destroy the proper identity of their biblical religion. This fact can be exemplified in the case of Canaanite agricultural feasts which the Israelites adopted. In these feasts we see another way in which biblical liturgy can impart depths to Christian living today.

Biblical liturgy kept humans right at home in the cosmos or material world where God had placed them to work out their eternal glory. It gradually became apparent to the Israelites that God fulfilled his promises and renewed the great redemptive acts of history by blessing them with the gifts of nature: with sun, rain, land and crops; with husband, wife and children. As a result, when the feast of the Pasch commemorated the exodus out of Egypt, the worshippers also thanked God for the creation of the world and for the gift of the barley harvest. In bringing the Israelites out of Egypt God made them, as he himself had confessed, "my special possession, dearer to me than all other people" (Ex 19:5).

God, of course, would always live up to his obligations which he had undertaken to create and protect his people. The barley harvest was considered a partial fulfillment of these divine commitments and its festival was joined to the feast of the Pasch. Pentecost, which liturgically renewed the giving of the law on Mount Sinai, looked upon the wheat harvest as a blessing of the law upon obedient Israel. The feast of Tabernacles originally celebrated God's care of his people in the desert and the conquest of the land; later it included the final harvest festival of the month of *Tishri* (September-October).

This aspect of biblical religion, attributing the gifts of nature to God's extraordinary, redemptive acts, makes them see the universe in a different way. Creation was not viewed as an exhibition of divine power but as a means of renewing the great acts of salvation. To leave a spiritual Egypt of sin and to enter a spiritual promised land of joy—such was the meaning of the Pasch. Through its celebration, therefore, the Israelites were experiencing the creation of a new heaven and a new earth. The liturgy possessed a "grace" by which this cosmos was already in the process of being established. Each present joy was a taste of the final messianic joy.

The liturgy, consequently, urged the Israelites to fulfill the divine command of controlling, using and enjoying all the material gifts of the world. Technological and scientific progress became an act of obedience to this divine command and manifested the glory of the risen Christ. Redemption theology, or passion-resurrection theology, of the New Testament continues this biblical tradition into our own day. According to the Bible, God will not destroy the universe but transform it. When the human family is completely transformed and redeemed then, as St. Paul wrote in Romans, the earth will no longer groan in travail.

The same power of love and obedience which raised Jesus from the dead will infuse new life into all who belong to Christ. Through the faithful, this transforming power will re-create the world. This power is at work even now. Miracles, which wondrously renew the weakness of nature and consecrate it totally to God's service and man's and woman's joy, are one part of this resurrection theology; another part is the role of Catholic hospitals and social services; still another, the vocation of parents, giving and sustaining life in the home. Nowhere is this eschatological moment more continuously and fully achieved than in the liturgy where everything material is lifted to the new grandeur for divine glory and human joy.

CONCLUSION

Who, then, is the person possessed of biblical depth? One who sinks the roots of the mind deep into the great, redemptive acts of the past, not to live in the past but to re-live the spirit of the past in the present moment. If we look continually to the liturgy, then doctrine will be seen, not as a life of Israel or a life of Christ, but as life *in* Israel and life *in* Christ. The great redemptive moments of the Bible are re-lived, and in this actualization of the past, God's promises of joy and glory are gradually fulfilled. In their fulfillment, the Christian is tasting even now the great joys of the eschatological age.

The liturgy opens the ages and includes every human reaction; it draws prayers and proclamations from the fullest human experience. Liturgical background, therefore, gives a depth of oneness with Christ's brethren everywhere. Only by being one with all in Christ can Christians truly distinguish the body of Christ. The liturgy can make them feel at home on this earth. Their roots are deep in every square foot of reality. By their own life in Christ, they are able to transform the universe into the new heaven and the new earth, the new creation of the risen Christ. This is the renewal, the *aggiornamento*, sought by Pope John XXIII.

Chapter Nine
Baptism: New Life

The first epistle of Peter makes abundantly clear that liturgy images life. Very respectable scholars have advanced the opinion that this epistle is no epistle or letter at all, but rather the baptismal ritual of the apostolic Church. However, according to the account, the setting of the ritual never remained long within the sanctuary. Church walls quickly vanished and the sidewalks of daily living stretched out before the early Christians. And then all walks of life converged again upon the place of worship, particularly upon the baptismal font. Today the lives of modern Christians pass through scenes contemporaneous with the apostle Peter. They too extend through ways familiar to Old Testament times, and then return to the last, suffering journey of Jesus upon earth.

How is it that this epistle can present the liturgy against a background so teeming with life? The question is especially important with regard to the liturgy of baptism. We must momentarily separate what St. Peter so richly combined at every step: the sufferings and the glory of Jesus; the trials and the triumphs of the Christian; the power of baptism in uniting Jesus and the Christian; divine life shared through a common life-blood.

According to the story, *Quo Vadis*, tears wore a groove in Peter's face. Historians dismiss that as legendary, but what cannot be doubted is the unmistakable stain of tears marking the pages of Peter's first epistle. Peter's thoughts in this letter are constantly returning to the sufferings of Jesus, his spirit is continually retracing the way of the cross. He never allowed that moment to blur, the moment when he heard the cock crow. "The Lord turned around and looked at Peter . . . He [Peter] went out and wept

bitterly" (Lk 22:61-62). He never ceased mourning that disgrace-
ful moment, but it was this very penitence which led Peter back
to his Redeemer. Peter made reparation by thinking continually
of the sufferings of Jesus. He himself possessed the spirit which
he ascribed to the Old Testament prophets, except that while they
looked ahead hopefully, he must look back sorrowfully.

We must not, however, over-emphasize Peter's pre-occupation
with the past; what happened once could be found again in the
liturgy. Peter appreciated the liturgical renewal of the past. His
appreciation, though at variance with St. Paul's style, was quite
similar to St. John's. Peter recalled the historical traditions about
the life, deeds and words of Jesus. It would seem that Peter could
not pull his eyes away from the scene in which he had deserted
Jesus. Twelve times within the space of five short chapters he
makes use of the *paschein* (to suffer), four times of the noun-
form *pathema* (suffering). This recurrence is very significant
when we recall that the verb is found only eleven more times in
the entire New Testament, the noun in only ten other places.

Without effort, Peter obeyed the summons directed to the
early Christians: "Christ suffered for you . . . and left an example
to have you follow in his footsteps" (2:21). Peter, however, made
his way to his suffering Jesus not only by silent prayer, but even
more persuasively by the example of his fellow Christians. It is
usually some problem or complaint within the Christian community which induced Peter to remember his Lord. Are domestic
servants bitter or moody over the severe attitude of their master?
They must think of Jesus, who, when he was reviled, did not
revile, when he suffered, did not threaten, and so they will return
to the shepherd and guardian of their souls (see 2:18, 23, 25).

When Peter wrote to his fellow Christians—"fellow priests,"
as he called them (5:1)—he was not so much instructing as reassur-
ing them. He truly admired the heroic endurance of these men
and women who were made "sorrowful by various trials" (1:6).
In fact, he seems to have felt a secret reaction of envy, poignancy
and delight when he addressed these words to them: "Although
you have never seen him you love him, and without seeing you
now believe in him, and rejoice with inexpressible joy touched

with glory" (1:8). Peter registers surprise at the temper of their faith (1:7) by using a special kind of negative. Peter did not employ the negative ordinarily found in participial clauses, but another kind of negative. It would seem that his words suddenly broke loose after long hesitation. The phrase should be translated, "*Never at any time* having seen him . . ." A quick reversal then follows: "still, you love him, and you exult with a joy too great for words." We can read between the lines this silent, wistful admission by Peter: "I saw him! In fact, I lived with him, conversed with him, became his confidant, and yet I failed him. I deserted him when he most needed me. But you have never seen him at any time, still, you love him . . ."

Peter again writes, "Do not be surprised, beloved, that a trial by fire is occurring in your midst . . . Rejoice instead in the measure that you share Christ's sufferings" (4:12-13). Christ is living again in the Christian community, so that the baptism experience is none other than a continuation of Jesus' own sufferings. Christians, therefore, are hallowing the Lord Christ in their hearts (3:15) whenever they display themselves "like-minded, sympathetic, loving toward one another, kindly disposed, and humble. Do not return evil for evil, or insult for insult. Return a blessing instead" (3:8-9).

Peter, privileged to work among Christians who lived in Christ, gained more for himself than he gave to them. He was able to make reparation for his desertion of the dying Jesus; by ministering to Christ, suffering, dying and rising triumphantly in the brethren, Peter can once more lay claim to that most honorable boast, of being a "witness to Christ's sufferings" (5:1). This inestimable grace was mediated to Peter through the Christian community; the prince of the apostles, therefore, addresses them as his "fellow priests" (5:1).

A closer study of Peter's expression "the sufferings of Christ" reveals a special nuance or shade of meaning. The Greek words penned by Peter (*ta eis Christon pathēmata*) refer to sufferings which lead to Christ or which consecrate one to Christ. In his classic commentary on Peter's epistle, Professor G. E. Selwyn translates the phrase: "the sufferings of the Christward road."

Charity and the apostolate involved Peter closely and admiringly in the lives of his flock and made him a witness of the suffering Jesus. Peter thus repaired his sin of denying and deserting the Lord. Was this the reason why he was moved to write those unforgettable lines: "Above all, let your love for one another be constant, for love covers a multitude of sins" (4:8)?

SYMBOLISM WITHIN LIFE AND LITURGY

Modern scriptural scholarship has discovered liturgical nuances in Peter's first epistle. Perhaps we should say, rediscovered, for it is now evident that Melito of Sardis (around A.D. 170), in a *Homily on the Passion,* and Hippolytus of Rome (around A.D. 200), in the *Apostolic Constitution,* explain Peter's use of the Greek *pasch-ein* (to suffer) as a reference to the Jewish Pasch, re-enacted in the Christian Eucharist. Biblical research is not only recognizing eucharistic references in the epistle, but it is uncovering vestiges, if not whole sections, of an ancient baptismal liturgy in the New Testament book. There is no agreement on details.

Minute precision over details, however, is probably over-demanding of the text. It is also over-taxing the Church's memory, so hazy about the details of the apostolic liturgy. At the very least, however, the epistle indicates many liturgical currents flowing through it. Just as its first formulation helped St. Peter, a further investigation of its liturgical depth will strengthen us. The meaning of baptism will indicate the meaning of life. The liturgy will enable us to return to our brethren and see in them the sufferings of Christ. We will then be prepared to find Christ more fully in the common liturgical celebration. Liturgy, like life, is composed of many symbols, but it is preparing for that moment when symbolism disappears and we are swept into ". . . praise, glory, and honor, when Jesus Christ appears" (1:7).

The epistle contains many references to the sacrament of baptism, along with an urgent exhortation to receive its sacramental benefits right now. The baptismal motifs must be investigated more fully. On nine different occasions the epistle actualized the mystery of redemption with the word "now"; we are involved right this moment in the sacred ceremony of baptism and thereby in the sufferings and resurrection of Jesus. "You are *now* saved," Peter writes, "by a baptismal bath . . . through the resurrection of Jesus Christ" (3:21). In the larger setting of this verse we are not only told of the water of Noah's flood, washing the world clean as does "its counterpart, baptism," but we read that Christ, after being put to death, "preached to the spirits of those who were in prison."

The interpretation of this last text has reference to the cross. Clement of Alexandria, Origen and Gregory of Nazianzus held out for some kind of conversion granted to the damned. An easier and certainly more orthodox explanation draws upon the baptismal symbolism. Following the thought of St. Paul in his epistle to Peter's converts at Rome, we can say that the catechumen, who strips off his clothes and walks down into the large baptismal font, re-enacts the passion and death of Jesus. Dying with Christ to sin, he is buried or imprisoned with Jesus (see Rm 6:3-11). As the baptismal words are pronounced over the submerged or buried candidate, it can be said that Christ is preaching to the spirit of one in prison, and by the power of his word engendering a new life within him.

This baptismal doctrine, it should be noted, is still surrounded with the reality of daily trials (3:16). If sacramental symbolism is to avoid the charge of superstition, it must always be a striking reminder and a strong container of real life. The sorrows which inevitably accompany Christian living also bury one in the death of Christ, but with and through Christ a new life rises within the baptized.

Another reference to baptism, this time more indirect but not so illusive, occurs in 1:22-23. Père Boismard (1956) prefers to call this section (up to 2:10) a post-baptismal homily, during which the celebrant explains baptism as a new birth through the word of God. Professors Cross (1954) and Preisker (1951) judged this section to follow immediately upon the pouring of water and the conferring of the sacrament. The Greek text is lapidary, the

words are blocked together like heavy chunks of marble, but the
theme of new life and of sincere love emerges in a simple and
appealing way:

> . . . you have purified [consecrated] your-
> selves for a genuine love of your brothers;
> therefore, love one another constantly from
> the heart. Your rebirth has come, not from
> a destructible but from indestructible seed,
> through the living and enduring word of God.

EFFECTS OF BAPTISM

An adequate explanation would involve many intricacies of
Greek grammar; through the various tones and tenses of the verb,
the Greek language says pithily what must be elaborately paraphrased in an English translation. The cleansing of the soul was
completed in a single moment, but its effects continue to be felt
ever afterwards. These conditions correspond very closely with
what has developed into the Christian doctrine of baptism. The
one act of baptism perfectly purifies the soul, but the Christian
must now live continuously within a Christian family. The effects
of baptism are felt primarily in a bond of love. In fact, there
is only one principal verb in the entire series, namely, "love
one another intensely." As Ceslaus Spicq points out in his remarks
on this verse, love is not a matter of precept but the effect of life
flowing from the fact of baptism.

While charity, according to St. Peter, is the primary effect of
baptism, faith or obedience to the truth is the most important
preparation. Faith itself purifies the soul, but this faith is not to be
considered an inherent knowledge of the truths of faith; it is,
rather, a disposition of humility and surrender. As St. Peter explains from the prophecy of Second Isaiah, faith is the realization
that:

> All flesh [that is, every human being
> without Christ] is as grass,
> and its glory [that is, its power

to achieve joy and salvation]
is as the flower of the field.
The grass withers, and the flower falls—
but the word of the Lord abides
forever (1:24; Is 40:6-8).

Faith, therefore, is that moment when a weak and sinful soul realizes through the preaching of the Gospel that God is near and will cleanse and strengthen it through the waters of baptism. This combination of humble contrition and obedient surrender on the part of man or woman, of the illuminating word and the cleansing water on God's part, is found in the Rule Book or *Manual of Discipline* of the Qumran covenanters. We read in this important document: "It is by the holy spirit of the community in his truth, that he [a member] can be cleansed from all his sins. It is by an upright and humble spirit that his sin can be atoned. It is by humiliating himself under all God's ordinances, that his flesh can be cleansed, by sprinkling with water of purification, and by sanctifying himself with water of purity" (1 QS 3:7-9).

It will be noticed that Qumran theology deftly combined the spirit within the community with the spirit active in "baptism"; obedience to God's truth with the cleansing power of water; humble need, with reception of the holy spirit. The background of Palestinian practice at Qumran and the doctrine of Christian baptism at Rome fill in the larger context of Peter's first epistle and help us to recognize elements of an early baptismal liturgy in its words. In each instance there is a convergence of faith, the word, purification or trial through water, a new life in charity.

The ceremony of baptism is reflected in still other features of First Peter. Obedience, love and sonship, stressed here by the prince of the apostles, remind us of Jesus' own baptism in the River Jordan. This act was undergone in obedience to the Father's will (Mt 3:15), was accompanied by the voice declaring Jesus to be "my beloved Son," and was intended to inaugurate Jesus' public ministry and the world's redemption. *"Lay aside* all malice . . . Crave, as newborn babes, pure spiritual milk"* (2:1-2). These words of St. Peter are not only an instruction to the newly baptized but actually contain the Greek word which later became a technical term at the baptismal ceremony, to "lay aside" or to "renounce" Satan.

The Trinitarian formula is repeated on several occasions (1:1-2; 1:3-12; 4:13-15). None of these references contain the actual formula of baptism, as in Matthew 28:18-20, but each develops the fuller meaning of the sacrament. The opening verses explain that the Christian vocation is:

> *according to the foreknowledge of God the Father*
> —the essential condition for baptism is
> to be called by God—
> *consecrated by the Spirit*
> —here we are reminded of the instrument
> and the ambient of the new life—
> *to a life of obedience to Jesus Christ and purification with his blood.*
> —one is henceforth absorbed into Christ
> and shares his obedient sonship.

The phrase "purification with his blood" recalls for Christians the scene of Calvary or of the Last Supper. St. Peter certainly includes these two moments of Christ's life within the scope of his words, but in them he also associates the blood of Christ with the theology of baptism. Because of his Jewish rearing, Peter quickly passes from the idea of life to that of life-blood. Throughout the Jewish Scriptures, blood indicated life, and because life belonged to God, blood could never be consumed. The sprinkling of blood upon any person was almost considered grafting that person onto God (Lv 17:11; 8:23; 9:22-24). The thought of such a person would henceforth be so motivated by divine energy that his words could be called the judgment of God.

Peter's thought moves back and forth from life and blood. He has told the early Christians that "you have been reborn." This new life, received in baptism, is none other than the vitalizing presence of the risen Christ. For instance, we read in another passage, highly liturgical in style and undoubtedly a portion of an early Christian hymn:

> Blessed be the God and Father of our Lord
> Jesus Christ,
> according to his abundant mercy,
> having begotten us [to a new life]
> [consecrated] to living hope
> [and] through the resurrection of Jesus
> Christ from the dead,
> to an inheritance, incorruptible and un-
> defiled and unfading (1:3-4).

God is blessed, because right at this moment his glorious re-demptive presence is manifest by new life within the believer. The baptized Christian bears within himself the living hope and the incorruptible inheritance of a heavenly existence. Just as the resurrection suffused a new life and a wondrous glory through the sacred humanity of Jesus, the same power is already at work within each baptized person. The assurance of sharing God's life quickly suggests the notion of blood. St. Peter allows the baptis-mal scene to widen and includes the covenant sacrifice and the paschal liturgy.

Obedience to the law and the sprinkling of blood recall the ceremony first enacted by Moses at Mount Sinai and later re-enac-ted in the liturgical renewal of the covenant at every Jewish Pen-tecost. We read in the book of Exodus: "Taking the book of the covenant, he [Moses] read it aloud to the people, who answered, 'All that the Lord had said, we will heed and do.' Then he took the blood [half of which had already been splashed on the altar] and sprinkled it on the people, saying, 'This is the blood of the covenant, which the Lord has made with you in accordance with all these words of his' " (Ex 24:7-8). The flow of blood between the altar and the people, between God and the nation, symbolized a community of life. Just as blood establishes a *one*-ness as it flows between the various parts of the same body or as it is shared through birth by different members of the same family, likewise, the blood ritual of Old Testament times symbolized a deeper, more mystic, but still very real bond of life between God and Israel.

Baptism constituted the Christian's blood ritual of the covenant. It sealed a community of life between God and the Christian. Humble obedience to the word of God prepared the catechumen for the cleansing, life-giving power of water and the word. In order to appreciate the full meaning of baptism, St. Peter refers to another blood ritual, the sacrifice of the paschal lamb. He leads up to this dramatic act of Old Testament faith, now encompassed within Christian baptism and the Eucharist, by insisting upon obedience and by promising a divine life. The steps of his thinking deserve attention.

> *so gird up the loins of your understanding*
> —just as the Israelites on leaving Egypt
> lifted up their long flowing robes and girded
> themselves at the waist, so as to march to
> the promised land without entangling
> encumbrances—
> *live soberly*
> —that is, renounce worldly lusts—
> *set all your hope on the gift to be conferred*
> *on you when Jesus Christ appears*
> —he is your Promised Land (1:13).

St. Peter then proceeds to advise the candidate for baptism: "You know that you were redeemed from the vain manner of life handed down from your fathers, not with perishable things, with silver or gold, but with the precious blood of Christ, as of a lamb without blemish and without spot. Foreknown, indeed, before the foundation of the world, he has been manifested in the last times for your sakes" (1:18-20). Just as in Egypt during the days of Moses, the blood of the lamb, sprinkled on the doorposts and lintels of the Israelites' homes, preserved God's beloved first born from death and inaugurated the march to the promised land, baptism begets new life, making the candidate God's beloved child and placing him at once within the heavenly existence of the risen Jesus.

Joy, life and fulfillment accompany baptism as they did the departure of the Israelites from Egypt. After speaking of Christ's blood, St. Peter writes: "It is through him that you are believers in God, the God who raised him from the dead and gave him glory. Your faith and hope, then, are centered in God" (1:21). These lines clearly imply, especially in their Greek form, that God is *now* raising Jesus from the dead, is *now* manifesting the glorious, redemptive presence of Jesus *at this moment* in a Christian who is being born to a life thoroughly Godward.

The blood of Jesus included more than the notions of joy and happiness. Redemption was certainly a life-begetting act, but to be a Christian implied more than the joyful experience of being conceived and born by the power of the divine word and the pouring of water. Baptism did not immediately waft the Christian into heaven; it left him in the midst of a hostile world, where even his own flesh contrived against him. Just as Christ could live only by battling unto death against pride, jealousy, hatred and intrigue, so the Christian must follow Christ's footsteps, courageously accepting the full consequences of life in God. Blood in Christ's case implied sorrow and death. Jesus had to put to death the weakness of the flesh and so transform his flesh into his glorious, risen body. This death resulted from the mighty surge of life (blood) battling every weakness and in death conquering the last obstacle.

Baptism warns Christians that if they share the same life, they must face the same struggle of life unto death, so that life may be eternally victorious. Christianity entails a death to disobedience and everything sinful, and this aspect was taught by St. Peter when he referred to Christ's precious blood. As a Christian struggles against sin and discouragement, in the words of St. Peter, he is making a "revelation of Jesus Christ." This statement is true, because the final victory and "goal of . . . faith" (1:9) are through the power of Christ's blood (that is, his life) now throbbing within the baptized person. Because Christ alone bestows the courage to follow the austere pilgrim existence of Christianity, every

Christian's endurance of suffering is a revelation of Jesus Christ living in him.

"Redeemed by the precious blood of Christ"—this phrase, drawn from the baptismal liturgy of the apostolic Church, always maintained its primary meaning of *life*. With Christ, all Christians shared one "life-blood" in God. On earth, however, this life was sustained amidst the desert austerities of opposition, suffering and even physical death. For Christ to share his life with us and be one with us, he had to suffer and die like ourselves, and so put to death all human obstacles to life. His followers must bravely face the same struggle. For this reason, St. Peter's expression, "redeemed by the precious blood of Christ," reminded Christians of sorrow and death, but never in a frustrating and gloomy way. Christ's death was a burst of life, overcoming the last obstruction to the full union of the human person with God. Baptism inaugurates a life which daily moves forward to a battle, confident that in each sorrow there is a more vigorous expression of the presence of the risen Jesus.

Because baptism engenders life and because life is pursued in the hostile surroundings of the world, St. Peter constantly returns to the difficulties and sorrows of daily existence. The liturgy forces the Christian to face up to the practical meaning of life. As Christians live in Christ, their sufferings become a Christward road. Pain reveals, in fact, the presence of Jesus crucified. It enables Christians, after any sinful betrayal of Jesus, to find their way back to the cross, and with Peter to become once again a witness to the sufferings of Christ. This witnessing, as Peter immediately adds, makes Christians sharers "in the glory that is to be revealed" (5:1). They are back again at the moment of baptism, this time with greater understanding and fuller appreciation. The life of the risen Savior is being received ever more completely. Christians are being vitalized always more richly with the life-giving blood of Jesus.

St. Peter concludes his baptismal liturgy with these words of an ancient Christian hymn:

The God of all grace, who called you to

his everlasting glory in Christ, will
himself restore, confirm, strengthen, and
establish those who have suffered a little
while. Dominion be his throughout the ages!
Amen (5:10-11).

Chapter Ten
Eucharist: Symbol of Life and Death

The Holy Eucharist is the bread of life, but inscribed upon it is a sign of death. The first Christians were not for a moment robbed of the memory of our Lord's sufferings even though the crucifix did not receive definitive artistic form until the sixth century. In the Eucharist, they found the most graphic representation of the sacrifice of Calvary. It is also interesting to note that the Romans referred to the sacrificial animal slaughtered in their own sacred ceremonies as *hostia*.

It was always the constant concern of the Church to associate closely the life-giving bread of holy communion with Christ's sacrificial death. Unfortunately, it is easy to forget that the bread received at our altars is sacrificial food. In order to appreciate the bread of life as such, attention must be directed to the scriptural theme of death and life. This theme is difficult to grasp, but its notion is essential to understanding the doctrine of the Eucharist.

There is not an exact time sequence that life comes first and then death, or that a person must die before he can live, although some scriptural texts may give this impression: "Whoever loses his life for my sake, will save it" (Lk 9:24); ". . . we were buried with him, so that . . . we too might live a new life" (Rm 6:4). Actually, death and life exist together like soldiers in mortal combat. When a person is succumbing to the blows of death, life is bursting forth. St. Paul writes: "I face death every day" (1 Cor 15:31). Yet, each "death" gives the Apostle greater right to exclaim: "The life I live now is not my own; Christ is living in me" (Gal 2:20).

There is always a war of elements when light strikes darkness, when hot air blasts against a pocket of cold air, when goodness confronts evil. Could anything take place when the light of God's Word appeared in this shadow of death? How could the darkness comprehend it? Christ's entire life was carried forward under the momentum of executing the will of his heavenly Father. The divine will was his life-giving food, but not to be eaten in peace. Jesus is pitted against people who do the works of their father, the devil. What happens when a man so selfless that he has nowhere to lay his head is sent into a world governed by the materialistic?

Can a religion of spirit and truth, which finds its greatness in interior virtue rather than in the first places at banquet tables, remain unmolested when it meets the self-canonized fraud? How long will a person survive who practices heroic love of enemies, when those enemies hate with a deadly hate? Christ solemnly explained that is why he came—to die! Struggle must ensue, when life meets the darkness of death in sin.

Yet, death did not destroy life but made it possible for this life to emerge more active and glorious. At no moment was Jesus more alive than when he was dying. His cry from the cross that it was finished was a triumphant declaration that here is the perfect expression of heroic obedience to the Father's will, of courageous attack on sin; most of all, of consummate charity for us. Yes, to die is to live.

This scriptural law of life and death must regulate the gift of life in the Eucharist. The fullness of life can come only through a death-inflicting sacrifice. To symbolize life, the Eucharist must bear the sign of Christ's death, for it was through and in the sacrifice of Calvary that Jesus was lifted up to the glory of heavenly life. The Eucharist must bring to mind that moment when Christ hung dying upon the cross. His mission of sending the Spirit of life to his followers began with his death. As the sacred symbol of the passion, the Eucharist plants in human hearts the cross of Jesus, in order that dying with Christ each one may participate in his heavenly life. We are ready to understand more clearly the linking of the eucharistic bread of life with the sacrifice of the cross if we are attentive to the scriptural association of these two aspects.

In clear and forceful words, Christ announces, "I myself am

the living bread" (Jn 6:51). In almost the same breath he adds that the Eucharist is the bread of death—"If you do not eat the flesh of the Son of Man and drink his blood, you have no life in you" (Jn 6:53). How can anyone eat flesh and drink blood, unless what they are eating and drinking has first been killed? The picture is disturbing, but our Lord insists that it is true. When he says plainly that this bread is "my flesh for the life of the world," his words carry the deeper meaning: here is my flesh laid down in sacrifice for the salvation of all humankind. The eucharistic sacrament is a mystery of faith. This bread will be a symbol and a mystic renewal of something in the face of which we stand in awe.

Christ gives a further explanation when he fulfills this promise of the bread of life. As he sits with his apostles at the Last Supper, the night on which he is to be betrayed, he makes his life-giving death an ever-present reality for all ages. Time with its past and future becomes an eternal present. Jesus is involved in the very act of delivering his body over to death and of shedding his blood in sacrifice. "This is my body to be given for you . . . my blood which will be shed" (Lk 22:19-20).

The earliest account of the institution of the bread of life is explicit in stressing the sacrificial character of the bread. Writing little more than twenty years after the first Holy Thursday, St. Paul told the Corinthians: "Every time, then, you eat this bread and drink the cup, you proclaim the death of the Lord until he comes" (1 Cor 11:26). The Eucharist places each Christian upon Calvary. Dying with Christ, the worshipper puts sin to death. That death is an heroic affirmation of life in all its fullness. Like Christ, the Christian is never more alive than when he dies at the moment of holy communion that Christ may live in him.

FOOD FROM THE SACRIFICIAL ALTAR

In the first three centuries of Christianity, everyone present at the renewal of the sacrifice of the cross partook of the sacrificial food. The practice of many communities directed each worshipper to approach the altar of sacrifice and receive the sacri-

ficial food in outstretched hands. After eating part of the consecrated bread the faithful were allowed to take home whatever
remained. However, even this privilege of private communion
at home did not rob the sacrament of its sacrificial character. The
Eucharist remained the sign of the cross, for this sacred food was
the Christian's abiding remembrance of Christ's death and a repeated participation in his sacrifice.

The pagan neighbors had a similar practice which transformed
their family meal into an act of religion. Meat purchased at the
market was considered sacrificial food. Before the animals were
sacrificed, certain ritualistic observances dedicated the animal to
the pagan gods. St. Paul faced this situation in 1 Corinthians
10:23-30. To eat such meat even at home was to become partakers
"of the table of devils." St. Paul asks: "Are not they who eat of
the sacrifices partakers of the altar?" However, "we have an altar
from which those who serve the tabernacle have no right to eat"
(Heb 13:10). From the altar of immolation the Christians received
their sacred food. The bread of life was Jesus' body and blood,
laid down in sacrifice. To the extent that sinful desires are crucified and destroyed, the heavenly life of Christ is imparted to the
Christians by the Holy Eucharist.

The tradition uniting sacrifice and sacrament continues in the
prescription of the Holy Week ritual that holy communion be
received only during the Mass of the Lord's Supper. At first, this
restriction may strike us as very unreasonable. Formerly holy
communion was distributed at frequent intervals before morning
Mass. But during Holy Week especially, the Church wants us
to be very conscious of the sign of the cross upon the eucharistic
food—with the same kind of awareness as Christ had on the first
Holy Thursday. As Christians gather at night in their own "upper
room" for the liturgical reenactment of the Last Supper, they are
to have one heart with the suffering heart of Jesus. With Christ
they are reliving his last moments on earth. To partake of the
sacrifice is much more than an external action. The bread of life
stirs up a strong desire to become as like as possible to Christ
in his grievous sufferings.

In order to understand better the actions and the words of

Christ in giving us the Eucharist as sacrificial food, the Old Testament is our "tutor in Christ." The ritual of the Jewish temple prepared for the Christian liturgy: "This is a symbol of the present time . . . imposed until the time of the new order" (Heb 9:9-10). The Pasch is certainly a type of Christ's death on the cross and of the Eucharist. And though it may be difficult to decide whether the typical sense can be verified in each detail of the paschal meal, the New Testament tradition consistently inserts the account of the holy Eucharist into the general context of the Pasch. These repeated allusions to the Pasch are like variations of a theme in a symphony. They provide a greater richness to our understanding of the eucharistic mystery.

In the days of Christ the words *passover*, *pasch* and *unleavened bread* were used without distinction. The three synoptic Gospels begin their account of the Eucharist with a reference to the feast of the unleavened bread. We read in St. Luke: "The feast of the unleavened bread known as the Passover was drawing near . . ." (22:1). St. John opens the public life of Christ with John the Baptist's announcement: "Look! There is the lamb of God, who takes away the sin of the world" (1:29). He again deftly touches upon the memory of the paschal ceremony before relating the miracle of the multiplication of the five barley loaves and the two fishes and the subsequent eucharistic discourse: "The Jewish feast of Passover was near" (6:4). The account of the Last Supper is introduced in St. John's Gospel with a brief but significant remark: "Before the feast of the Passover, Jesus realized that the hour had come for him to pass from this world . . ." (13:1). St. John concludes his passion narrative with another reference to the paschal lamb: "These events took place for the fulfillment of Scripture: 'Break none of his bones' " (19:36).

The mere mention of the Pasch should remind us, as it did the early Christians, of all the particulars of this holiest of nights. At the beginning of the paschal meal a Jewish child at table asks the father: "What does this rite of yours mean?" Each holy communion should draw forth a similar question from the Christian, since the bread of life is received in the midst of a paschal sacrifice. The Mosaic law prescribed the order of ceremony for this "night of vigil for the Lord." Its details can teach Christians the deeper meaning of their paschal meal. These details are outlined carefully in chapter 12 of Exodus.

This association with the paschal celebration reveals the full meaning of our eucharistic ceremony. Jesus is the lamb of God, acclaimed as such by John the Baptist and by the Baptist's disciple, John the Evangelist, who refers twenty-eight times to the lamb in Revelation. Also, in Hebrews and in First Peter we are told that Christ, our paschal lamb, "through the eternal spirit offered himself up unblemished to God" (Heb 9:14), for "you were delivered . . . not by any diminishable sum of silver or gold, but by Christ's blood beyond all price, the blood of a spotless unblemished lamb" (1 P 1:18-19). Our Egypt of sin and oppression is dead and past. Like the Israelites we begin a new life, as we eat the bread of life.

After the slaughter of the paschal lamb and the sprinkling of its blood, the ancient Jewish family prepared for the sacrificial banquet. The lamb was roasted and served with unleavened bread, wine, bitter herbs and wild lettuce. The family took part as though ready to set out on a journey: with long oriental robes tucked up, with sandals on their feet and with staff in hand. The bitter herbs were a final farewell to the heavy misery and dark discouragement of the Egyptian slavery. They were about to set out on the journey towards the promised land of Palestine.

Christians also sit down at the table of the Lord to eat their sacrificial meal. Their lamb has been slaughtered, and its blood has been sprinkled across the lintels of their hearts. As the Christians look at the table set before them, the cry of John the Baptist echoes in their hearts, with tones of sorrowing, grateful love: "Look! There is the lamb of God, who takes away the sin of the world!" Not only is Christ their paschal lamb: he is likewise their bitter herbs. Christians could never completely forget the bitter taste of sin and its crushing burden of discouragement, even though Christ had taken all this bitterness upon himself. "For our sakes God made him who did not know sin to be sin" (2 Cor 5:21). Engraved across our paschal meal is the sign of the cross. The Jews had been told, "This shall be a memorial feast for you."

Christians commemorate the memorial of the passion and death, the price of their liberation from the Egyptian slavery of sin.

As they eat this sacrificial food, St. Peter admonishes them to "gird up the loins of your [their] understanding" (1 P 1:13). Christ is food for the long, wearisome journey, traveled "in darkness and in the shadow of death." Like Elijah in the desert of Sinai, Christians must rise from the table and march in the strength of this food to a promised land where in joy eternal they will celebrate the marriage supper of the lamb. From the bread of life they will absorb the stamina to withstand the sorrows of life and the burning heat of their "Sinai desert." They must die daily to sin and imperfection and rise to newness of life in Jesus Christ. The bread of life, therefore, is really the bread of death to every form of sin and human weakness. The Eucharist inscribes the sign of the cross upon the souls of Christians, so that each is entitled to exclaim, "I bear the brand marks of Jesus in my body" (Gal 6:17).

The Christian family, gathered around the sacrificial banquet, is a "chosen race, a royal priesthood, a holy nation, a people he claims for his own" (1 P 2:9). St. Peter wrote, in a context redolent of the paschal ceremony, ". . . become holy yourselves in every aspect of your conduct, after the likeness of the holy One who called you" (1 P 1:16). This holy people is sanctified by the spirit of charity. "Because the loaf of bread is one, we though many we are, are one body, for we all partake of the one loaf" (1 Cor 10:17).

This lamb, standing as if slain before the eyes of those who pierced him by their sins, must be wholly consumed. The sacrifice will continue until the last fragment has been eaten. Each holy communion is a continuation of the paschal sacrifice. And if we are asked what this rite means, we can reply, "This is the Passover sacrifice of the Lord." The bread of life is the food of love because the sign of redemptive death is engraved upon it. Although the first Christians did not place a crucifix above their altar, they recognized the sign of the cross in the Eucharist. They lived the words of St. Paul, "Everytime, then, you eat this bread and drink this cup, you proclaim the death of the Lord until he comes."

HOLY EUCHARIST: SYMBOL OF GLORY

On Easter morning the sacred body of Jesus, marked with the scars of the nails and lance, rose triumphantly from the dead. His glorious resurrection illuminated the eucharistic sign of the cross with joy, peace and victory. The silence, born of Good Friday's sorrow, was quickly driven out by the bells of Easter Sunday morning. That the mourning over Christ's death was cut this short never made the early Christians feel ill at ease. St. Paul had written, "Christ our passover has been sacrificed. Let us celebrate the feast . . ." (1 Cor 5:7-8).

In this same spirit of joyful sorrow and sorrowing joy an Old Testament prophet, Zechariah, had announced the day of the Lord. At first, his words reverberated like victorious bells, tumultuously ringing out their news: *Haec dies*—"that day which the Lord has made." Zechariah repeatedly proclaims the triumph of God "on that day." However, the peal of bells stopped without warning, and the toll of single, mournful strokes began as he said, "In that day I will pour out . . . a spirit of grace and petition; and they shall look at him whom they have thrust through, and they shall mourn for him as one mourns for an only son" (Zc 12:10). Then, just as suddenly, sorrow again turned into joy and Jerusalem was described as the center of God's paradise on earth, "In that day living waters shall go forth from Jerusalem" (see Zc 12-14).

This theme of sorrow and joy, of death and life, meets us on almost every page of the Bible. The quick interchange of darkness and light in biblical thought leads us to fuller understanding of the mystery of the Eucharist. God is not the God of the dead, but of the living, for all are alive in him. The institution of the Eucharist, as related in St. Luke's passion-resurrection narrative, begins with the darkness of the agony in the garden but closes on a different tone: "He left them and was taken up to heaven. They fell down to do him reverence, then returned to Jerusalem filled with joy" (Lk 24:51-52). Time slows down to a dead halt, and at once eternity emerges: "You put to death the Author of life. But God raised him from the dead" (Ac 3:15). The words "lifted up" or "raised" technically mean to be swept up to victory and glory. It is used often in relation to Christ's ascent to the cross. "And I, once I am lifted up from the earth, will draw all men to myself."

The cross provides a means of journeying upward to heavenly glory. The darkness of Calvary is only for a moment. In quick succession St. John writes: "It was *night*. Once Judas had left, Jesus said, 'Now is the Son of Man glorified and God is glorified in him'" (Jn 13:30-31). The Eucharist, drawing our thoughts upward to Jesus upon the cross, is simultaneously lifting us up to the heavenly triumph of the Son of Man. From all eternity the cross was surrounded with the glory of heaven. St. Peter confessed, "Into these matters angels long to search" (1 P 1:12). When "that day" of Christ's death was over, heavenly glory joyfully received his scarred, crucified, but triumphant body. Next to the throne of God is the "Lamb standing, a lamb that had been slain" whom thousands praise with a loud voice: "Worthy is the lamb that was slain to receive power and riches, wisdom and strength, honor and glory and praise!" (Rv 5:6, 12).

The glorious triumph of the lamb was foreseen by Christ as he sat with his disciples in the upper room and instituted the holy Eucharist as a memorial of his passion. The contrast of death and life, of darkness and light, appears in his final discourse. It was on the night in which he was betrayed, that Christ celebrated the feast of the Unleavened Bread. Christ was a lamb, not only doomed to death, but also destined for exaltation. "Now," Christ said of the hour of his passion, "is the Son of Man glorified" (Jn 13:31).

During the Last Supper, a mysterious atmosphere of joy and peace pervaded the room. The Eucharist was to be a memorial, not only of sorrow and death, but also of joy and life.

> If you truly loved me, you would rejoice . . .
> All this I tell you that my joy may be yours
> . . . Because I have had all this to say to you,
> you are overcome with grief. Yet I tell you
> the sober truth; it is much better for you

> that I go . . . you will weep and mourn but I
> shall see you again; then your hearts will
> rejoice with a joy no one can take from you
> (see Jn 14-16).

Years later when St. John was composing his Gospel, that "now" was a present reality. Christ had come. Through the gift of the Spirit, St. John tasted the joy unspeakable of the paschal mystery in each Mass and communion. The joy of the resurrection is evident throughout the entire fourth Gospel; each event of Christ's life, but especially his sacrifice on the cross and its memorial in the Eucharist, is seen transfigured with glory.

Jesus himself also looked upon the Last Supper as the foretaste of a heavenly banquet. Each synoptic Gospel echoes these words of Christ: "I will not eat again until it is fulfilled in the kingdom of God . . . I tell you from now on I will not drink of the fruit of the vine, until the coming of the reign of God" (Lk 22:16, 18). A study of the Jewish paschal meal helps to unravel the mystery of joy contained in the memorial of the passion. For the Jews, the feast of the pasch celebrated freedom from hardship and oppression; it pointed ahead with hope to a new life of enduring happiness. The greatest of these joys came from an anticipated union with God in peace and holiness. Fittingly enough, therefore, the Jews interrupted their paschal meal with the singing of the *Hallel* (Pss. 113-118). In the time of our Lord, Psalms 113-114 were chanted before the repast. Psalms 115-118 after it. The Last Supper began as the usual Jewish paschal meal. Earlier in the day Jesus had sent Peter and John, saying, "Go and prepare our passover supper for us" (Lk 22:8).

The first pasch in Jewish history was the day when God fulfilled his promise, "I will stretch out my hand, therefore, and smite Egypt by doing all kinds of wondrous deeds there" (Ex 3:20). "I have come down to rescue them [you] from the hands of the Egyptians" (Ex 3:8). Since Egypt had become a synonym for the state of sin, that day marked the beginning of Israelite independence from sin and its evil oppression. A new life, therefore, lay before the nation. The Lord said to Moses and Aaron in the land of Egypt, "This month shall stand at the head of your calendar; you shall reckon it the first month of the year" (Ex 12:2). The slave camps of Egypt opened wide their doors, and hearts were free to sing this song to the Lord, composed by Moses and Miriam:

> Who is like to you among the gods, O Lord?
> Who is like to you, magnificent in holiness?
> O terrible in renown, worker of wonders . . .
> In your mercy you led the people you
> redeemed (Ex 15:11, 13).

This "day of the Lord" signaled the beginning of a journey towards "a good and spacious land, a land flowing with milk and honey" (Ex 3:8). At the end of the exodus there awaited the Israelites the reward of life with God in the promised land of Palestine. The pasch was intended to provide the people with strength for this journey. They were instructed: "This is how you are to eat it: with your loins girt, sandals on your feet and your staff in hand, you shall eat like those *who are in flight*" (Ex 12:11). Stretching out before them was the triumphant way of the Lord. Each subsequent paschal meal vibrated with the spirit of the first pasch. The participants chanted these words, "This is the day the Lord has made." In the strength of the food eaten at the meal they were to rise up and march towards the fulfillment of all God's promises.

Wondrous deeds of God would accompany this new exodus from sin, which led towards the revelation of the glory of God. Reclining at the Last Supper, the apostles sang about making "straight in the wasteland a highway for our God" (Is 40:3). It was the melody flowing rhythmically from the heart of every Jew as he partook of the paschal lamb:

> The sea beheld and fled;
> The Jordan turned back.
> The mountains skipped like rams,
> The hills like the lambs of the flock
> (Ps 114:3-4).

The Last Supper was the last paschal meal ever to be celebrated under the Mosaic law and the first under the new dispensation. As our Lord reclined with his disciples in the upper room the mystery of the passion-resurrection began to be enacted. Christ could announce the inauguration of a new covenant, since the promises and hopes of the old covenant were now being accomplished. Here was the beginning of a new era. "This," He solemnly declared, "is my blood of the new covenant." The words of Christ sounded a trumpet call, summoning his followers to leave the oppression of sin and to march with him towards the promised land of heaven. As people in flight from sin, they must follow the way of the Lord which they find in the footsteps of him who is the way, the truth and the life.

With good reason Christ wanted the apostles to rejoice. This paschal meal was more than a commemorating of a past event—the exodus of their forefathers out of Egypt. They themselves were setting out on a journey. This was a day of independence, the start of a new life. Christ told his disciples, "I am indeed going to prepare a place for you, and then I shall come back to take you with me, that where I am you also may be. You know the way that leads where I go" (Jn 14:3-4).

When St. John recorded this discourse of our Lord, the apostles understood the meaning of this mystery of joy, hidden in the words of Christ. The pentecostal Spirit had revealed where Christ had gone in order "to prepare a place for you." For Jesus, the "exodus" or journey led along the way of the cross. Wondrous acts of God attended this last earthly journey of Christ. As he was being lifted up upon the cross, he was rising to heavenly glory.

"I am coming again, and I will take you to myself." Each Mass celebrated by the apostles was a partial fulfillment of this promise of Christ. It signaled the beginning of a new journey, along the way pointed out by Jesus in his way of the cross. As the early Christians celebrated their paschal meal, God was saying once again: "You shall eat like those who are in flight." "This is the day of the Lord." "Rise, take up your cross and follow in the blood-stained footsteps of Jesus Christ."

This journey was possible, since the bread of life infused within their hearts Christ's life of heroic obedience and self-sacrificing charity. The Eucharist struck a blow of death in the souls of the apostles, and it continues to be the bread of death to all their followers. Christ's presence in the Eucharist can tolerate neither sin nor the least imperfection. The warmth of his charity breaks the cold of selfishness. His obedience sweeps away the forces of disobedience. The poverty of Christ destroys every desire except the one concern to love God.

The journey is not yet over. The cross is not the goal. It is simply a sign post. The Israelites rose from their paschal meal not simply to lose themselves in a desert of heat and thirst. Their intention was to pass through the desolate waste of the Sinai desert to reach the promised land. But in the desolate desert the revelation of God took place. God was present for a blinding moment atop the majestic peaks of Mount Sinai, and the memory of his glory urged them to push forward till they arrived at the land of God in Palestine.

The breaking of the bread of life lifts Christians up upon the cross, and through the cross they participate in Christ's heavenly glory. For a moment they are swept upward in joy, for never before have they felt so close to the presence of God. The cross is their Mount Sinai, and the earth shakes at the revelation of God's glory. They must never lose the cross, for in the cross is life. Life and death, happiness and sorrow, can and actually do exist together for people of faith who realize the meaning of the Eucharist.

Although Christians remain pilgrims on earth, they share the joy of eternal life with each eucharistic celebration. The way of the cross leads Christians to union with Christ, who is marked with the scars of crucifixion, but is at the same time glorified and risen. Eating the bread of life which is their paschal lamb, Christians joyously sing: "Let us be glad and rejoice, and give glory to him; for the marriage of the Lamb has come." This marriage is the union of Christ with all Christians.

Still other features of the Jewish paschal meal imparted a spirit of joy to the Christian passover sacrifice. The Mosaic law prescribed that the entire household gather at the banquet table, with the father at the head. There was to be peace, unity and contentment as all broke the same bread, drank from the same goblet of wine and mingled their voices in the great song of praise. Outsiders who participated became as members of the family. "If a family is too small for a whole lamb, it shall join the nearest household in procuring one and shall share in the lamb." Unity was part of the pasch. It was natural that Christ should pray for a spirit of unity at his final paschal supper.

> That all may be one as you, Father, are
> in me, and I in you; I pray that they may
> be [one] in us, that the world may believe
> that you sent me. I have given them *the glory*
> you gave me that they may be one . . . Father,
> all those you gave me I would have in my
> company where I am, *to see this glory of mine*
> (Jn 17:21-22, 24).

To eat the Christian pasch, we must belong to the household of which Christ is the head. We must experience a bond of familial love with every other member of our household. No one seated at this table can be as a stranger or a foreigner. All are united like branches of the same vine, as we drink from the one cup of Christ's blood. "Many will come," Christ had prophesied, "from the east and from the west, and will find a place at the banquet with Abraham and Isaac and Jacob" (Mt 8:11). Here in the eucharistic bond there is neither east nor west, border nor breed nor birth. The peace of Christ reigns everywhere among people of good will. Such peace of all persons with one another is a sharing in heavenly glory. Seated at the table of the Lord, the members of God's household are able by faith to behold Christ in glory, as he had promised.

To be present at this agape or love feast, one's garments must be washed in the blood of the lamb. The forgiveness of Christ must have removed all stains of hate, jealousy, selfishness and sensuality. This redemption from sin has come through the blood of Christ. St. John is very conscious of the role of blood in the paschal liturgy. Since the Jewish pasch gave a prominent place to the blood ritual, it is not surprising that the importance of blood is stressed in the New Testament passover. As the blood of the paschal lamb had once brought deliverance from Egypt and salvation from death in the days of Moses, the blood of Christ brings glory and union with God.

The full meaning of the blood ritual comes to mind when we recollect that for the Jew blood symbolized life. "The life of every living body," Leviticus declares, "is its blood" (Lv 17:14). Blood belongs to God in a particular way, for the reason that life is God's special property. Whatever is consecrated by blood is solemnly dedicated to God. The blood of the paschal lamb, sprinkled upon the doorposts of the Israelites' homes, sets apart the occupants of that home. Their life belongs to God. God calls his chosen people "a kingdom of priests, a holy nation," "my special possession, dearer to me than all other people" (Ex 19:6; 1 P 2:9). The blood ritual unites God and his people in a new mysterious bond of life.

Christians celebrate their paschal sacrifice, the Eucharist, with the realization that the days of shadow and prefigurement are past. Through the gift of faith God has commanded light to shine out of darkness and has granted enlightenment "that we in turn might make known the glory of God, shining on the face of Christ Jesus" (2 Cor 4:6). The Christian is totally consecrated and united to God, not by the blood of goats and bulls but by the blood of Jesus Christ. St. Peter writes, "You were delivered . . . by Christ's blood . . . the blood of a spotless unblemished lamb" (1 P 1:18-19). "How much more will the blood of Christ, who through the eternal spirit offered himself up unblemished to God, cleanse your conscience from dead works to worship the living God" (Heb 9:14). The blood of Christ unites the worshipper with the triumphant Christ of Easter Sunday morning.

The joyful significance of the Eucharist, the Christian pasch, cannot be adequately understood without allusion to many Jewish ceremonies. The New Testament writers, and especially St. John, reveal such richness of thought that they pass quickly from one

Old Testament rite to another. "Whatever promises God has made have been fulfilled in him" (2 Cor 1:20). All the Jewish liturgical acts were ". . . but a shadow of things to come; the reality is the body [casting the shadow] of Christ" (Col 2:17). Nonetheless, the apostles looked upon the Eucharist primarily as a paschal sacrifice.

In the Eucharist the Christian is lifted up to the mystery of the cross. The bells toll the death of "him whom they have pierced"; then quickly, but not unexpectedly, the bells ring out a joyous *Alleluia:* "He has risen." The way of the cross is an elevation to glory. Christians can begin and end their eucharistic sacrifice with the words of our Lord, "Father, the hour has come. Give glory to your son . . . that he may bestow eternal life on those you gave him" (Jn 17:1-2).

The sign of the cross appears upon the eucharistic, sacrificial meal. This is a sign of sorrow and mourning; the lamb of God has been slain. Yet, this divine sorrow does not exclude joy; instead, it gives a foretaste of a glorious banquet of heavenly joys. The Christian pasch is not so much the descent of heaven upon the earth but rather the earthly is lifted up to the heavenly. "For Christ, our passover, has been sacrificed. Therefore, let us keep festival!" The *eschaton* or final day has arrived—at least for a moment. The glorified Christ is in our midst.

The consecration and communion sound the notes of the angels' trumpets, announcing the *parousia* or triumphant presence of Jesus. He who went into a distant country to obtain a kingdom for us has returned. "When Christ your life appears," St. Paul writes, "then you shall appear with him in glory" (Col 3:4). At each Mass, Jesus is summoning his followers, "Come, rise from the dead. This is the day which the Lord has made." Forming one family with all Christians and looking to the risen Christ at the head of the table, all worshippers begin a new, heavenly life with each eucharistic repast. Consecrated with the blood of the lamb, they sing the triumphant *Hallel* of praise, sung by their forefathers:

> The joyful shout of victory . . .
> 'The right hand of the Lord has struck

with power . . .'
I shall not die, but live, and
declare the works of the Lord . . .
This is the day the Lord has made;
let us be glad and rejoice in it . . .
Blessed is he who comes in the name of the Lord . . .
The Lord is God, and he has given us light
(see Ps 118).

Chapter Eleven
The Psalms: Heart of the Liturgy

If you pick up your Bible and open it at the center, you will find the book of *Psalms*. Perhaps it is one of those unexplainable accidents of history that the psalms are printed at the heart of the Bible. In biblical circles, however, *accidental* is a very uncongenial word. Does anything ever happen haphazardly in a world where one says to God:

> O Lord, you have probed me and you know me;
> you know when I sit and when I stand . . .
> Even before a word is on my tongue,
> behold, O Lord, you know the whole of it.
> Behind me and before me, you hem me in
> and rest your hand upon me (Ps 139:1-6).

It is more in keeping with biblical practice and, therefore, more theologically correct, to say that God put the psalms at the heart of the sacred writings on purpose. But how did God manage to do that? And why? Questions such as those are rightly asked, not just by the full-time scholar, but by everyone, Jews and Christians alike, who value God's word as their comfort and delight, and, according to Pope Pius XII's expression of faith, as a "heaven-sent treasure . . . [and] most precious source of doctrine."

The answer to these questions will reveal how old and tried are the goals sought in the liturgical renewal: popular participation in worship; adaptation to regional needs; absorption of local customs; respect for all sacred traditions. All these matters are closely inter-related. Culture and tradition, though the most prized heritage of the past, are also at the heart of contemporary thought and represent the most spontaneous expression of life in the present. Modern life, for its part, is ever influencing and modifying this culture and so preparing its own heritage for the future. Today's Christian community has been formed by the ancient word of God and is never so vitally and so profoundly alive as at the moment of liturgical worship. At that moment the Church places herself prayerfully before God and publicly expresses her longing and hope, her sorrow and contrition, her devotedness and love, her life in and for Christ, through the hymns, readings and creeds of Scripture. In the celebration of Mass and the sacraments, Jesus Christ, through his minister, speaks biblical words in the midst of the Christian assembly.

The Church's liturgy, during the patristic and medieval period, was continually open to adaptation. Surprisingly true to ancient form, the liturgy adopted many different languages and customs, so that what was once the daily attire or private prayer of the people became the sacred vestments and official liturgy of the Church. This Church, adapting and modernizing, was not only the Church closest in point of time to Jesus and the apostles, but it was also most intimately in contact with ancient Scriptures. Later, unfortunately, this sensitivity to local and changing needs was lost by the Roman liturgy. Vatican II's efforts to revitalize this ancient spirit can be guided and aided by a study of the Bible, and especially of the psalms.

To understand the psalms, the heart of the Bible, one must appreciate the place and the function of the heart in the human body. The heart is at the center of human life in any number of ways. If the heart did not send sixty to seventy beats of blood each minute to the finger, foot, and brain, these organs would not only stop functioning but, in fact, would corrupt and disintegrate. The brain could never think nor could the stomach and intestinal tract digest food without the nourishment which the heart continually circulates through the body. The heart thus sustains life in every area of the body.

It is just as important to note, however, that the heart itself reacts most delicately and most sensitively to the least breath of activity on the surface of human existence. The heart, as we sometimes express it, "hammers" away with fierce strokes in the midst of excitement, "races" to catch hold of hopes and goals, "freezes" in a grip of deadly fear, "beats" regularly and quietly under normal work-loads, "skips" beats and irregularly repeats during times of excessive demands. The psalms, the heart of the Bible, act in a similar way. This phenomenon was very evident in Old Testament times.

The psalms kept the Scriptures alive in biblical times. They, too, reacted most sensitively to every phase of life. This statement must be understood against a larger background of events and traditions. According to the Bible, the initial spark of life came from the word of God; as this word was spoken in the soul of the Amorites and Hittites (Ezk 16:3), children of God came into existence. These men and women, once no different from any other "wandering Aramean" (Dt 26:5), were transformed into the Lord's "special possession, dearer . . . than all other people" (Ex 19:5).

So great was the change in the very first one to hear God's word that God gave him a new name: Abram was thereafter to be called *Abraham*. God's word changed an impulsive, hot-tempered Moses into the "meekest man on the face of the earth" (Ex 2:11 ff; Nb 12:3). Moses became an excellent leader because he had learned how to take orders from God and listen to his word. Through God's word to Abraham and Moses, the Bible was already coming into existence, not so much, if at all, a book to be studied, but rather a divine word to be proclaimed by priest or leader and a response to be sung by the entire congregation.

The earliest parts of the Old Testament were composed according to a rhythmic pattern, so that they could be sung as one sings a ballad today. The measured and moving style of the ballad is just what one would expect since it was the custom to recite these stories of God's greatest redemptive acts at ancient sanctuaries. Almost all the geographical sites mentioned in the Bible were famous for their shrine or sanctuary. God first spoke to religious leaders like Abraham and Moses at these holy places, and here the people congregated to hear the same divine word spoken to them. The Bible thus took shape in a setting of public worship.

Originating in sanctuary prayer, the early historical sections of the Bible not only followed the rhythmic cadence of song, but were frequently interrupted with prayer refrains, homilies, and longer hymns (e.g., Gn 9:6-7, 25-7; 12:1-3; 14:19-20; ch. 22; 48:15-16; ch. 49). This word, as proclaimed and sung, became the liturgy and the Bible simultaneously. Many of the songs and prayers, especially the more popular ones, were being assembled in hymn books.

These books were not formed from papyrus sheets, much less from printed pages, but rather from another and different product of the ancient Near East, the fiber of the people's tenacious memories. This fact bears considerably on the study of the psalms. Most biblical people did not read or write, but they were highly appreciative of exquisite lyrics and elaborate folklore; they greatly valued a carefully formulated rhythmic style. It was not only very conducive to the majesty of public worship, but it was also an extremely helpful memory aid.

One aspect of this oral transmission is very important for a liturgical study of the psalms. While a copyist carefully followed a master sheet, eloquent speakers or conscientious prayer leaders always felt the need and mood of their audience and adapted themselves to the intuition of the moment. When the sacred traditions were changed and the hymns sung, there was a natural tendency to actualize them by slightly adapting them to make them more contemporary, thus involving the worshippers more personally and immediately.

What has been stated about the origin and the transmission of the Bible can be applied to the psalms as well. Every great moment of salvation-history was relived in the psalms. Even if we lost the entire Bible, except for the book of Psalms, we would, nevertheless, possess enough material to reconstruct Bible history. The call of Abraham and the wandering of the patriarchs; the Mosaic covenant and its demands; the journeying through the desert and the conquest of the Promised Land; the coronation and the exploits of David; the threats of the prophets and teaching of the priests; the advice of the wise men and the prayers of the poor, public and private; long and short sentiments of devotion—

all these great and small moments are concentrated at the heart of the Bible in the psalms. The psalms speak God's great deeds to each new age and succeeding generation, thus creating and sustaining the ongoing life of God's children.

The psalms teem with life-giving power because they followed the laws of living organisms. The law of life is one of open receptivity and generous bestowal, of fertile contact and continual cross-breeding of adaptation to environment and resistance to hostile forces, of vitalizing the old and absorbing the new. What the psalms give of life they have received; the psalmists were instrumental in repeating the great moments of salvation-history because they were fully receptive to the first great word of God.

At prayer, the Israelites discovered the meaning of their life. It would be false to claim that the singing of psalms cleared up life's mysteries for them in the same way as the Palestinian sun suddenly banished the darkness of the night. Mysteries remained in their lives but somehow or other the worshippers realized that what was most mysterious about God was the power and love of his presence. "In your goodness, O God, you provided . . . for the needy" (Ps 68:11). It was a delight for the people to live within such mystery.

By contemplating the past, the community found a sense of direction in the present and a way into the future messianic age. By reliving God's redemptive acts in the present, Israel was enabled to appreciate personally what God had done in the past. The wonders of faith, however, remained, enveloping the past, the present and the future. Such mysteries must first be experienced before words, even the most sacred, can communicate their message. The chanting of the psalms in the sanctuary liturgy was the beat of the biblical heart, sending enlightenment to the mind, strength to the will, a sense of devoted faith to the whole congregation. But only on condition that every element of life remain in close contact with the psalms could the power of that heart be effective.

The liturgical renewal of salvation-history was accomplished especially through the recital of Scripture and the singing of the psalms. As the faithful, therefore, looked at the whole panorama of God's great deeds, they declared, almost ecstatically, that they were beholding the face of God. We hear the assembly joyfully crying out in a hymn of praise: "Consider the Lord and his strength; seek his face constantly" (Ps 105:4 CS). By attending to God's presence in Israelite history, the worshipper was viewing all the delicate facets of the divine personality. God, of course, has no face, but he does have what the human face symbolizes and reveals, a character. In God's case this character is of extraordinary, infinite versatility. Through contemplating the divine activity in Israel's history, the worshipper communicated with God and was granted an overwhelming sense of God's immediate presence.

The psalmist had to personally relive salvation-history before he was able to appreciate its mysterious meaning and detect the face of God reflected upon its surface. There were other conditions which the psalms insist upon. First, no moment or setting was more favorable for the reception of God's merciful grace than the time of sanctuary worship. The phrase, "seek the face of God," actually came to mean, "to worship" or "to offer liturgical service to God." That, in fact, is the translation found in the New American Bible for Psalm 105:4.

The other condition for grasping the true sense of salvation-history put a special demand upon the psalmist. He, or the singer, was required to so adapt or modulate the words that the worshippers instinctively realized they were right at the center of what was happening. This qualification certainly did not demand that each psalm be rewritten before every liturgical service. Changes were made carefully, slowly, but *changes were made*. Early Christian liturgies followed this same practice of retouching psalms and readings in order to make the past meaningful for their own liturgical assembly. God's former redemptive acts were integrated in such a way with those happening right now that each threw light upon the others. A typical example of this type of modification found among the ancients occurs in Psalm 105. As the psalmist narrates—or rather, relives—the plagues of Egypt, he sings that God:

> . . . struck down their vines and their
> fig trees and shattered the trees
> throughout their borders (v. 33).

A very pedantic reader could stiffly assert that an error exists here in the Bible. According to Exodus 9:31-32, the thunder and hail did not destroy vines and fig trees but rather flax and barley. The narrator of the Exodus account is very careful to point out that "the barley was in ear and the flax in bud. But the wheat and the spelt were not ruined, for they grow later." Evidently—so the charge might go—the later author of the psalms was badly misinformed about agricultural produce in Egypt. In his ignorance he spoke of Palestinian instead of Egyptian crops!

We know now, from the liturgical study of the psalms, that their composers did not write out of ignorance but out of personal piety. The author of Psalm 105 was declaring that the Israelites were driven back into Egypt by their sins. This was a religious, not a geographical, journey. Sin gave them the character of a hardened Pharaoh. God allowed sin to take its toll; only thus could the people ever learn to be faithful to God and to enjoy peace.

> He sent the darkness; it grew dark
> but they rebelled against his word
> (Ps 105:28).

Sorrow and destitution were intended to develop a poor and lowly spirit, contrite for its sins, dependent upon God. Once the Israelite realized his lowly state, he became one of God's "chosen ones," "led forth . . . with joy" (v. 43). He took his place among the hungry ones, satisfied "with bread from heaven." Famine or sickness or loss of friends were the plagues which freed him from Egypt and mysteriously led him back to God's promised land.

Psalm 105 is not unique in this pattern of liturgical modification to environment and needs. An inspired singer, speaking for the entire congregation, added this prayer to Psalm 51, asking God to repair the ruins of Jerusalem:

Be bountiful, O Lord, to Zion in your
kindness
by rebuilding the walls of Jerusalem
(Ps 51:20).

This psalm, actually a personal prayer for pardon, has undergone careful scrutiny within the last few years, and we can now
recognize within its lines an anthology of earlier prophetical
preaching. Its phrases are drawn from the prophecies of Isaiah,
Jeremiah, Ezekiel and Deuteronomy. The voice of great reformers
speaks to sinners of a later age. In the spirit of the psalmist the
Christian liturgy today applies this psalm to us, especially on
penitential days, particularly during Passiontide.

Example after example can be drawn from the psalms to show
the openness of the ancient liturgy to changing circumstances. A
brief study of Psalm 22 will show that it originated as the prayer
of a deeply peaceful but particularly lonely sufferer. Long, solitary days, darkened by sickness and perhaps by prison confine-
ment, finally ended, and the saintly man offered a poem to the
temple as a votive gift of thanksgiving. What he laid in the hands
of the priests was Psalm 22.

The second stage of the psalm's history began with its growing
popularity among the people. Many generations of suffering men
and women found that it poignantly expressed their sorrow, faith
and consolation. The psalm acquired its place in the public liturgy.
The third stage imparted a messianic meaning to the psalm. Because salvation always came through divine mercy upon the
suffering, *the* great event will have to come about in the same
way. The messianic people must first be a suffering people. At this
later date, some notes of the newly emerging resurrection theology crept into the psalm (22:30-31).

The fourth and final stage of Psalm 22 came from its New
Testament application to Jesus. In him suffering humanity lived
and triumphed. In the spirit of its composition, this psalm can be
appreciated today and its redemptive power released only when
the Christian feels a close bond with all his suffering members.
Only in the mystical Christ can the real Christ be found. The

original author and later singers of this psalm remind us that it can be understood only by reading it in the context of those nameless numbers of innocent sufferers among the people of God. Charity is essential, therefore, for understanding this and every psalm. Hence the necessity, as mentioned above, of group worship, where charity can be manifested and where that knowledge which love alone communicates can be received and given.

The psalms so spirited the daily lives of God's people that almost every possible human reaction appears in their lines. The psalms, like the human heart, vitalize every activity of a person, and are therefore closely associated with that person's body, words, thoughts, actions. A brief survey may indicate how the psalms are clothed with every psychological state. In them we find expressed:

> —hopes, born of quiet waiting (Ps 131) or issuing
> from anguish (Pss 42:10-12; 130)
> —frustration and despair (Pss 89:47, 50)
> —sorrow (Ps 12)
> —loneliness of an individual (Ps 22); or of a
> group (Ps 123)
> —pride or complacency which needs correction
> (Pss 44:7, 18-23)
> —impetuosity (Ps 44:24-25)
> —boundless joy (Pss 47:2; 95)
> —serene and quiet joy (Ps 133)

Many liturgical acts surround the psalms with full participation or involvement of the worshippers. These actions did not originate from priests giving orders but from people spontaneously entering into the sacred service. The congregation:

> —clap their hands (Ps 47:2)
> —shout joyfully (Pss 47:6; 66)
> —offer holocausts and vows (Ps 66:13)
> —process with song and musical instruments like
> timbrels, ten stringed instruments, lyres,
> harps (Pss 68:26; 92:4)

—kneel or prostrate (Ps 95:6)
—listen to prophetic discourse (Pss 50; 95:7b-11)
—carry on melodious dialogues (Pss 24:7-10; 50)
—sing refrains (Pss 8; 68:2; 136)
—dance (Pss 149:3; 150:4)
—set a sacrificial banquet (Ps 23:27)

THE PSALMS OF ANCIENT ISRAEL

It is a truism that the Bible must be read in the spirit of the writers. One cannot begin to understand the psalms without understanding the more important elements of Hebrew life. A plant uprooted dies; a word pulled out of context falls apart. To understand the psalms, you must go back to ancient Israel and accompany the Israelites to the temple for worship. Walking along with them, you must watch as they identify themselves with the people along the way. You must listen attentively as they speak about their neighbors, their family, their king, their God. You must note their reaction when the sacred word, *God*, is first mentioned. You will be impressed by the way the memory of their ancient forebears—Abraham, ·Moses, David—frequently rises to the surface of their thinking. The Hebrew people will remain strangers to you unless you learn something about them. A psalm, separated from its liturgical context, loses its freshness and vitality.

One of the elements of Hebrew life is the Israelites' sturdy sense of oneness with all God's people. At the temple, the Israelites did not squirm with embarrassment, as moderns do, when their personal praise and petition to God were absorbed into community prayer. They felt it an honor and a blessing to belong to this holy nation whom God called, "my special possession, dearer to me than all other people" (Ex 19:5). To be saved from affliction, they forgot their own personal sorrow and thought of the affliction of the nation, for it was the nation's sorrows, as God had said to Moses, ". . . which I have witnessed . . . Therefore I have come down to rescue them" (Ex 3:7 ff.).

Totality thinking is the term which modern biblical students give to this mentality. Totality thinking so controlled the emotional reactions and thought-patterns of the Israelites, that the biblical account frequently shifts from the individual to the group and back again to the individual. One instance of this shift is found in the Patriarchal stories in which later tribal history often mingles with the lives of individual persons. Many examples of this totality thinking can be found, but none is so clear as Adam and Eve, who represent for the Israelites not only the parents of the entire human race, but also every individual man and every individual woman.

Such totality thinking did not make nameless individuals out of persons nor did it rub off the individualistic features of faces. Despite this sense of unity, it was individual leaders, conspicuous for courage and saintliness, who typified the nation. The history of the people is told in the framework of biographical accounts: Abraham, Jacob, Joseph, Moses, Joshua, David and the great reforming kings. This fusion of the person with the nation and conversely of the nation with the individual allowed the sacred author extraordinary freedom to move from one to the other. The Suffering Servant of the Lord is the nation, as the nation relives the covenantal role of Abraham, exhibits the meekness of Moses, endures the desolation of Jeremiah, undergoes the excruciating tortures of the exiles. Just when the individual servant seems absorbed into the nation, the nation finds its true identity in individuals. In this type of thinking there is a preparation for the New Testament doctrine of the Mystical Body of Christ.

A second distinctive mark of the ancient Israelites necessary for understanding the psalms is their faith in a personal God. This concept was developed already in the opening chapters in the context of Catholic spirituality. It is the most basic feature of Old Testament theology. When the Israelites prayed, they knew that their words did not bounce against a wooden block. They did not run the risk—as did their neighbors—of their God being too busy or too moody to listen (1 K 18:27). Yahweh was genuinely interested in his people. His intervention in their lives, at the same time, was never a quick impulse but was always controlled by sovereign love. God was reliable as a rock (Ps 18:2-3), sympathetic as a shepherd (Ps 23). Yet, God was eminently differ-

ent from every human friend, because God would forgive not
once or twice but again and again. As he confessed through his
prophet Hosea:

> I am God and not man,
> the holy One present among you;
> I will not let the flames [of your sins]
> consume you (11:9).

God was truly almighty and transcendent:

> For as the heavens are high above the earth,
> so surpassing is his kindness towards
> those who fear him (Ps 103:11).

Nothing, the Bible had to admit, was so transcendent in God as
his love. At the same time, divine love, more than anything else,
narrowed the distance between heaven and earth, bringing God
and humans so close that man and woman could eavesdrop on
divine soliloquies (cf. Gn 2:18; 18:14).

Very fittingly, then, did the God of Israelites call himself
Yahweh, which means, "I am he who is always there." God's name
could never be communicated in the letters of a word; it could
be known only in the mystic experience of his presence through
the years of a person's life. God revealed himself, therefore, by
being there in the redemptive acts of his outstretched arm and in
the liturgical renewal of these same acts in sanctuary worship.
God, accordingly, was known as the Lord who called each generation in their father Abraham (Is 51:1 ff), or as "the Lord, your
God, who brought you out of the land of Egypt, that place of
slavery" (Ex 20:2), or again as the Lord who by a solemn promise to David made an everlasting covenant of love with you
(see Is 55:3).

In community worship the individual was caught up into the
mystery of the divine election of the people and was protected
by the powerful arm of God's love. The liturgy renewed the great
redemptive acts of Yahweh towards the nation, and therefore at
liturgical prayer the worship was caught up most vitally into the

saving power of divine love. In public prayer the worshipper felt individually drawn towards the personal God of the people. Nowhere did anyone find the personal, loving acts of God so close, so absorbing, so effective as in the sanctuary liturgy.

This term, *sanctuary*, brings us to the third important feature of Hebrew life which is needed to appreciate the psalms. Even a rapid reading of such books as Genesis, Numbers, Joshua, Judges, Samuel and Kings leaves a clear impression of the prominent place occupied by the sanctuary in Hebrew life. In fact, almost all history pivoted around the sanctuary. In the patriarchal narratives the tribe moves from one shrine to another: Shechem, Bethel, Hai, Hebron, Beer-sheba, Kadesh; in the desert days of Moses, the Ark is the center of activity; in the period of the Judges, every national threat or local disturbance summons the people to the sanctuaries of Gilgal, Mizpah, Shechem, Bethel, Dan or Shiloh. This image of a sanctuary-centered life becomes even more pronounced in post-exilic Israel. Ezekiel, Malachi and Joel; Ezra, Nehemiah and Maccabees locate the heart of Hebrew life in the Jerusalem temple.

The sanctuaries, therefore, were the spot where each and every Israelite felt most keenly their union with God and God's people, their sharing in God's redemptive acts towards the nation, their confidence of survival in an ever more hostile environment. On pilgrimage to Jerusalem the Israelites walked quickly, their steps almost dancing. We read in the psalter:

> I rejoiced because they said to me,
> 'We will go up to the house of the Lord'
> (Ps 122:1).

A fourth and final element needed for fully understanding the psalms—or, for that matter, for understanding any other part of the Bible—depends on an accurate appreciation of Hebrew grammar, and especially of the laws of the Hebrew verb system. It was not that the psalmist felt obliged to conform to grammatical laws, for no such Hebrew grammatical system existed in his time, nor, indeed, in the time of St. Jerome's translation of the Bible. However, today's Hebrew grammar represents our attempt to formulate rules about Hebrew thought patterns and modes of expression. Based on long study, the resulting rules are reliable guide posts to an understanding of the psalms.

Hebrew grammar reveals a method of thinking wherein time, with its past, present and future, is secondary. This phenomenon constitutes a problem difficult for us to grasp. What absorbed the psalmist's attention was his present, personal involvement in life's happenings. Instead of describing an event as past or future, it was described as complete or incomplete, desirable or undesirable, intense or reflective, or as setting off a chain reaction. As God's redemptive acts were commemorated in the liturgy and proclaimed in the psalms, the worshipper relived what happened long ago. What happened centuries before his time was still happening, and the worshipper was personally involved in the saving act of God. Smoothing the differences between past and present, the Hebrew verb system put God's saving activity into the "now" moment.

SUMMARY

Once we bring the four preceding elements of Hebrew culture into our reading of the psalms, we can begin to understand them better and have a deeper appreciation of them on their own terms. However, we started out seeking an answer to why and how the psalms are at the heart of the Bible. The historical reason has not been given, nor will it be given. It is still locked within the secret possession of many, many closed centuries. But after all, the problem is more theological than historical. The psalms are to Israel—both the Israel of Old Testament times and the chosen people of the present age—what the heart is to the human body: the center of life. All salvation-history flowed to this center and found expression in the psalms. These sacred songs and prayers, in turn, brought nourishing and healing power to every area of life.

The liturgy constitutes the heartbeat of the psalm. The sacred melodies were composed for choral recitation and public worship. As people stood in the presence of God, they not only contemplated the face of God in all his wondrous deeds, but God looked at his people just as they were in their hopes and defeats, in their sorrows and joys. People are never more honestly and nakedly themselves than when they stand in God's presence. The psalms had to reflect all the moods and needs of every changing generation, otherwise, the heart would die. With the heart silenced, the faith of the people would collapse. Because the psalms are so very human, they bring the spirit of God, or rather, the beat of God's heart into every moment of human activity. When this is finally achieved, then the eternal liturgy of the new heaven and the new earth will bring all the elect into the fullness of his life.

Chapter Twelve
The Psalms: Prayer within Reality

The human body throughout the changing years of growth and development maintains a combination of consistency and continuity. These two elements are necessary for responsible adult behavior. The Bible, too, maintains this balance of consistency and continuity in its life. Israel steadily found her identity in the faith-conviction that she was God's chosen people, redeemed by him from slavery and assured of his continual protective presence. In his love she found courage to seek the future with hope (Dt 7:6 ff.; Ho 11; Is 44:1-8; Rm 9:1-5). Strength flowed into the system, not by a satisfying contemplation of past achievements, but rather, by courageous expectation of the future. Second Isaiah sang out his faith: "Those who wait upon the Lord renew their strength" (Is 40:31).

The Bible reflects consistency within change, for it tells of Israel's being transformed from a semi-nomadic style of life to an agricultural and even an urban existence. Government underwent change, at times abrupt and revolutionary—as when David established a royal dynasty in place of the more democratic form of the Judges. The same David and his son Solomon were responsible for a radical transformation in liturgical practice, in building a temple as a fixed abode for the Ark of the Covenant, which up until then had roamed with the wanderings of the people. All the while, the historical-religious traditions which found their way into the Bible were living within these changes and, like the human body, absorbing their effects.

The human body can survive only within the real world of earth and fresh air, fire and water, shared within a family and community. Because God is real and, in fact, can be contacted

only within the real, his presence is somehow incarnated within
the real environment of his people's life. A passage of Second
Isaiah speaks of this reality:

> For just as the rain and the snow
> come down from the heavens,
> And do not return there
> till they have soaked the earth,
> Making it fertile and sprouting with life,
> giving seed to him who sows,
> and bread to him who eats,
> So shall my word be
> which goes forth from my mouth;
> it shall not return to me empty;
> Instead, it accomplishes what I desire
> and achieves the purpose for which I send it
> (Is 55:9-11).

Though God's ways and thoughts are said to be as far above
the ways and thoughts of human beings as the heavens are above
the earth, nevertheless, God's ways and thoughts do not remain
suspended like majestic clouds in mid-air, to be admired in wonder
from afar. In the Bible, God's thoughts return to him in a totally
earthly way. They return clothed not only in human language,
but also within the fabric of human history. Whatever is real
finds its way into the Bible and eventually into the heart of the
Bible, the psalms.

This quality of reality may explain why the psalms seem to be
such unreal prayers or, at least, such uncomfortable prayers for
many of us moderns. When we pray, we are accustomed to appear
before God scrubbed clean and dressed up in our Sunday best.
Our prayers, accordingly, fit the occasion. We arrive at prayer
polite, reverential, noble, pure, devout, grammatically correct,
musically in tune, even majestic and pompous. We normally place
ourselves before God not as we truly are (and as God truly sees
us to be) but rather, attired in our make-believe Halloween
costumes.

Not so the psalms! It is true, majestic paeans like Psalms 96-99 proclaim God's glorious royalty. Wonder and honor are parts of the real—but not the only part and certainly not its ordinary part. Discouragement and threats, anger and curses, monotony and routine, quiet relaxation, stately philosophical moments—in fact, all of life—pulses within the psalms. Above all else, the psalms are honest. If a person feels that God is distant, or even asleep during the storms of life, he or she can shout with the psalmist, "Lord, wake up!" (Ps 44:24) just like the disciples rudely shook their master, Jesus, out of sleep (Mk 4:38). If a person or community burns with anger, they curse. If Israel judges that she has received a raw deal from God, she puts her problem plainly before God as in Psalm 44.

Another part of the difficulty in understanding the psalms derives from the common problem of making sense out of life. If the psalms are perplexing, it is because life is that way. Prayer does not seek to disentangle international crises or personal problems. Nor does the psalmist propose to give a philosophical discussion on the subject of pain. In the psalms one prayerfully places oneself realistically in God's presence. Or, as in Psalm 69, one expresses the search for what is already too close to be seen. In the agony of loss we sense the ecstasy of union:

> You know my reproach, my shame and my
> ignominy:
> before you are all my foes.
> Insult has broken my heart, and I am weak;
> I looked for sympathy, but there was none;
> for comforters, and I found none
> (Ps 69:20-21).

The psalms are not to be identified simply with surface facts of reality. The psalms plummet to the depth of reality through the insights of faith—the profound conviction that God is truly present—and then hammer back at life with new hopes and aggressive demands. Not all the psalms equally respond to God's redeeming and inspiring presence. Not even the saints live always on the same high pitch. In this context, we can ask: are there degrees of inspiration within the various passages of the Bible? To take this question one step further, are all one hundred and fifty psalms equally inspired? If not, must we feel obliged to make equal use of all of them? These questions deal with the nature of inspiration in some of its more controversial areas.

The psalms, and for that matter the entire Bible, voice in a human way the hopes and ideals, the questions and the problems, the discouragement and even the curses prompted by God's presence and expectations within the real. Inspiration of the Bible, then, is the common faith of all persons, articulated by one person of uncommon insight and ability. An inspired passage becomes part of the Bible when all men and women sooner or later agree that this one person "spoke God" for them and not simply to them. It is the community through its leaders who decides the question of "canonicity" or of what belongs in the Bible. Moreover, if the community can respond to God's inspiring and sanctifying presence in varying degrees, the reflection of this inspiration in the Bible will manifest itself in various degrees.

The comments above have been a rather simplistic way of explaining the present-day scholarly pursuit for the "social character of biblical inspiration." However, it seems to be a necessary explanation before continuing the subject of the psalms. Chapter 5 of Vatican II's document on revelation implicitly adopts this newer position about the social character of inspiration.

If some parts of the Bible (Nb 1; Dt 7:2) and of the psalms (Ps 110:5-6; 137:9) may be less inspired than others, can we (in fact, ought we) omit these minimally inspired sections from our Christian liturgy and ordinary prayer? Are some psalms very inspired and yet too historically conditioned by ancient names and outmoded styles to be suitable for contemporary prayer, especially when this prayer is to draw the worshippers into full participation? These questions are serious, especially in their implications.

Let us never reject such sections out of ignorance. Let us never measure the Bible by our standards, but always be ready to ponder anew what we cannot understand or appreciate about the Holy Scriptures. Further, where God seems to be less present —in life or in the Bible—we need to reflect a longer time. Keeping such psalms in our prayer prods us into a more intensive search for God where we need more desperately to find him—in the difficulties of life. If we pray only when it is easy to find God on our own terms, we will be badly prepared to seek his presence on other people's terms or to search for him in his seeming absence. Maintaining all the psalms, at least in the Church's public liturgy of the Eucharist and the Divine Office, may become a powerful incentive to faith in God in the totality of the real. Prayer includes a search beyond the obvious if it is a prayer of faith.

The psalms, as has been alluded to already, can seem to hinder full liturgical participation. Some days we come to the Eucharist, or we begin the Divine Office, happy and thankful in spirit, and we are asked to recite some sorrowful lament or dreadful complaint like:

> Save me, O God,
> for the waters threaten my life;
> I am sunk in the abysmal swamp (Ps 69:2).

Just as surely on another day when we happen to be sick or depressed or harassed by problems, the official liturgical prayers call upon us to sing:

> Let the heavens be glad and the earth rejoice;
> let the plains be joyful and all that is in
> them (Ps 96:11-12).

The temptation is to substitute another liturgical text and to question anew the appropriateness of the psalms for prayer today. Should we not instead question our own narrow-mindedness and face up to the challenge of changing and adapting ourselves to the greater world of reality in the liturgy and the psalms? When we are very joyful we ought not to forget the poor and the depressed. On the other hand, when we are suffering pain and feel miserable, do we have to cover the entire world with our shroud of mourning? In the liturgy we are asked to unite ourselves with the whole Church and the whole world. Like Jesus, we are to open our arms to embrace all men and women. Like Jesus on the cross, our own welcome to the world may be achieved only through the impalement of open arms upon a cross of violence. The psalms, moreover, embrace centuries of human experience and so force our prayer out of the prejudicial confines of narrow, personal circles. The psalms can liberate us as they plunge us into the human emotions of all our brothers and sisters of all centuries in Jesus.

PSALMS OF PRAISE

Praise is a wondrous acclamation of God's redemptive acts as these occur over and over again among us his people. Praise gives nothing to God. Praise is a burst of wonder at what is happening because of God's presence. Praise is the recognition through faith of what is real in its deepest, most personal aspects. What everyone can see in nature, the sunrise or the sunset, or in history, the liberation of an oppressed people from slavery, Israel sees with the laser beam of faith. Such a religious perspective enables Israel to experience a still more profound reality. God is acting now because of a love-bond (such is the sense of the Hebrew word *hesed* in Ps 136), uniting Israel and God as blood-relatives in one "tribe."

Because praise gives nothing to God but simply and joyfully acclaims reality, praise does not demean God nor ourselves. To picture heaven, or for that matter, to perform the liturgy as though God would be some despotic, proud potentate who delights sitting upon a glittering throne to receive the fawning adulations of his subjects, is a caricature totally unbiblical.

The ecstasy of praise releases the greatest amount of energy without necessarily producing anything or getting anywhere. In praise faith plummets through the wonder of the real, and the soul is overawed into silence. Praise is the mighty leap of love into a wonder beyond rational control and intellectual explanation. Because the hymn of praise does not give the reason why but rather acclaims that God is mighty in his goodness, this type of psalm may seem to get nowhere. It ends where it begins. At times the conclusion repeats the introduction. For the singer of hymns, reality is wonder beyond analysis. Where science may be satisfied, as determining how the earth was formed, faith never exhausts the wonder of it all:

> The wonder of such knowledge slips beyond me.
> Should I rise on the wings of dawn
> and make my home at the farthest horizon
> of the sea,
> Even there your hand rests upon me
> (Ps 139:6, 9-10, CS).

The hymn of praise delights in announcing the wonders of life. Death, suffering, penance, and all such moments of loss never enter the hymn of praise—at least in so far as these sorrows afflict God's chosen people. Biblically, Yahweh is a God of life, not of death. Frequently, the psalms protest the inability of the dead to praise God. But this is found in the prayers of supplication, not in the hymns (Pss 6:6; 30:10; 88:11-12; Is 38:18).

God's gift of joy to his people raises a serious question. Ordinarily in the lives of people, life, joy and the good things of this earth frequently distract from God. Yet, from God's viewpoint, life and joy are the only proper manifestations of his presence. Normally, we seek out the help of a spiritual advisor when we are beset with difficulties, not when everything goes well. The request most frequently heard by a priest or teacher is not: everything is wonderful, so tell me about God, but rather, everything is terrible, where is God? Can it be that our difficulties of sensing God's presence in joy make the hymns of praise seem inappropriate for worship today? In this case, perhaps the liturgy, maintaining these psalms against our feelings, exerts a corrective action and reaches deep down into our sub-conscious, enabling us to recognize that the Lord is a God of life.

Biblical religion also possesses a forward vision. Its golden age was not placed in the bygone days of long ago, never again to be fully regained, nor was its religion a frantic attempt to run with what can be salvaged out of the collapsing house of the past. Israel's messianic age always extended from the now into the future. The past was the topic of prayers and recitals because promises came from the past to sustain the present moment as it looked to the future. The past, therefore, was being continually relived as the narratives and hymns and law—in fact, everything which constituted Israel's religious traditions—were being re-read and actualized in each new age.

The hymns of praise achieved this actualization of the past in many ways, and all the while the assembly was being drawn ever more actively into a full re-living of Israel's momentous redemptive acts. And that re-living is not simply a repetition but a new experience within an integrally new setting. "Re-living" is understood here as the way in which grandparents live in the lives of their grandchildren. Some of the means enabling the hymns to actualize the past are the following:

(a) The hymns tend to make a great use of participles, a verb form which bypasses any mention of "time," past, present, or future, and simply extends the action content of a verb into a continuous happening, as in Psalm 136.

(b) Many directions for liturgical actions accompany the hymn: sing, shout, clap the hands, clang the cymbal, pluck the harp, blast the trumpet, touch the lyre with the rhythmic dance of the bow, yes dance with all the rhythm of your body, march in procession, lift your arms, bow, kneel and prostrate against the ground, offer a sacrifice, and assemble around a table for a sacred banquet. See especially Psalms 149-150, but also Psalms 68:26-28; 92:4; 95:6; 98:4-6. Accordingly, Israel was responding now as she participated at the moment of worship in God's redemptive act.

(c) Another aspect of Hebrew grammar enters our consideration of the contemporaneity of the hymns of praise. Contrary to all Western, Indo-European languages, the Hebrew verb did not primarily express time but the mood of the speaker or writer. The speaker referred first of all to an action complete or incomplete, simple or intense, causing a chain reaction or rebounding back upon the subject.

(d) Finally, Israel's special name for God, "Yahweh" (which is normally translated "Lord), can best be explained as the verb "to be" in the continuous, incomplete tense. Whatever the Lord accomplished in Israel's history remained incomplete until all Israelites—perhaps men and women everywhere—would participate in the redemptive action. The past became a promise, sustaining the present in its link to the future. As Fr. Albert Gelin described the divine name "Yahweh" spoken by Israel, "Yahweh" is a prayer of faith, "Be there always with us"; and spoken by God, "Yahweh" is a promise full of hope, "I am he who is always there with you."

This "now" aspect of the hymns of praise was so important that sacred traditions were changed and modernized. For instance, in Psalm 105:33 God still saves his people by the plagues against their enemy, though not as he did in Egypt, destroying flax and barley (Ex 9:31), but rather, by striking down vines and fig trees, the produce of Palestine. This example is not used for its own sake. Rather, it is a biblical reminder of what can and ought to be done today in Christian worship. Changes ought not to be made in biblical readings abruptly and on the spot; but, nonetheless, changes can be made carefully, prayerfully, ahead of time in planning each day's liturgy. The Bible presents a community response to reality. The Sacred Scriptures reflect life, yet not simply life as it has been or is, but also life as it can be and ought to be. In the biblical mirror, reality is caught between the "is" and the "ought to be," and this tension precipitates action.

PSALMS OF SUPPLICATION

The other type of psalm most clearly indentifiable in literary style with the hymns of praise and most frequently encountered in the psalter, is the prayer of supplication. The major themes of the two types of psalms are at opposite poles, however. The hymns of praise never allude to what totally preempts attention and emotions in the supplicatory psalms: sin, suffering, cursing, death. These tragic experiences may be vaguely and distantly implied when the hymns celebrate the triumph of Yahweh and Israel over their common enemies, but Israel exults in joy, untouched by the ravages of war and the upheavals of nature.

Despite these inherent differences, both categories of psalms have a similar literary structure and are united basically in the faith of Israel. The literary form of both types can be compared as follows:

Hymn of Praise	*Prayer of Supplication*
Introduction . . . Call to praise and worship God.	Call to God for help.
Central part . . . Motivation for praise, "Indeed," but not the reason "why."	Expression of pain, dejection and hatred of enemy; petitions for help; but not the reason "why" God allows suffering.
Conclusion . . . Repetition of the call to praise.	Repetition of the call for help or anticipated thanksgiving.

Not only is there a similarity in literary form in the hymn and the prayer, but there is also a common, basic attitude of faith in the central section of each. Neither type progresses logically with human reasons. Instead, each demonstrates a basic faith in God who is present and acting. This conviction cannot be proven nor adequately explained; it must be experienced. Because the encounter with God happens at a profound depth within the human psyche and with such intensity, it bursts the confines of grammatical sentences and rational words. In view of this innate force seizing the soul, a person remains in wonder or in agony. Solace or relief comes more in the sheer ability to sustain this experience than in the intellectual satisfaction of explaining it.

To appreciate the faith of the psalmist when confronted with suffering, we must do what he or she never did—seek some reasons and attempt some explanation. We must start with the premise that divine goodness is the basic ingredient in the mysticism of the psalms; only it is present in different ways. In the hymns of praise the psalmist is swept beyond words in the wonder of God's goodness, while in the prayers of supplication pain has left the worshipper so far behind this goodness as again to be speechless. Very important to Israel's theology is her strong faith that Yahweh not only lives, but can be acclaimed as "a compassionate and gracious God, slow to anger and rich in kindness and fidelity . . ." (Ex 34:6-7). Moreover, if the word "Yahweh" is to be explained as "He who is always there" then he must be present as he really is, a Redeemer who is kind, gracious and forgiving, driving away pain and threats to life.

Israel could not countenance a god of suffering nor a god of death. Their Canaanite neighbors, on the other hand, even named one of their gods, *Muth* or *Moth*, which is the ordinary Hebrew-Canaanite word for death. The mythologies of the ancient Near East possessed stories about the gods dying and rising again. These myths were actually a rationalistic explanation, personalistic and pre-scientific, but all the while highly intellectual, for answering the problem of how suffering and joy, death and life can co-exist. There were separate gods for each experience, or at least separate moments in the career of a single god.

Israel never resorted to such rationalistic subterfuges. She confessed that Yahweh was always there, present with the full force of his life and goodness, even when she could not say how. The prayers of supplication never identify suffering with God. This is true even when Israel felt obliged to cry out to an absent God and believe that her cry was heard. The suffering prisoner who composed Psalm 22 asks with poignant amazement, even in broken grammar, "My God! My God! Why have you abandoned me? Far from my salvation (be) the roar of my words . . ." In many other passages such as Psalms 6:6; 30:10; 88:11-12; 113:17; Isaiah 38:18, we hear the lament that the dead cannot praise God nor even contact him. Yet, all the while, Israel confessed that Yahweh's gracious fidelity was stronger than even the blood-bond within a family. Isaiah wrote, "Fathers declare to their sons, O God, your faithfulness." Again, this same faith, looking into the mysterious face of death, was left without an answer, "For among the dead no one remembers you (nor) . . . gives you thanks" (Ps 6:6). It seems that what the Bible denies explicitly, it maintains implicitly.

Another insight for understanding Israel's attitude toward suffering in relation to God can be found in her ritual for mourning the dead. It is far too elaborate to describe here, but we know that professional mourners, sometimes very jealous of their position (cf. Mt 9:24), could be hired so as to conduct the service properly. The important thing to note, however, is that the ritual remained entirely profane, outside the realm of sacred liturgical ceremonies. Moreover, the classic and moving elegies of Israel's literature, like David's lament over Saul and Jonathan, do not mention the name of God (2 S 1:19-27). The high priest, as the one closest to Yahweh and most representative of God's presence, was not permitted to mourn even his father and mother (Lv 21:11). All other priests, while granted some exceptions, must obey the prescription, "None of you shall render himself unclean for any dead person among his people" (Lv 21:1). Contact with a corpse, even to be present in the same home with it, rendered a person unclean for sanctuary worship. These laws are found in the priestly tradition of the Pentateuch and therefore reflect a post-exilic spirituality and not just an early superstitious stage. Even today on the Mount of Olives in Israel, an elaborate system of Hebrew signs directs the path of the *kohanim* or priests so that they will not inadvertently defile themselves by any of the cemeteries on the mountain. Death remained outside the sanctuary of the living God.

Very consistently, then, slaughtering an animal destined for sacrifice was by no means a sacred act. The ritual in the early chapters of Leviticus relegates the killing of the animal to the lay person who brings this offering. Slaughtering was a necessary but not a sacred act. The lay person, once having killed the victim and carefully drained the blood from the corpse, presented these items to the priest who then initiated the sanctuary ritual. Blood was never offered to God. As symbolic of life and the unity of life among the many members of the one body, blood was sprinkled on the altar and at times on the people to announce, and thereby to intensify, the oneness of life and holiness in the community with God, or to manifest that sin has been forgiven and reunion with God achieved (cf., Lv 17:11; Ex 24:6-8; Lv 16).

This consideration of life and death in relation to the Israelite liturgy brings up the delicate and important topic of atonement. It is summarized this way:

> Since the life of the living body is in
> its blood, I have made you put it on the
> altar, so that atonement may thereby be
> made for your own lives, because it is
> the blood, as the seat of life, that makes
> atonement (Lv 17:11).

Blood makes atonement in that it instills, maintains and strengthens life where life had become weak or was threatened with death. Atonement is achieved when those with "good" blood, most of all God, unite with others in need of purer blood to expel "disease." One person's good health cannot substitute for another's bad health. Only in the closest bond of life can one healthy member of the body come to the aid of another sick member.

Atonement is achieved by union, not by substitution. Strictly speaking, therefore, Jesus did not suffer or die for us—that is, in place of us—because we still suffer and must die. By suffering and dying Jesus united himself with our suffering and dying, and in that most intimate bond, his obedience to the Father's will surges through us, and we rise to a newness of life in his resurrection (cf. Rm 6:1-14).

In the psalms of supplication we find a union of the saint and the sinner, of the living and the dead, of the suffering and the joyful, of the faithful and the desperate. Because the psalmist believed, he had problems with his faith; because he believed firmly, he absolutely would not accept evil; because he believed with love, he was compelled to cry out to God who had seemingly abandoned him. Let us ponder for a moment the psalm already mentioned which sums up most poignantly the inexplicable, mystic nearness of a distant God:

> My God! My God! Why have you abandoned me?
> Far from salvation be the roar of my
> words!
> O my God, I cry out day by day, and you
> answer not;
> night by night and there is no relief for me.
> Yet you are the one enthroned in the holy place,
> O glory of Israel!
> In you our fathers trusted;
> they trusted, and you delivered them.
> To you they cried, and they escaped;
> in you they trusted, and they were not
> put to shame.
> But I am a worm, not a man . . .
> Be not far from me, for distress is near;
> I have no one to help me (Ps 22:2-7, 12, CS).

Converging together in this psalm are all the real components, good and bad, of the Israelite community. Because the psalmist was plunged so totally into the lives of sinful people, he suffered, and he suffered more fiercely because of his greater goodness. Yet, this goodness produced a psalm which would sustain the discouraged and the sinful down through the ages until Jesus himself took refuge within its words. Once again we find the example of atonement by union, whereby goodness, submerged within evil, provides the strength of new blood to purify the evil, revivifies the personal and achieves the new resurrection.

A final necessary consideration in understanding the psalms of supplication concerns the difficult question of suffering being associated always with sin. In the Bible, sin is removed, not by good persons' substituting their prayers for the evil in the sinner but rather by uniting themselves so closely with the sinner, that goodness drives out wickedness and all are purified. This process of purification does not preclude suffering. Forgiveness, suffusing an ever greater goodness within the soul of the sinner, causes more suffering.

An example in the physical order might clarify this point. An otherwise healthy person, with strong vital organs, suffers far more from poison in the system than does someone with a bad heart, poor circulation, weak lungs and who has other organs giving out. The latter person can quickly lapse into a coma and suffer very little. Theologically, to use an analogy, we see that the presence of goodness causes ever more suffering within a person or community, for it strengthens the body in ejecting evil more vigorously. A loving and faithful spouse suffers more from an unfriendly word from his wife than a playboy does about his adultery. Suffering, then, is not so much punishment as it is purification. The silence of God leaving the sinner at "peace" with sin is the worst punishment of all; for then the sinner is comatose.

The silence of God is broken and he speaks his word in Sacred Scripture. As this word, like God himself, lives across generations of people, the blood-bond of union extends also through the centuries, backward as well as forward. For this reason the Bible, which reflects God's intervention in history, seems to defy the laws of chronological history. In the Bible we discover that Moses or David or Jeremiah are continuously alive and their words are always living. Modulated to fit new times and generations, we find in them atonement by union, not substitution.

Once sin is committed, evil is released across the centuries, backward and forward. No one, even in the past, can be fully at rest, if anyone, even in the future, is sick and sinful. The power of goodness, ejecting this sin, comes from all directions. Hopes for the future purify as much as nobility inherited from one's forefathers. Later generations can repay for the gift of life (if that were ever possible) by atoning for the sins of their parents; present generations can sustain the hope that their children's children will correct the mistakes and sins of today. From this consideration, we can conclude that sin always brings suffering somewhere across the centuries, and that suffering always implies sin somewhere in the genealogical tree. "Suffering" here is qualified to mean the purifying force of goodness ejecting evil.

The prayers of supplication in the psalter bring to us the faith and perseverance of our forefathers, challenging our consciences to measure up to their goodness, sustaining us in our sorrows lest we lose faith. Such goodness from the past keeps us from becoming comatose and so induces more suffering in our personal lives as well as in our communities of faith. These ideas also bring us into contact with a number of important theological questions: original sin, merit and indulgence, prayers of petition for others, the suffering souls in Purgatory. If studied in the context of atonement by union instead of substitution, these traditional expressions of faith need not be denied. Rather, they can be enriched when expressed in contemporary terms.

SUMMARY

In conclusion, the psalms of praise and supplication express the universal hopes and ideals of the human race. They also open up new avenues of approach to contemporary situations because they touch people in the everyday situation of their lives. It is important to remember both these aspects when deliberating on the moral practical need of celebrating the liturgy with certain types of groups, each with their own unique situation. At the same time, because they are universal, the psalms touch people in their own specific here and now reality in a way that transcends time. And we, after considering these facts, are now better able to take a closer look at that reality itself in the concluding chapters of this book.

● **PART FOUR**

"Whom shall I send?" "Here I am, send me."
Isaiah 6:8

Call and Response—a dialogue between
Yahweh, Lord, and his people.

GENESIS · 32 · 29

MEDITATIONS FROM A SKETCHBOOK

Say not, "I am too young"...
whatever I
command you,
you shall
speak...

If you are called, reply,
"Speak, Lord, for your servant is listenin

and carrying out my design to shatter the enemies who have risen against us...

Judith 13:5 O, Lord God, now is the time for aiding your heritage...

the word of God is a two-edged sword

The Lord will
have Sisera
fall into the
power of
a woman

Deborah
was judging Israel
She used to sit under
Deborah's palm tree
and the Israelites
came up to her for
judgment

I have grasped you by the hand;
I formed you and set you
as a covenant of the people
a light for the nations

here is my servant, my chosen one, in whom I am well pleased. he shall bring forth justice to the nations

why is it, o sea, that you flee? o Jordan, that you turn back?

Let me now sing of my friend,
My friend's song concerning
his vineyard...

You, too, come along to my vineyard,
and I will pay you what is fair...

Open to me the
Gates of JUSTICE
הללו
the joyful shout
of VICTORY —
the right hand
of the LORD
has struck with
POWER

I WILL ESPOUSE YOU TO ME FOREVER... I WILL ESPOUSE YOU IN RIGHT AND JUSTICE... I... IN LOVE AND IN MERCY... I WILL SAY YOU ARE MY PEOPLE...

אמת חסד צדק שלום

MEDITATIONS FROM A SKETCHBOOK - LILLIAN BRULC

• PART FIVE
THE CHALLENGE

*— Let the coming generation be told
of the Lord — Psalm 22*

Chapter Thirteen
God's Approach to the World: Incarnational

The Scriptures portray God coming to us in earthly trappings and as absorbed in historical movements. This is not a pantheistic statement. Rather, it is an affirmation of God's providence.

> If I go up to the heavens, you are there;
> if I sink to the nether world, you are
> present there.
> If I take the wings of the dawn,
> if I settle at the farthest limits of
> the sea (Ps 139:7-10).

Isaiah recognized God incarnated in the brutal power of Assyria. In the preaching of this prophet, God called Assyria "My rod in anger, my staff in wrath" (Is 10:5). When Habakkuk questioned how God could be present in the wicked Babylonian invaders, God simply replied: "The just person lives by faith" (Hab 2:4).

This incarnational presence of God is a mystery of faith; often God is camouflaged in strange garments exerting a redemptive, supernatural power. To know God—and that knowledge, according to St. John's gospel, is eternal life—a Christian must look for God where he is present. He has no other choice. And because God takes the incarnational approach towards human beings, they must seek God in the same way. Faith is a person's incarnational approach towards God. By faith a person sees beneath the surface of human events and adores the presence of God.

One might prefer that God come in the wondrous establishment of a world empire or in mystic abstraction. The Sadducees and Pharisees wished the former type of transcendent Messiah. When God came to them incarnate in flesh, suffering and dying, they shouted, "Blasphemy!" They had forgotten the message of the theophany granted the prophet Elijah: God was present neither in the mighty wind nor in the earthquake nor in the fire. Only at the "sound of the gentle stillness" did Elijah wrap his face in his mantle before the God of Israel (1 K 19:11-13). God came, silenced and incarnated beneath the weight of human earthliness.

God's incarnation in human affairs involves world history in a travail of tension and agony. From within, God impels the world to develop into something beyond itself, to reach a fulfillment exceeding its native capacity and even its highest desire (cf. Ep 3:19; 1 Jn 3:20). God's incarnational approach incites a kind of transcendental agony at the heart of existence. God within the world, like Jesus walking among men and women, seeks to lift the human world beyond its capacity and dreams, and this initial uneasiness is triggered into struggle and hostility by the world corruption of original sin. That which must be transformed has been contaminated at its heart. Once this struggle unto death broke out between God and the powers of darkness in history, the *world*, the *earth* and the *flesh* became biblical synonyms for weakness, hate and rebellion.

Each time God and a person meet in the union of faith, the transcendental agony begins all over again for that person. Christians, through the presence of Jesus Christ, transcend and transform their sinful flesh. In the process, this sinful flesh (*sarx*) evolves into the risen body of Christ (*soma tou Christou*). Christians stay at the front line of a gigantic messianic struggle whose outcome transcends human powers of goodness or evil. They will become either beasts of the earth (cf. Rv 13:11) or children of God. Even though the incarnational approach must remain the point of departure, Christians spring at once into a transcendental battle: "the mystery of iniquity" (2 Th 2:7) opposing the mystery of the Word of God made flesh.

By looking at the Scriptures in order to determine more exactly how God is incarnate within the world and how his presence precipitates an agonizing struggle of transformation, we can unravel some elements of the mystery of Christians facing the world. From what God has done, men and women learn what they must do in order to find God. Technically, the incarnation refers specifically to God becoming human, but it can be used in the wider sense of God's presence and activity in and through creatures. The Word-made-flesh is but the climax of a long, incarnational approach. God made the world in such a way that at its heart there always pulsed a drive towards renewal and re-establishment in Jesus Christ. St. Paul said all things ought to be re-capitulated in Christ. The most important element of this world is humankind, the center of God's incarnational presence and transcendental purpose. Created to the image and likeness of God, men and women have always sought the fulfillment of this ideal—to be like God.

CREATED THROUGH CHRIST

According to the Scriptures, God's incarnational approach began at the moment of creation, and he has never deviated from it since. Once he had created the universe, he was continually within it, sustaining it, healing it, transforming it. Even the work of creation, as described in chapter 1 of Genesis, came about, not so much by God's issuing orders from majestic heights, but rather by his placing the seed of his word within a growing, evolving mass of matter. "And God said, 'Let there be light . . . firmament . . . earth'." This word of creation, like every word, flows from God's deep center and reveals his secret thoughts. It reached its fullest expression in man and woman, for there it could be received into heart and mind to be cherished and obeyed. To create them to his own image, God breathed his own divine life into them. The imaging of God, therefore, began from within and gradually diffused itself outward across the surface of human activity. So intimate was God's incarnational presence that God and his human family communed and entered one another's thoughts. God thereby elevated people and their world to unde-served heights of knowledge, love and loyalty.

From the very start of all things, God placed within creation a faint resemblance of himself, a feeble stirring of his own life. Creation could never be at rest afterwards. It felt an impulsion to reflect its Maker perfectly, to reunite its scattered remembrance of him into one resplendent image. This unrest of world existence was like the scintillating buoyance of youth, exhilarating in strenuous exercise, relaxing after expended effort. Like the giant sun, it began once more to joyfully run its course (Ps 19:6).

Sin, however, struck at the heart of the first man and woman, invading that deep, personal area where divine life resided. After that, the woman and her offspring struggled with the serpent and his offspring (Gn 3:15). The forces of darkness met with more than human strength to corrupt man and woman's divine life into a proud revolt to be "like God," knowing [and controlling] good and evil (Gn 3:5). These forces have continued to strive for human hearts ever since. The human family, for its part, was involved by its own guilt in a titanic struggle. It desperately needed clear direction and extraordinary strength in order to keep on the path of God's approach toward itself.

The Old Testament called this divine assistance "wisdom." Wisdom was not distinct from that loving, directing power of God, first manifested at creation. Wisdom, according to Proverbs:

> . . . was poured forth.
> at the first, before the earth . . .
> When he established the heavens [wisdom sings]
> I was there,
> when he marked out the vault over the
> face of the deep . . .
> Then was I beside him as his craftsman (Pr 8:23-30).

Because of sin, however, wisdom took the form of discipline and law: coercing, encouraging, reasoning, punishing, rewarding. Wisdom pronounced innumerable prescriptions in the Book of Proverbs. These laws not only came from God but also revealed his presence. Through them, a process of redemptive activity was in progress.

He who finds me finds life . . .
[wisdom announces]
all who hate me love death (Pr 8:35).

Sirach carried this theme of "wisdom . . . creation . . . redemption" one step further. He imparted a distinctly Israelite tone to divine wisdom by identifying its laws with the *Torah*. He wrote this personification of Wisdom:

> From the mouth of the Most High I came forth
> and mistlike covered the earth.
> In the highest heaven did I dwell,
> my throne on a pillar of cloud.
> In the holy tent I ministered before him,
> and in Zion I fixed my abode . . .
> in Jerusalem is my domain.
> All this is true of the book of the Most
> High's covenant,
> the Law which Moses commanded us
> (Si 23:3-4, 10-11, 22).

The creation of the universe, then, was the first step toward the erection of the Jerusalem temple. History was always moving forward toward the day when the temple liturgy would be solemnly enacted and the priestly instructions clearly proposed. This steady progress resulted from the incarnational presence of God at the heart of world existence.

The rabbis further developed this notion. We are told in their literature that the *Torah* was older than the world and instrumental in creating it. "The world," declared Rabbi Udan, "was created for the sake of the *Torah*." The *Torah* so controlled the work of creation that it actually lived within the created world. It represented the incarnate presence of God. It pulsed as a divine élan within the universe, continually striving for the complete expression of itself. The *Torah* was the masterful word of God, creating, sustaining, perfecting and achieving. After the world struggle of the Messianic era, the *Torah* would be fully observed and then, as it were, re-absorbed into God in the everlasting "age to come."

Both the Old Testament and the rabbinical traditions portrayed God *almost* incarnate in the world, in order to elevate the world to divine, transcendent glory. The New Testament, for its part, erases that word "almost" and announces that the Word of God has actually become flesh to dwell in our midst. With the arrival of the fullness of time, "God sent his son, born of a woman" (Gal 4:4). St. Paul wrote the earliest theology of redemption, an approach quite different from St. John's, for example. The Apostle of the Gentiles overlooked the historical aspects of Jesus' ministry, and from the revelation of the risen Christ on the road to Damascus, this thought slowly moved back to that eternal moment, before time, when God was on the verge of saying: "Let there be light . . . firmament . . . earth" (Gn 1). Skilled in the Scriptures and trained by the rabbis, St. Paul presented the incarnate approach of Jesus Christ against a background of wisdom, *Torah*, creation and redemption.

The full theological synthesis of the apostle's thought emerged only in his later mature years. By that time Paul had passed beyond the early stage reflected in Thessalonians where the imminent *parousia* of the risen Lord absorbed his attention. He had left behind the larger but still limited concern of Corinthians, Galatians and Romans. In those, his "great epistles," the vision of the mystery of Christ had expanded to include not only the future *Day of the Lord*, but also the Christian's present sharing in Christ's risen life. But even this vision did not match the definitive achievement of Colossians and Ephesians. In these last two epistles, Paul's interest swept from eternity to eternity. It moved back to the moment "before the foundation of the world" and from that point swung forward to the "recapitulation of all things in Christ" where all "appear with him in glory" (Ep 1:10; Col 3:4). In this, his final statement, St. Paul sees the beginning of the incarnate approach of the Son of God, not with his birth at Bethlehem, but with the initial act of creation.

Somewhat abruptly in chapter 1 of Colossians, St. Paul inserts an early Christian hymn. It praises God who has

> rescued us from the power of darkness
> and brought us into the kingdom of
> his beloved Son. Through him we have
> redemption, the forgiveness of our
> sins (Col 1:13-14).

This liturgical song accumulates reasons why redemption in Christ Jesus evokes wonder and praise. Jesus who redeemed us by his death-resurrection is acclaimed:

> image of the invisible God,
> the first-born of all creatures.
> In [or, by] him everything in heaven
> and on earth was created . . . all were
> created through him and for him . . .
> It is he who is head of the body, the
> Church; he who is the beginning, the
> first-born of the dead, so that primacy
> may be his in everything (Col 1:15-18).

In this hymn, the redemptive work of Jesus Christ is like the wide span of a circle. It began in the silent majesty and transcendent glory of the invisible Godhead. Jesus Christ was the resplendent image or *eikon* of the divine. In this glorious reflection St. Paul contemplates God the Redeemer. In his theology, this eternal "Christ" overflows into the universe.

The glory of God shines from the bosom of the Trinity, wondrously and perfectly imaged in the beloved son, Jesus Christ. Through him it is refracted into the creatures of the universe. Thus it happens that "all things in the heavens and on the earth, things visible and things invisible . . . stand created through and for him." St. Paul deliberately employs the perfect form of the Greek verb, denoting an action already achieved in its fullness, whose effects continue to be felt: "all things stand created." Christ is the mediator or the workman through whom Almighty God creates and continues the work of creating. Paul uses another perfect tense of the verb in the following verse: "The universe owes its coherence to him."

It is very difficult to explain how Jesus exercised a "mediatorial function . . . in creation." St. Paul's language here is liturgical and poetical. Poetry, however, does not destroy the reality in Paul's words; it simply attests that strictly rational categories of thought cannot contain nor communicate the full truth. The poet, like the mystic, judges intuitively and speaks symbolically. With liturgical language Paul does away with the barriers of past and future, in order to involve the worshipper in a divine redemptive act now taking place. This Christological hymn written by St. Paul quickly moves from first creation to the death of Jesus and even beyond Calvary to the final re-creating; from Christ the *Alpha* to Christ the *Omega;* from the beginning to the end.

Some kind of efficient and exemplary causality seems to be attributed to Christ. Scriptural and philosophical scholars variously interpret this passage. Some, while admitting its difficulty, have suggested the following interpretation: in him all things have been created as in their supreme center of unity, harmony and cohesion; he gives to the world its sense, its value and therefore its reality. He is, as it were, the foyer, the meeting-point where all the threads of the universe and all its generative powers meet and coordinate. Whoever has an instantaneous point of view on the whole universe, past, present and future, sees all beings suspended ontologically in Christ, definitively intelligible only in him.

When St. Paul calls Christ the "image *[eikon]* of the invisible God," he places our Lord prior to Adam and all other persons. Christ is the image; all others are made according to that image. God expresses himself totally in this one, perfect reflection, Jesus Christ. Through this image God's reflection spreads wide, like the colors of a spectrum, in the act of creation. What was fully in Christ, through Christ is divided and shared with all the parts of the universe.

Paul repeats this idea when he refers to Christ as "the first-born before every creature." It is clear from this phrase that Christ is not a part, not even the first part of creation. He is the one by whom and according to whom the universe begins its existence. It would be long and tedious to give all the supporting texts, but there is a direct line of thought, connecting Paul's phrase, "the first-born before every creature," of Colossians with Proverbs 8:22, "The Lord begot me, the first-born of his ways," and from Proverbs back to Genesis: "In the *beginning* God created the heavens and the earth" (Gn 1:1).

The Hebrew word in Proverbs, translated "first-born," is identical with Genesis' "In the beginning." With the help of Proverbs the rabbis concluded that wisdom or the *Torah* was the first-born of all creatures, and they then interpreted Genesis to mean, "According to the *Torah*, God created the heavens and the earth." In creating, God scattered the reflective brilliance of the *Torah* throughout the universe, and, therefore, through obedience to this *Torah*, the universe will reach its final, perfect stage. The *Torah* was instrumental both in creating and in redeeming. The idea of "redemption" must be included here in speaking of creation, because as creation continues, it is constantly overcoming many sinful obstacles. To the extent that the *Torah* wins obedience, the power of God's word achieves the full effect for which he sent it.

With ease Paul could make the transition to Christ, the "Wisdom of God," the new *Torah*. Christ possesses all the fullness of the Godhead; he is the perfect image of the deity. He is the "mystery of God, Christ, in whom every treasure of wisdom and knowledge is hidden" (Col 2:2-3). All of these descriptive phrases must be understood dynamically, in the active way of God creating, God redeeming, God fulfilling, God glorifying. Such is Christ.

The Old Testament and especially its rabbinical interpreters came as close as possible to making the law and the wisdom of God a divine person, one with God yet distinct from God in its emanation through the universe. St. Paul took that step, which, perhaps, was just a hair's breath away from the position of the rabbis, but a hair's breath which flung him into the tumultuous mystery of Jesus Christ. He does not tire of calling Christ and his redemptive work "the mystery which has been hidden from eternity in God" (Ep 3:9).

Paul summed it up this way: "In Christ the fullness of the deity resides in bodily form. Yours is a share of this fullness" (Col 2:9). This well-known passage brings to the surface of human words three most sublime mysteries: the divinity of Christ, his work of redemption and our divine life of grace. As we remember not only Paul's rabbinical training but also the totally existential order of the biblical narrative, we conclude that for St. Paul Christ is divine because he exercises the fullness of God's redemptive power. "Of his fullness" (*to pleroma*) signifies Christ's divinity in the existential, rather than in the essential order. It has the same sense as meant in the Johannine Prologue, "Of his fullness we have all had a share" (Jn 1:16). The implications of this statement will be explored in the next chapter.

Chapter Fourteen
Christian Approach to the World: Incarnational-Transcendental

Books can and will continue to be written on each Pauline statement in the Scriptures. In this chapter, however, a conclusion will be proposed, not to settle all discussion, but simply to indicate the consequences of one orthodox line of thought for the subject at hand: the Christian's confrontation with the world. When St. Paul contemplates the divine Christ, living "before the world began" (Ep 1:4), he sees the fullness of all divine activity, from that of God creating in the first moment of time all the way down to that of God recreating in the eschatological moment. The universe comes into existence, not only God-stamped but truly Christ-stamped. God creates in Christ by extending the radiance of Christ's being. What is scattered always seeks unity. Water, drawn from the ocean and scattered through the land, again seeks the ocean. Water roars with fierce power against rocks and canyon walls which obstruct its path. Its energy mounts to an almost unlimited degree when it is locked behind colossal dams.

The image of Christ, spread across the universe, always sought the fullness from which it came forth. Once sin set up barriers, the image fought and battled to express itself adequately, and this struggle continued across the endless stretch from Adam who was a son of God all the way to Jesus, the new Adam and the perfect son of God. In Jesus Christ dwelt "the fullness of the Godhead bodily." Like water stored behind a mammoth dam, the full force of God stirred within the bodily frame of Christ Jesus, truly an infinite reservoir of energy. This water of divinity poured into Christ and pounded against the walls of flesh. The full redemptive glory of the Godhead strove against the binding, restrictive, even hostile power of human *sarx*. It broke through these barriers in his death-resurrection.

The death-resurrection of Christ was accompanied with the triumphant cry: "It is perfected! It is finished!" And yet, as this fullness is received into the Church, the body of Christ, it is not yet perfected nor is it yet finished. This is not to say that the Scriptures need correcting, but that we tend to have an inadequate understanding of the Scriptures. What happened in Christ is happening in the mystical Christ. The redemptive-creative work of God—what the Bible sometimes calls his "glory"—is over with, but one must linger while pronouncing these words, for the work is still passing over and through the Church. The Church is just as truly Christ as the Christ who died and rose again. The Church, fully understood, is the real Christ now existing.

We face, therefore, a redemptive-creative work, fully accomplished and yet somehow still being accomplished; a redemptive incarnation which has totally transformed the human and lifted it to the transcendent glory of heaven and at the same time a redemptive incarnation still filling up "his body [that is, Christ's body which is] the Church" (Col 1:24). These good tidings of "the unfathomable riches of Christ," according to St. Paul, are "the mysterious design which for ages was hidden in God, the Creator of all . . . now through the Church made known . . . and thus carried out in Christ Jesus our *Kyrios*" (Ep 3:8-11).

What has happened in Christ Jesus, therefore, had already existed, hidden in God before creation. Creation proceeds from God, one with the redemptive accomplishment of Christ Jesus, and what Jesus did is now made known—that is, is now being done—through the Church. God took the incarnational approach in order to lift the earth to transcendent glory. He is still approaching that way, and we can meet him and be united with him.

St. Paul's theological synthesis, formulated in Colossians and Ephesians, seems to have originated in the liturgy of the apostolic Church. The place of the liturgy in relation to the life of the Christian has been taken up in a previous chapter. It will be considered here from the aspect of God's incarnational approach towards humankind. What St. Paul drew from the eucharistic worship of his day can be relocated in the eucharistic worship of our own day. The Eucharist is truly an *anamnesis* or remembrance of God's incarnational approach towards men and women. The Eucharist also consecrates our earthly life as a path towards God. God and his people meet "incarnationally" in the Eucharist, and in that encounter the human family rises to participation in God's transcendent life.

With the background already given on liturgy, we can look at the Old Testament and restrict our consideration of the liturgy to the feast of the Paschal Lamb. During its celebration, Jesus instituted the Eucharist. The Pasch beautifully embodies the incarnational approach of God. The feast began in thoroughly human circumstances and in later history continually absorbed new details of Israel's very human existence. At times, the events appeared so insignificant, even so unworthy of God, that long prayer and strong faith alone could see beneath such a tawdry surface and detect God's redemptive presence.

The Pasch began with the exodus out of Egypt. It is difficult to say what this occurrence meant to the Egyptian people. They probably attached very little importance to it; they did not even judge it important enough for their official records. The exodus made little or no dent upon the Egyptian economy. In no way does it seem to have injured the morale of Pharoah's soldiers, and it assuredly did not topple the reigning dynasty. Even for the Israelites involved in the first exodus, the event seemed a hectic combination of fear, panic, silence, stealth, grumbling and despair (Ex 14:10-14). Only when the waters closed in to separate them from their Egyptian pursuers, did the Israelites sing triumphantly to God their Savior (Ex 15:19-21). Then almost immediately they began grumbling all over again (Ex 15:24; 16:3).

In and through all this humanness God performed one of his mightiest redemptive acts. Time and prayer were necessary before the people of God grasped the inner reality of this event. The exodus gradually became the elaborate festival of the paschal lamb; a ritual by which the people sought to express externally the divine meaning of the first saving act of God. The human imperfections and sins of the Mosaic days were forgotten and the redemptive act of God was lifted to the surface. Without the liturgy the exodus would probably have been forgotten and its details erased from memory in the same way that Egyptian sands and winds have worn down and silenced other seemingly greater events of history. However, the fact remains: Israelite liturgy would have remained silent and meaningless also had it not reached out to re-enact the deeds of salvation-history. Its very life was the continuing existence of what God once performed at a given moment of time. The liturgy, as we have seen, does not commemorate and renew the achievements of scholars, or even the definitions of rabbis and Church Fathers. It commemorates and renews the redemptive acts performed by God in human history.

In this process we can detect the incarnational approach of God to people and of people to God. The liturgy reaches within a human event, discards the surface elements of politics, selfishness and short-sightedness and lifts to popular vision the transcendental presence of God. Through it the people of God are enabled to adore God their Savior and to re-experience the salvation event. The liturgy of a later age clothes this divine act of salvation with the human wrappings of contemporary civilization. After the Israelites, for instance, had conquered Palestine and settled down in their new homeland, the exodus liturgy was modified. It had begun as a vigil of fear and silence; it continued during the desert days as a nomadic festival of freedom. Joyful features slowly appeared in the liturgy; the worshippers began to recline peacefully. No longer did they eat standing "like those who are in flight" (Ex 12:11). In Palestine they added the ritual of unleavened bread to thank God for the yearly deliverance from hunger at the spring harvest festival. Deliverance from oppression was no longer a throwing off of Egyptian chains but was seen as an emergence from the threat of famine.

Centuries later during the Babylonian exile, when they were again oppressed in a foreign land, the paschal liturgy expressed their faith in a new exodus. They still proceeded across a desert where springs flowed marvelously with water and where the entire route was a way prepared by the Lord (Is 40:3; 43:16-21).

The incarnational aspect of God's approach did not stop here but continued, always assimilating new elements of Israelite life until the fullness of time came. At that moment the paschal lamb absorbed and literally transformed the bread, wine and lamb of the New Covenant. The liturgy today, as in the past, reflects the daily life of the people and, in fact, is that life in its deepest reality, for it repeats anew the historical meeting of God and his people.

The liturgy, like human life, changes on its surface; but at its heart it remains the same. In the case of the Pasch, the liturgy renews the great mystery of the exodus, the passage of God's people from sin to grace, from oppression to freedom. There is a continuity in the celebration of the Pasch from the days of Moses until the time of Christ and into our own day. It is evident that the Pasch is not so much a line which extends through the ages but a point around which the ages revolve. Each event is a redemption from darkness, need or oppression, and therefore each in its own way is an exodus.

Most important for our Christian understanding, however, is the realization that the first act of creation was dynamically related to the Pasch-exodus event. It too was a redemptive act of God, for as creation continued its work through the centuries, it struggled against darkness and sorrow. This aspect of creation in the paschal mystery was to continue and reach its fullest expression in Christ, our paschal lamb. Christ, crucified and risen, was to die and through that death rise to new life. The paschal celebration of his death-resurrection re-enacts this mystery in the Church, until all of us are re-created in eternal life. The incarnational approach of God will involve the liturgy in changing history until time and space are transformed into the transcendent glory of the eternal, new creation.

Now, as always, the liturgy receives its initial exterior form and its abiding interior significance from the events of history. But through the centuries, the liturgy has sloughed off many accidental details of historical events, so that only the most important features were dramatized. In this pruning process it becomes clear that God is at the heart of history, saving and gladdening his people. "God at the heart" means God incarnate within his people so that through God's presence the people feel the beat of a divine mode of life. God slowly enables the world to transcend its greatest hopes and to evolve into a new paradise.

STRUGGLE IN THE PROCESS

Throughout history, however, all things did not run smoothly. Obstructions and hindrances were encountered. Sin diminished the life of the people and sometimes healing was necessary before transformation could take place. Healing was accomplished through expiation. Expiatory sacrifice was nothing other than a people's profound and contrite sense of sin rising to the surface of consciousness and expressing itself liturgically. Even though every individual person and nation began life carrying the seed of sin deep within themselves, still, a long time elapsed while that seed grew and thrust its vicious power into the level of consciousness. Still more time passed before conscience admitted its guilt and repented.

Experience shows that everyone lives exuberantly at first. It is only later that we recognize the weakness of the flesh. This law of life is true of Israel and of the Church. The Apostles, in Acts, began their ministry repeatedly announcing that they were witnesses of the resurrection. They touched very quickly, almost apologetically, upon the passion and death of our Lord. But as they courageously manifested the power of the risen Savior in a world of flesh, all kinds of difficulties appeared within and without the community, and slowly they admitted the necessity of suffering with Christ in expiation of sin.

The same process is evident in Old Testament times. Israel began an independent national existence when she burst from the womb of the Red Sea and beheld the glorious theophany of Mount Sinai. For a long time afterwards—in fact, for longer than six hundred years—expiatory sacrifices and sufferings held little or no place in the Israelite ritual. Serious offenses were punished according to the southern tradition of Leviticus with death or a form of excommunication. The northern practice is embodied in the Shechemite liturgy of covenant renewal. In this latter ritual the levitical priests proclaimed great blessings and threatened dire curses but gave no attention to expiation for serious sin. It seems that the ceremonial included some type of public confession of sin. This formal begging of God's forgiveness presumed that the worshipper was contrite, already freed of any hateful disposition towards God and wholly intent on adoration. True, Leviticus speaks often enough of "sin offerings," but the context of these references shows clearly that these sacrifices were offered for unintentional faults and various sins of inadvertence.

Israel always recognized her desperate need for divine assistance. Without God she would have rotted in Egypt, dried up in the desert and starved amidst Palestinian famines. These, however, were the days of her youth. Israel hoped and dreamed; great victories were taking place: the exodus, the covenant, the conquest, the establishment of the Davidic dynasty. The liturgy, like Israel's life, rang with vibrant *hallelujahs*.

The prophets Amos, Micah, Isaiah, Zephaniah, Jeremiah and Ezekiel cleared the way for the elaboration of expiatory sacrifices. "The day of the Lord," shouted Amos, was to be "a day of darkness" (Am 5:18). Zephaniah added dour words of lament: "A day of anguish and distress, a day of destruction and desolation" (Zp 1:15). Jeremiah taught that God had first "to root up and to tear down, to destroy and to demolish" before he could be ready "to build and to plant" (Jr 1:10). Wondrously enough, God was in the midst of all this agony. He cries out in Hosea's words: "My heart is overwhelmed, my pity is stirred" (Ho 11:8).

In one of the boldest passages of the entire Bible, God cries out through Second Isaiah:

> You burdened me with your sins,
> and wearied me with your crimes (Is 43:24).

The phrase, "You burdened me"—from the Hebrew verb *'abad*—literally means "you have made a servant of me." This phrase becomes even more startling when we recall its close connection with Second Isaiah's theme of the Suffering Servant of the Lord—in Hebrew, *'ebed Yahweh*. God was somehow with his people, a servant with them as they experienced the humbling effects of sin. The four songs of the *'ebed Yahweh* reach the climax of humiliation and exaltation in chapter 53. The servant is a lamb slain "for the sin of his people"; "he gives his life as an offering for sin."

The hymns of Second Isaiah and especially the Suffering Servant laments in Is 40-55 may have been composed for liturgical assemblies or else they were strongly influenced by Israel's liturgy. Once more the liturgy voices the deep sorrow and re-enacts the tragic experience of the people. The painful groan of sorrow sounds within the syllables of another liturgical book: Lamentations, composed most probably in Palestine for services at the site of the devastated temple. Adoration and joy continue to hold the dominant role in Israelite liturgy, but God has surrounded himself with a new feature of human life—the expiatory sufferings of the wicked and especially of the innocent. Hereafter, expiatory sacrifices, fasting and other penitential rites were firmly fixed in the ritual.

The New Testament evidences how Jesus thoroughly united himself with a sinful world and most bitterly experienced the sin-consciousness of the human race. He was enfolded in the *sarx* or flesh of human weakness. "He has suffered," we read in the epistle to the Hebrews, "and has been tempted" (Heb 2:18). So completely human did he appear that St. Paul wrote: "for our sakes God made him who did not know sin to be sin" (2 Cor 5:21). "God sent his Son in the likeness of sinful flesh as a sin offering, thereby condemning sin in the flesh" (Rm 8:3). According to Pauline theology, that last statement can be reworded to read: Jesus condemned and overcame our sin by becoming incarnate in our flesh. If Jesus had withdrawn to a remote solitude, he never would have suffered in any way, much less died on the cross. But the law of the incarnation drove him to be thoroughly immersed in the affairs of men and women, surrounded by their jealousy and hatred and finally overcome by their death. Jesus, of set purpose, struggled with the powers of darkness so that his divine life might destroy them.

These two superhuman forces—the Son of God and the offspring of the demon—eventually locked in deadly combat. So close was the burning breath of sin upon Jesus that St. Paul pictures the struggle as a battle waged in the flesh of Jesus where sin was condemned. The more fierce the struggle, the more strenuously was the Spirit of God manifested in Jesus. His death was a mortal blow to *sarx* (flesh) forever, and the triumphant Messiah rose from the dead, "crowned with glory and honor" (Heb 2:9). He who had become incarnate in *sarx* destroyed *sarx* that a new body might emerge transcending human possibilities.

Jesus is our model and master; he teaches the Christian how to face the world, how to become completely incarnate in the world. And through the apostolic Christian alive in Christ Jesus, the new Adam, the world can transcend its present sinful condition and be reconciled to God (cf. Col 1:20). Only in Christ can the Christian accomplish this heroic feat. Of himself, the Christian is part of the world of *sarx*. In Christ, the Christian becomes a new incarnation where the Spirit dwells; and as once in Jesus, so now the Spirit cries in each Christian, "Abba, Father!" (Gal 4:6).

"If the Spirit of him who raised Jesus from the dead dwells in you," wrote St. Paul, "then he who raised Christ from the dead will bring your mortal bodies to life . . ." (Rm 8:11). In that particular section of Romans, St. Paul hastens to add that "we are children of God . . . heirs with Christ, if only we suffer with him" (Rm 8:17). This suffering is most keenly felt, not so much by inflicting self-denial from without but by allowing the Spirit within to move outward and transform the rebellious *sarx* into the obedient body of Christ, *soma Christou*.

Nowhere does the body of Christ struggle so energetically against its weakness and sinfulness as in the Eucharist. There it proclaims the passion and death of Jesus. It renews the moment of mortal combat between flesh and spirit in the death of Jesus. Once again as in Old Testament times, the life struggle of God's people is most intensely and most vitally experienced in the liturgy. Some passages taken from the eucharistic text in First Corinthians (11:23-34) relate directly to this theme.

In the text Paul writes, "Everytime, then, you eat this bread and drink this cup, you proclaim the death of the Lord until he comes!" (1 Cor 11:26). Paul answers the questions of how the

Eucharist preaches the gospel and witnesses to the world the death of the Lord in the following verse where he hints at his own personal insight into "the body of the Lord." He complains that the Corinthians are eating the bread and drinking the cup unworthily, and this is why they eat and drink "without recognizing the body" (1 Cor 11:29). The last phrase is crucial. It provides the clue for appreciating the Pauline doctrine of the Eucharist as the renewal of the death of Jesus. What was this body which the Corinthians did not distinguish or recognize?

Using modern terminology, would we claim that the Church of Corinth denied the presence of the body and blood of Jesus in the Eucharist? Not if they were instructed by Paul. Earlier in First Corinthians he had written, "Is not the cup of blessing we bless a sharing in the blood of Christ? And is not the bread which we break a sharing in the body of the Lord?" (1 Cor 10:16). We can dispose also of another possible solution. The Corinthians, gathered for the eucharistic banquet, did not become so intoxicated as to be unable to distinguish consecrated bread from other morsels of food. Though revelry and sensuality were prevalent later in Christian history, they do not seem to have been a regular abuse at the eucharistic meal at this time. St. Paul nowhere condemns the Corinthians for this kind of sacrilegious reception of the body of the Lord. The final solution must be discovered from the general context of First Corinthians. The body of the Lord which the Christians failed to recognize was the body of Christ, *the Church*.

At Corinth, the body of Christ was being torn by boasting, jealousy and schism. Here is where the Christians separated into those "of Paul," and those "of Apollos," those "of Cephas," and those "of Christ." And Paul retorted, "Has Christ, then, been divided into parts?" (1 Cor 1:11-13). The Greek expression, *ho Christos*, refers to the total Christ as he now exists. St. Paul, in chapter 12, calls the Christian Church simply, "*ho Christos.*" "You, then," he writes again in the same chapter, "are the body of Christ" (1 Cor 12:12, 27). The pronoun, *you*, is plural, i.e., *all of you* are the one body of Christ.

Returning to the eucharistic passage of chapter 11, we can

draw some conclusions. When the Corinthians quarrel and split apart, when they boast as if their gifts were independent of the Spirit inhabiting all the brethren, when jealousy blinds their eyes from seeing distinctly the goodness of others, they are no longer capable of distinguishing the true body of the Lord. Christ simply cannot be adequately and realistically known if he is separated from his full body, the Church. Unless Christians correctly approach the world of their neighbor, they cannot recognize God's presence in the world, a presence which constitutes the true and total Christ.

It can be seen now how the eucharistic celebration "proclaims [or preaches] the death of the Lord until he comes!" To celebrate the Eucharist worthily, the Corinthians must forgive and forget offenses against one another, they must endure humiliations and persecutions from outsiders. They must conquer and put to death the rebellious flesh around and within them. The members of the Church assembled for the eucharistic ceremony witness publicly to what they truly are—Christ alive, and by that life constantly dying as the Spirit overcomes the weakness of rebellious flesh, their *sarx*.

Can we go a step further and say that the assembly of the Church does more than symbolize the humiliation and the death of Jesus on Calvary? Because the Church and the eucharistic body are mysteriously the one body of Christ, can we claim that the eucharistic ceremony is a renewal or commemoration of the passion and death expressly because the Church is undergoing sacrifice and death? It certainly does endure the suffering and the dying of Jesus in its members. And the same Holy Spirit who led Jesus courageously forward to struggle with and conquer the weakness of flesh now dwells within the body of Christ, the Church. This Spirit of Christ impels the Church, as St. Paul wrote in Romans, to "put to death the evil deeds of the body" and so to "live" (Rm 8:13). St. Paul, this time in Second Corinthians, expressed it this way: "While we live we are constantly being delivered to death for Jesus' sake, so that the life of Jesus may be revealed in our mortal flesh" (2 Cor 4:11).

We cannot separate the death and the life of Jesus in his body the Church from his body in the Eucharist. What happened to Christ's body in the moment of passion-resurrection, not only constitutes the eucharistic body of the Lord but also happens today in his body the Church. And the sufferings or joys experienced by the body of Christ, the Church, at once react upon the eucharistic body of Christ. There is only "one body and one Spirit" (Ep 4:4). This is the full eucharistic-mystical body of Christ. It applies as a basis for later theological thought on the Mass as well.

The Mass is truly the sacrifice of the dying-rising Christ, the one sacrifice of Calvary continuing now. What Christ accomplished through the Spirit on Calvary he now continues to do through the indwelling Spirit in his mystical body. The sufferings of Christ now in his body which is the Church demand a sacrificial presence in his eucharistic body. When the Church no longer needs to suffer in overcoming *sarx*, then the transformation of all into the full body of Christ will have been completed and the Eucharist will no longer be celebrated. The eschatological moment will have arrived.

To participate intelligently and religiously in the Eucharist, the Christian must be able to recognize the true body of Christ, his full body. This recognition must necessarily be vital and experiential, so that the Christian participates by living faith in the one body of Christ, sharing its struggle against sin that the fullness of the God-head may be realized. In order to accomplish this, men and women must be as completely incarnated in the world of their neighbor as Christ is. This participation, like the incarnation of Jesus, leads to a passion and death; as it continues the mystery of Calvary, the Church undergoes the dying of Jesus and thus completes the eucharistic celebration as a full renewal of Calvary. Incarnate in *sarx*, the Christian transcends it by being transformed through the indwelling Spirit into the glorious body of Christ. Each putting to death of sinful *sarx* means that at that moment there is a new burst of life in Christ Jesus.

Until the final age of the world recapitulates all things in Christ, something will always be lacking to the body of Christ. St. Paul writes,

Even now I find my joy in the suffering
I endure for you. In my own flesh I fill
up what is lacking in the sufferings of
Christ for the sake of his body, the church.
(Col 1:24).

The parallelism here is striking. Paul's sufferings are identical with "what is lacking of the sufferings of Christ." Sufferings borne "for you," he tells the Colossians, are being endured "for the sake of his body, the Church." The sufferings of Christ continue in his body, the Church, until all the weakness of its *sarx* is transformed into the glorious *soma Christou*.

Just as the great redemptive act of Calvary was absorbed into the liturgy, transforming the Jewish paschal sacrifice of deliverance from Egypt into the Christian sacrifice of the body and blood of Jesus Christ, so the continuing acts of the sufferings of Jesus in his Church are drawn into the liturgy of the Eucharist, proclaiming today the death of the Lord until he comes. Only those who recognize the true and total body of the Lord can adequately perform this liturgy. Once more we are reminded of St. Paul's statement: "In him everything in heaven and on earth was created, things visible and invisible . . . all were created through him, and for him" (Col 1:16).

Chapter Fifteen
The Process of Humanization

The tasks of the apostolate seldom, if ever, find us in the enviable position of having limitless resources, creating exactly what we want, with no opposition in the way. Likewise, God himself rarely appears as creator in the Sacred Scriptures, omnipotently summoning life with nothing existing ahead of time to interfere with his plans. Instead, when God enters the history and pages of the Bible, he meets a people plagued with many problems and frustrations: Abraham, "a wandering Aramean," sterile and propertyless; the children of Jacob, slaves in Egypt; the twelve tribes divided and overrun by Philistines in the land of Canaan. In fact, once the first two chapters of Genesis are left behind, sin dogs the footsteps and infests the very nature of every person in the Bible all the way down to the time of Jesus when people seemed like "sheep without a shepherd." The work of God in the Bible is as is the work of the apostolate today, a redemptive rather than a creative process.

Creation, in the strictest sense, is an omnipotent act reserved to God alone; redemption is a kindly deed in which men and women participate with God as co-workers. Salvation starts after humankind has marred the creative work of God. It patiently brings to fulfillment, despite all barriers along the way, the hidden potential which God created within the dreams of a people. The apostolate, therefore, is the long process of accepting people as they are, yet continuously challenging them to reach for their hopes. The result is humanization.

Acceptance and challenge are the two important attitudes found in the biblical process of humanization. The Bible shows humanization as being realized because of the genuinely good values found within world cultures. It also shows humanization being challenged because of God's "secret plan" stirring within still greater hopes for the future (cf. Ep 3:1-13).

In this chapter, three aspects of humanization in the Old Testament will be examined: first, the basic biblical principles of humanization; second, some of the human or "secular" values religiously accepted by the Bible; third, the prophetic confrontation: condemning what has become too formal and top-heavy in human achievement and reviving the spirit of each person because of the greater hopes God has implanted in the human heart. Through this process salvation turns out to be a way (and how important is that word *way* in the Bible) of improving human attitudes towards life here on planet earth. There is no other way of preparing for eternal life hereafter. Jesus made this very clear in his sermon about the final judgment: "Come . . . Inherit the kingdom prepared for you from the creation of the world. For I was hungry and you gave me food . . ." (Lk 25:34-35).

THE PRINCIPLE OF HUMANIZATION

Within the process of humanization, as accepted and then challenged, a basic pattern is continuously at work in the Bible. It can be described both from an historical and theological viewpoint, the latter being closely intertwined with the first. Historically, human evolution usually follows a two-stage program. It begins with some type of military, political or economic conquest of one people by another. This subjugation by external violence is never permanent unless, through a second stage, the conqueror adapts himself to the local climate and geography. But even more important at this stage is his adaptation to the customs, values and general life style of the conquered people. The military conqueror must allow himself to be conquered culturally.

Examples reach back into world history. Rome defeated Greece militarily but was itself conquered by Hellenistic culture, and so was able to secure a longer lease for the Roman Empire. And even though barbarian tribes from Europe and Asia swept through and toppled Roman dominance in the world, they, in turn, eventually succumbed to Roman culture, spoke Latin, and were governed by Roman jurisprudence. We can look also at the other side of the coin. In some respects, might not the failures we have sustained in our own day be instances where this second stage of humanization was, at least in a derived sense, ignored? The failures of the United States in Vietnam, France in Algeria, Belgium in Zaire are just a few examples of an unwillingness or inability to become an integral part of the human landscape.

The only way in which the second stage of cultural reconquest can be avoided lies in the horrendous policy of deportation or extermination of a conquered people. Soviet Russia may be attempting the solution of deportation by removing all persons of leadership ability from such countries as Lithuania, Estonia and Latvia. In the past, European settlers in North America exterminated the indigenous Indians and transplanted their own culture to the United States instead.

The history of Israel in Old Testament times followed this normal two-stage process, but with God's people there was also a unique third stage, that of prophetical challenge.

Although there are many hypotheses to explain how Israel took control of Canaan, practically no scholar disputes the fact of a military conquest. In a series of armed expeditions, Israel first obtained a foothold and then extended her control over more and more of Canaan. The long story is compressed and religiously interpreted in the books of Joshua and Judges, and in First Samuel, chapters 1-7. No one, it seems, secured Israel's power over the land more forcefully than King David, who broke the back of the Philistine invaders, absorbed scattered pockets of Canaanite population, and formed friendly alliances or trade agreements with those at a distance. Examples of the latter are the seaport principalities of Tyre and Sidon (1 S 8-1 K 2). And Israel, the military victor, was reconquered culturally by the vanquished Canaanites.

In the process just described, however, some serious questions can be raised in regard to the basic principle of humanization. One of them concerns the matter of violence. In the Bible we find the spread of revealed religion being closely aligned with military conquest and external violence. In fact, a great part of the biblical narrative attempts to justify or at least to celebrate liturgically the acquisition of the land by the sword. In the book of Joshua, chapter 1, the right to the land is traced to a special divine promise, while most of chapters 2 to 6 are derived from later liturgical celebration at the well-known sanctuary of Gilgal. Even from a cursory reading of Joshua, chapters 1 through 10, one will quickly spot such cultic allusions as sermons and instructions, confessions of faith, solemn processions, liturgical "shouts," and the sounding of the ram's horn.

Any attempt to reach back to the reasons behind these liturgical celebrations and theological justifications raises most embarrassing questions for biblical scholars. Does God directly sanction and ordain such violence? I do not think so. However, I am convinced that God always expects his people to live within reality. Most unfortunately, "wars and the rumors of war" (Mk 13:7) belong to the real world of human life. Like the Bible, the Church, too, has always shown herself willing to come to terms with reality and to seek the Spirit of God within reality. The Church does not pretend that Communism is non-existent. At the same time, while being one of Communism's most consistent opponents, the Church has maintained diplomatic relations with countries like Cuba, Poland and Hungary. The Church has always placed military chaplains in the armed forces on all sides of world conflicts. Charity works within the real and does not wait for the ideal circumstances. When help is needed, charity acts at once and leaves theological justification and ornate liturgies for a later date.

The basic principle of humanization, as applied to Israel in the Bible, reads, then, like this:

1. Israel conquered Canaan militarily.
2. Canaan, the vanquished, conquered Israel culturally.
3. Israel, in turn, conquered Canaan religiously.

HUMANIZATION, RELIGIOUSLY ACCEPTED

So completely did Israel adopt the culture of Canaan that we are unsure even of the precise language or dialect spoken by Moses. The Patriarchal and Mosaic traditions were translated into the language spoken by Canaanites and adopted by Israelites. From these same culturally rich people Israel derived her alphabet and a new urgency about preserving written documents in popular style. The esoteric forms of hieroglyphics or sacred picture-writing used in Egypt and in Mesopotamia, where the origins of the biblical people lie, were less available to people in general. Only a few highly trained persons mastered the art of writing. Alphabetic writing reflects the more open character of a people willing to argue even with God. From Canaan Israel also learned to farm, to build homes and city walls, and to construct sacred edifices like sanctuaries and temples. When Israel was transformed from semi-nomadic wanderers of the desert to a sedentary people working the farm lands and vineyards and settled in permanent villages, Canaan provided the know-how.

Outside influences also shaped the styles of government and social organization within Israel. Just as earlier in the days of Moses the covenant was modeled upon the familial type of tribal structure, this same Mosaic covenant was revised in the book of Deuteronomy, as mentioned in chapters 4:44–11:32, to reflect still more closely what is known as the *Hittite Suzerainty Treaty*, normally used in Lebanon and Syria, north of the land of Israel. In fact, practically every biblical law can be found outside Israel in other pre-existing law codes. While the spirit and organizing principle of Israel's law code were vastly superior, all the details were already at hand and did not have to be dictated by God.

One of the most important humanizing factors absorbed by Israel from the surrounding ancient Near East was her peculiar tribal organization. According to the primary law of this social structure, no one possessed security and total rights unless they had been incorporated into the genealogy and "blood stream" of a people. A boy or girl was never adopted simply by a father or mother, but rather by grandparents and great grand-parents and all the ancestry. A good example of this tribal procedure is found in the case of the Kenizzites, who earlier belonged to the line of Esau, the twin brother and jealous protagonist of Jacob (Gn

25:23-24; 27:41). Later they were "genealogized" into the line of Jacob's son Judah (1 Ch 4:13; Gn 29:35). Only in this way could the Kenizzites, a foreign people, come to enjoy the privileges and promises of the Israelite nation.

Because the blood bond was so essential to tribal organization and security, primary obligations flowed from it. Members of a family *had to* come to the aid of one another: buying a brother or sister out of slavery (Lv 25:47-55), regaining a dispossessed property for the clan (Lv 25:23-34), executing the murderer of any member of the family (Nb 35:9-29), marrying a brother's widow who had not yet borne a male child so that the first son could carry on the name of the deceased husband (Dt 25:5-10). The Hebrew name for this blood bond and its concomitant obligations is gō'ēl, the very word which was later applied to God by Second Isaiah in chapters 40-55 and became frequently translated, *redeemer*.

Important consequences flow from the fact that Israel was culturally conquered by the indigenous people where she lived. We turn for direction to the document of Vatican II on the *Missionary Activity of the Church*, entitled *Ad Gentes*. Frequently, in various contexts, this declaration repeats the need of adaptation to local culture and customs (nos. 6, 9-10, 16, 19, 21-22, 25). A statement typical of so many others reads:

> This duty [of following Christ along "a road of poverty and obedience, of service and self-sacrifice" ;o. 5] is one and the same everywhere and in every situation, *even though the variety of situations keeps it from being exercised in the same way*. Hence, the differences . . . are *due to the circumstances in which this mission is exercised . . .* For although the Church includes within herself the totality or fullness of the means of salvation, *she does not and cannot always and instantly bring all of them into action* (no. 6, italics added).

> [The laity of the young church are to express their new life in Christ] in the social and cultural framework of their own homeland, according to their own national

traditions. *They must be acquainted with this culture.*
They must heal it and preserve it. They must develop it
in accordance with modern conditions, and *finally* perfect
it in Christ" (no. 21).

Missionaries, then, so far as they can with God's grace, follow
Christ in poverty and self-sacrifice. Because they appreciate the
richness of revelation in the Word made flesh (Col 2:9; Jn 1:14),
they are impelled to obey the command to "make disciples of all
the nations ... [and to] teach them to carry out everything I have
commanded you" (Mt 28:19-20). Yet, there are a series of steps
to be taken; the Church "does not and cannot always and instantly
bring . . . [the fullness of the means of salvation] into action."
This gradual development is accented in another statement which
refers to being *"finally* perfect in Christ."

The Old Testament's interaction with non-biblical culture
offers directions how to proceed step by step. Some truths of
the Christian faith are non-negotiable. Yet, these absolute require-
ments should be carefully weighed and accurately stated, lest one
infringe upon the adaptation called for by Vatican II.

The Bible will specify further the general principles of Vatican II about culturalization:

(1) God normally does not reveal culture and styles of civili-
    zation. These human factors pre-existed and were accep-
    ted by Israel (though she later critically judged and trans-
    formed the "secular" culture). We, too, need to be
    convinced that the Church today must be "indigenized"
    or culturally conquered before she will be in a position
    to judge and transform.

(2) Because the human condition or culture of any people
    includes their scale of values, these, too, must be accepted.
    In fact, no work of the apostolate or of charity will suc-
    ceed unless the Church seeks first to know and always
    to respect the primary values already existing among a
    people. In biblical times, to have imposed immediately
    such important values of contemporary culture as indi-

vidual freedom and monogomy would not only have disrupted the whole social economic structure, but it would also have destroyed the great value and overwhelming strength of the *gō'ēl* family bond.

Today the Church, with its cultural standards and scale of white, western and generally middle class values, must avoid the temptation of demanding these same values at once of a people whose cultural background may be very different. For example, one group of people may be freer in individual sexual practices (illegitimacy may not carry the same stigma of disgrace nor be as disruptive of family life as in another culture) and yet far more demanding in family care (it might be unthinkable to put children in orphanages or "up for adoption" or to incarcerate the elderly in nursing homes).

In responding to either group, we should first seek out *the more important* values and *their integral relationship.* In this way lines of authority and social stability are maintained; a strong setting is provided for securing what is best and for correcting what is harmful. Each true value should be seen, according to Vatican II, "as a sort of secret presence of God." Missionary "activity frees [these] from all taint of evil and restores [them] to Christ its Maker . . . And so, whatever good is found to be sown in the hearts and minds of men, or in the rites and cultures peculiar to various peoples, is not lost. More than that, it is healed, ennobled, and perfected for the glory of God, the shame of the demon, and the bliss of man" (AG, no. 9).

(3) Apostolic and charitable undertakings should begin with the primary values emphasized by a people within their own proper culture. These ought to be accepted, appreciated and strengthened, so that they become the pivotal points for discussing, purifying and transforming all other areas of their life.

HUMANIZATION, PROPHETICALLY CHALLENGED

Israel remains rather unique in world history for many reasons. One of these was her extraordinary sense of identity and continuity back to Moses in 1240 B.C., and possibly to Abraham in 1850 B.C. No other nation or people on earth can document its continuous history over such an expanse of time, crisscrossing so many cultures in human evolution. Culturally we can explain this exceptional phenomenon by the intimate tribal solidarity exemplified under the term, *gō'ēl*, or blood bond, but this reason does not suffice. Other ancient Near Eastern people, like the Canaanites, Babylonians and citizens of Mari also possessed the same tribal unity, and all have disappeared from history as distinct units.

And so we come to the third stage in Israel's humanization. While Israel conquered Canaan militarily and was in turn conquered by Canaan culturally, nonetheless, Israel was practically the only nation in world history to overcome her cultural conqueror religiously. This exceptional spirit was manifested particularly in the "classical" or "writing" prophets, persons like Amos and Hosea, Isaiah and Jeremiah. These must be distinguished from the earlier "charismatic" prophets who stressed the miraculous and visibly heroic and never left a written record of their preaching (cf. 1 S 10).

The "classical prophets," as explained already, were persons (1) who were so fully and consistently a member of their community and (2) so perceptive and articulate (3) that as a result they bring the internal challenge of the community's conscience—its divinely inspired hopes and ideals—to bear upon the external form of the community's life style and work. When, therefore, external forms of culture, whether these be in business or government, relaxation or religion, tend oppressively to suppress the interior pulsation of the spirit, the prophet cries out in protest: "Hear the word of the Lord!"

The prophet Amos challenged the formalistic way of obeying the law and destroying the person. Because the law demanded debts be paid, a poor man was being sold into slavery for the price of a pair of sandals (Am 2:6). Because God had promised to bless his people, Israel came to view the wealthiest, most cultured persons as being the holiest, even if they abused the needy as did the obese women of Samaria (Am 4:1), and reveled in drunken sensuality as did the effeminate men of the same city (Am 6:1-7). Amos challenged their theology and turned it around against them. For the very reason that they were God's favorite ones, Amos concluded that God would punish them all the more (Am 3:2) and change their great "messianic" day into darkness. Only a remnant would survive—but survive they would.

Hosea, a contemporary of Amos, began with the agricultural fertility customs of Canaan. He never rejected the Canaanites for the obscene immorality they practiced in these rites. Rather, he was to transform them by demonstrating in his own life God's love for Israel. When Hosea's wife Gomer repeatedly proved to be unfaithful, even to the extent that he was unsure of the paternity of the children (Ho 1:9), he could have wallowed in the fertility orgies at the sanctuary. He could rightfully, within the law of Israel, have divorced her and remarried (Dt 24:1-4). Yet, mysteriously and agonizingly, he felt compelled to forgive her over and over again and accept her back at his side (Ho 2:4-25).

Hosea's interior compulsion towards forgiveness and reconciliation seemed totally irrational until he himself realized that "thus the Lord loved Israel!" (Ho 3:1). What Hosea had heard year by year in the liturgical celebrations of the sanctuary, and what may have seemed irrelevant and monotonous at the time, now made its impact upon him. Hosea felt called to forgive more than would be normally expected or even be judged humanly possible. Divinely inspired, Hosea was able to speak of the Lord as the "Spouse of Israel," and from this divine example the prophet could now uphold the dignity of marriage and its extraordinary possibilities of holiness.

Other prophets reacted more directly within the politics of the time: Isaiah of Jerusalem at the time of the Syro-Ephramite league (Is chs. 7-12), Nahum at the collapse of the great Assyrian capital, Habakkuk at the moment of the Babylonian threat. In each instance, the prophet responded totally within the culture of the age and place, never intending to destroy it but seeking to transform it to new purity and divine expectation. It was when human means were activated to the full and the cultural conquest of Israel seemed complete that a prophet could realize even more was expected. It could be accomplished only by faith, surrendering oneself to God unconditionally and, like Hosea, following the intuitive demands of love.

Israel's prophetic challenge to the humanization process strikes relentlessly at our conscience. The message is as stern as love. In this context, the words of Jesus begin to make sense. "Whoever will save his life (that its cultural expression may never be challenged) will lose it (as did all of Israel's neighbors), and whoever loses his life for my sake (and in faith surrenders to the interior expectations of the spirit) will save it (as did Israel and her greatest son, Jesus). For what profit does he show who gains the whole (secular) world (of culture) and destroys himself in the process"? (Lk 9:24-25).

We can recognize the heroic expectations of God emerging within our human culture. Values, no matter how good they are, must be challenged to become still better, if they are to survive. To speak more concretely, it must be admitted that the most difficult goal of the apostolate is to tell good people that they are still not good enough. God has even greater hopes and more expansive dreams for his people. These dreams are the stuff of hope and their fulfillment is the work of faith. This faith, however, is not a luxury. It is an essential quality for living eternally. The just person lives by faith (Heb 2:4; Rm 1:17).

Almost as crucial as faith for the apostolate is the ability to discern the prophetic moment. To challenge people too soon is to crush the true values within their culture; to wait too long allows stagnation and corruption to set in. The determination of the right moment comes only after appreciating the genuine goodness within a culture. Because it is a good, one can challenge it to become still better. Neither the Bible nor the Church creates culture and civilization. Therefore, in meeting any new life style, the Church must patiently wait and learn the native values within the culture. The Church must allow herself, like Israel in the Old Testament times, to be conquered culturally. Once the genuine goodness of a culture is appreciated from within, then God's greater expectations can be preached to government and labor, to entertainment and art, to education and religious expression. The time is ready for the prophetic challenge.

Prophets must be thoroughly a part of their age and place in life, and yet they need to be so personally absorbed in God that they can forcefully speak his will for greater holiness. The prophetic role within the apostolate means that the Church must first know well the great secular advances in social work and health services, in education and counseling. At the same time, the Church must be able to challenge that culture when it succumbs to stuffy professionalism, top-heavy or impersonal bureaucracy, individual aggrandizement, financial obsessions, and similar diviations and corruptions.

The Church's role in the apostolate of charity can be reduced to three main assertions, corresponding to the three stages of humanization in the Old Testament:

(1) No matter how violent may be the military, political, or social revolution at times, the Church must remain within the real and seek to make the situation more livable in every way possible. These must be the days of giants and martyrs and perceptive diplomats (such as we see required in the delicate and intricate interaction of the Church with Communism).

(2) The Church must seek to appreciate and preserve local customs and the unique system of values in the native culture. Improvements must follow the indigenous life style and its special traditions. Moral problems must be solved normally within the local scale of values.

(3) When culture has evolved to an advanced stage and the Church has been thoroughly acculturated, prophets must rise up within the Church to challenge a people who feel humanly independent of God and put their supreme value in the external system and outward appearance. The Church now undertakes a new role, usually to preserve the spirit and to maintain the importance of the individual person.

In stage one, humanization is a struggle for existence; in stage two, it is religiously accepted, defended and enriched. In stage three, it is challenged, even under the threat of death, that it may rise beyond human expectations to newness of life in Christ Jesus.

Chapter Sixteen
Reconciliation and Original Sin

The theme of reconciliation in the Bible involves us in theological questions which tend to divide Christians. Any study which traces reconciliation back to the beginning at once touches the volatile topic of Adam and Eve, that time of original rebellion of people against God and each other. The sensitive issue of original unity and hereditary sin, therefore, must be approached carefully, even indirectly. Entering through the back door might allow us to relax and investigate related issues with more objectivity. And when the facts are sorted out, we then can apply our conclusions and seek reconciliation for the more quarrelsome issues.

We must, first of all, face the fact that the story of the fall of the first man and woman remains an isolated incident in the margin of the Old Testament. It is mentioned once in the Hebrew text, only two more times in the Greek Septuagint. The New Testament allusions are restricted almost exclusively to Paul who contrasts the first Adam and the new Adam, Christ. The classic text, of course, is Genesis, chapter 3. Another important text of Genesis, often neglected in the study of original sin, is the story about the Tower of Babel in chapter 11. The entire human race had been destroyed by the flood according to Genesis 7-9. Noah, through his three sons, became a new "Adam" or founder of the human family (Gn 10). The harmony between the sons was first ruptured by Ham's ridicule of his drunken father (Gn 9:18-29), followed by the punishment of a world-wide dispersion at the Tower of Babel. The pattern of unity-sin-separation is apparent.

After chapter 11 of Genesis, references to Adam and Eve and the paradise story are almost non-existent. The only other important use of the motif occurs in Ezekiel 28:11-19 where the future collapse of the seaport metropolis of Tyre is announced as an expulsion of the perfect one "from Eden, the garden of God." Many details of the paradise story are woven into the account. It is apparent that these details are literary symbols, the common property of story-tellers in the ancient Near East. If they are not taken as strictly historical facts in Ezekiel, then we must ask if the traditional doctrine about original sin and reconciliation in Christ demands an historical interpretation of the same details in Genesis 2-3.

After Ezekiel's time (593-570 B.C.), the first paradise and its occupants hardly concerned anyone. The few allusions come and go quickly. In a passage of Second Isaiah, the return from exile will be across deserts transformed into beautiful country "like Eden . . . and the garden of the Lord" (Is 51:3). It is well to note how the hopes for the future are read back into the beginning rather than modeled upon it. The same literary style of a "throw-back" was already at work in the passage from Ezekiel just mentioned. Other vague references to Eden or to the Garden of God are found in Genesis 13:10; Isaiah 11:6-9; Ezekiel 31:8-9; 16-18; 36:35; Joel 2:3; Psalm 8:6-9. However, no idea of an original fall is included.

After Genesis 3-4, the sin of Adam and Eve is not mentioned until the Book of Wisdom, composed in Egypt in the Greek language about the year 50 A.D., some 1200 years after Moses and 950 years after David. We read in Wisdom 2:23-24:

> For God formed man to be imperishable;
> the image of his own nature he made him.
> But by the envy of the devil, death entered
> the world
> and they who are in his possession
> experience it.

This passage seems to exempt the just from the dreadful sentence of death. Only those people in the possession of the devil experience it. The following chapter of Wisdom presents the death of good people as something entirely different from the death of the wicked. The dreadful kind of death which entered the world by the envy of the devil does not seem to touch the innocent. In fact, in a later chapter, the sad results of Adam's sin seemed to have been removed entirely: wisdom "raised him up from his fall, and gave him power to rule all things" (10:1-2).

Another sapiential book, Sirach, or Ecclesiasticus, written by the master of a Jerusalem school for noble youths (51:23), makes only one reference to Eve and one to Adam. "In woman," he wrote, "was sin's beginning, and because of her we all die" (25:23). This passage is part of Sirach's suspicious attitude towards women (see also 1 Tm 2:14). In Sirach 49:16, on the contrary, Adam's "splendor" is praised "beyond that of any human being." Sirach does not trace the origin of sin back to the garden of Eden, for he speaks gloriously of that place in 24:23-26. Sin is rooted, instead, in each person's creaturehood and evil inclination (Si 17:24-27; 18:6).

Even in the New Testament direct references to the original sin of Adam and Eve are rarely encountered. The best-known text occurs in the Epistle to the Romans:

> Therefore, just as through one man sin
> entered the world and with sin death,
> death thus coming to all men inasmuch as
> all sinned . . . much more did the grace of
> God and the gracious gift of the one man,
> Jesus Christ, abound for all (Rm 5:12, 15).

It should be noted that while death comes from Adam, its penalty must be incurred or reaffirmed by the personal sin of each individual (see also 1 Cor 15:22, 45-57). Other New Testament allusions to Genesis 3 are vague. In Revelation or Apocalypse, chapter 12, only a theology of struggle and victory can be deduced; nothing is clearly proposed on original sin or world corruption.

The texts, then, about an original sin of Adam and Eve are so scarce and so insufficiently integrated with the larger theological patterns of any biblical writer or tradition that it is not possible to draw any outstanding conclusions from them. In order to appreciate the necessity of repentance and reconciliation in Christ, therefore, we must look beyond the doctrine of original sin to the larger context of the Bible and study the attitudes of the people. After doing this, we can return again to the subject of original sin.

GOD'S REDEMPTIVE PRESENCE

One of the special ways of God's redemptive presence can be found in the optimism of the sages. Wisdom literature tended to reflect a moderate to optimistic attitude towards human nature. The sages do not write with the supposition that all men and women are, in general, corrupted. God shares the divine secret of his wisdom with men and women in their daily pursuit of life. Enlightened by God, the obedient person is already participating in a secure, everlasting joy. See such sapiential psalms as Psalms 1; 19:8-15; 119. Compared with most other parts of the Bible, the sages strike one as "enlightened humanistic gentlemen" with secular interests in the world which was regarded as being good. This attitude is reflected most strikingly in the principal sapiential book, Proverbs.

Holiness, in the sapiential books, was identified with the practical handling of everyday needs and problems in the remembrance of God's presence.

> The Lord permits not the just to hunger,
> but the craving of the wicked he thwarts.
> The slack hand impoverishes,
> but the hand of the diligent enriches
> (Pr 10:3-4).

According to this passage those persons succeed who work consistently and industriously. Such is the overall plan of God. No special savior or messiah is required, only a prayerful remembrance that

> The fear of the Lord prolongs life . . .

> The Lord is a stronghold to those who
> walk honestly (Pr 10:27, 29).

The sages, we must note also, recognized a master plan at the heart of life which no amount of human effort could fully understand or adequately control. The secret but pervading presence of wisdom so personally affected everyone's life that the editor of Proverbs allowed wisdom to speak in her own name:

> From of old I was poured forth,
> at the first, before the earth . . .
> When he established the heavens, I was there . . .
> There was I beside him as his craftsman . . .
> So now, O children, listen to me;
> instruction and wisdom do not reject
> (Pr 8:22-33).

Such passages present wisdom as mysteriously at home with the creator from the beginning. Christians sometimes see in this passage a foreshadowing of the Word, the second person of the Holy Trinity. Such an interpretation leaps beyond the intention of the Old Testament, but it does point out a conviction at the heart of the sapiential theology: men and women cannot save themselves. Ultimately they must submit in faith to the mystery of God in their daily personal lives.

The reader of this literature must remain always ready for a completely new experience. No one really becomes wise, for, in the final analysis, God determines the fabric and design of each person's life. Redemption and reconciliation for the wise man do not consist so much in overcoming sin through penance, priestly acts or messianic deliverance, but rather in a humble realization that the full appreciation of life is a divine gift. Reconciliation is achieved when God's wisdom unites the hopes and labors of all persons. This mystery, not any "original sin," lies at the heart of redemption.

Another way God's redemptive presence was evidenced can be found in the liturgical reconciliation of hopes. The optimistic view of the sages—that the reconciliation of all goodness was at hand for any industrious person who lived in the fear of God— was not totally acceptable, even to all the wise men. It was challenged by such eloquent poets as Job and Ecclesiastes. According to these writers, life included sorrows and frustrations inexplicable on any terms and not to be explained away as a mystery hidden away with God before creation. The answer of Proverbs 8:22 ff. was not sufficient. And the priests and prophets presented even greater objections to the sages.

The liturgy, in the priestly tradition, emphasized the *mirabilia Dei*, the wonders of God. God must intervene in extraordinary ways, not only to harmonize all goodness within the wondrous plan of salvation, but also to prevent Israel from falling over the precipice of extinction. According to sanctuary worship, the good life presumed much more than the honest, boot-strap efforts of a God-fearing person. Sanctuary worship reflected God's response in biblical history at such serious crises as Abraham's pitiable condition without land or heir (Gn 15; Is 51:1-3), Israel's slavery in Egypt (Ex 1-3); Israel's forty years of desert wandering (Nb 14:32-33; Dt 2:7; 8:2), repeated oppression in the days of the Judges (Jg 2:6-23), exile of the northern kingdom (2 K 17), and finally of the southern kingdom (2 K 25; Lm).

Each crisis was remedied only by God's special redemptive acts, which formed the basis of Israel's official religion. This sacred history inspired many of Israel's classical creeds (Dt 26; Jos 24), liturgical hymns (Pss 95; 105; 114; 136) and prayers (Pss 44; 60; 106). These crises and tragic moments were attributed at times to Israel's sins, but not always, and certainly not to any original sin of Adam and Eve. Abraham's sterility and Israel's slavery in Egypt were not due to any infidelity or disobedience, yet these two redemptive acts of God in Israel's favor did reach to the origins of the nation and the roots of her faith.

Sin certainly entered into the priestly or liturgical tradition of the Pentateuch (Gn 6:9-13), but not as any sort of inherited weakness. In fact, the priestly account of creation in Genesis 1:1-2:4a says absolutely nothing about any primeval sin or any expulsion from paradise. And when another priestly tradition, the deuteronomic source of the north, explained God's redemptive acts in Israel's favor, it attributed the necessity of God's intervention to divine love and the Lord's fidelity to earlier promises made to the forefathers (Dt 7:7-11).

Israel's liturgy, then, emphasized the people's dependence upon God, not just to survive, but to fulfill hopes of extraordinary proportions. Reconciliation was a matter of uniting sublime hopes with prosaic reality. Because the task was complicated by the weakness, selfishness and sinfulness of the people, it was possible only through God's intervention. Put simply, redemption according to Israel's liturgy was not a war against original sin but a prayer to fulfill extraordinary hopes through God's special intervention.

The sense of personal sinfulness and community guilt evolved in Israel principally through the preaching of the prophets. These extraordinary religious leaders, whose pure hearts perceived the real possibilities of goodness within Israel, were saddened and angered by their nation. Seeing it lulled to sleep by rigid formalities and external righteousness, they could not remain silent once God revealed to them the possibilities of something far better:

> The Lord God does nothing
> without revealing his plan
> to his servants, the prophets.
> The Lord roars—
> who will not be afraid!
> The Lord speaks—
> who will not prophesy! (Am 3:7-8; cf. Jr. 20:9).

The prophets reacted against the false holiness which inclined the people to think they could oblige God to fulfill his promises and wondrously intervene on their behalf. Israel considered herself a chosen people with a divinely assured future. God, they maintained, would even resort to miracles to save them; they had little to do beyond enjoying themselves and performing their sacred ritual (cf. Am 4:4-5). Amos responded that the true Israel is only the remnant, those people with genuine personal integrity

(Am 3:12; 5:1-3, 15). The *Day of the Lord*, moreover, will not break necessarily into splendor, preached Amos. Rather, chaos first will whirl it into a *Day of Darkness* (Am 5:18). God first must purify them by the ordeal of cleansing fire. As the prophetic momentum increased, these preachers announced the total destruction both of the northern kingdom of Israel (Am 4:1-3; 7:17) as well as the southern kingdom of Judah (Jr 7; 26).

In one important way the prophets reacted like the sages: they announced God's demand of interior holiness and moral integrity, seemingly within the normal ability of anyone who believed in God's presence. This idea is summed up in Micah:

> You have been told, O man, what is good,
> and what the Lord requires of you:
> Only to do the right and to love goodness,
> and to walk humbly with your God
> (Mi 6:8).

But in achieving the goal of the remnant—a people just and pure and strong—the thought of the prophets was independent of that found in the wise men. And here was the source of some violent conflicts between the two groups (cf. Is 5:19-21; 29:14-15; Jr 18:18; Ez 7:26). The prophets failed to recognize what the wise men found in human nature—an innate ability through the fear of God to arrive at *shalom*, the perfection of God's mysterious hopes.

According to the prophets, God must sweep away all the externals which supplied the ingredients of Israel's proverbs and liturgical songs. God would allow an entire nation to convulse over the horrendous experience of military invasion and defeat and a consequent mass deportation. In this ordeal, the innocent suffered equally with the guilty Israelite. In fact, good persons endured a greater interior agony. They would take their flesh between their teeth, demand an audience with their Maker and ask, "Why?" Psalm 44 prayed from the struggle of faith:

> You marked us out as sheep to be slaughtered;
> among the nations you scattered us . . .

> All this has come upon us, though we have
> not forgotten you,
> nor have we been disloyal to your
> covenant (Ps 44:12, 18).

We can now begin to recognize the real problem of original sin. The effects of sin had become so deeply rooted in the people Israel that everyone from their birth became involved in the purifying process of suffering.

We find something inconsistent here about the prophets. At the same time they announced the whirlwind of chaos sweeping away both the innocent and the wicked, they also traced the guilt of individual sinners who must bear the responsibility of their own misdeeds. They insisted that troubles were not to be blamed on any kind of inherited community guilt. Both Jeremiah and Ezekiel, key Old Testament prophets, ordered the people never again to repeat the proverb:

> Fathers have eaten unripe grapes,
> thus their children's teeth are on edge
> (Jr 31:20; Ezk 18:2).

Those who feel teeth on edge and their lips smarting from bitter pain have eaten the sour grapes, not grandpa! The prophets would not allow sinners to escape personal responsibility for their misdeeds. Yet, in another prophet's words, God did not separate the good from the evil, the wheat from the chaff (Mt 13:29-30), but allowed all to die violently or to be marched pitilessly into exile.

In the midst of this suffering by good and evil persons alike, another prophet found a solution. It is written down in what are called the *Songs of the Suffering Servant:* Isaiah 42:1-7; 49:1-6; 50:4-9a; 52:13-53:12. Because innocent persons have learned the lesson of sin, through suffering they can help the guilty in their pain and lead them to a reconciliation:

> The Lord God has given me
> a well-trained tongue,
> That I might know how to speak to the weary

a word that will rouse them.
Morning after morning
he opens my ear that I may hear;
And I have not rebelled,
have not turned back.
I gave my back to those who beat me,
my cheeks to those who plucked my beard;
My face I did not shield
from buffets and spitting (Is 50:4-6).

This pattern of the innocent suffering among the guilty that all be saved opened the door to the idea of universal salvation. In the *Songs of the Suffering Servant*, the salvation of the gentile nations reached its clearest expression. Israel, who suffered from the rapacious invasions of foreign powers, was thrown into total involvement with the gentiles, thus bringing them the possibility of holiness and a saving knowledge of the one God-savior.

It is too little, he says,
for you to be my servant,
to raise up the tribes of Jacob,
and restore the survivors of Israel;
I will make you a light to the nations,
that my salvation may reach to the ends
of the earth (Is 49:6).

The prophets arrived at this theological notion by refuting the easy, simplistic idea that a chosen people must be automatically saved because of divine promises. Yet in the theology of innocent suffering, the prophets presumed the centuries-old attitude that a blood-bond united Israelites with the firmness of one body and many members. Sin which originated in one person at once took its toll of suffering from all others in the family or tribe. Israel's traditional understanding of tribal or blood relationship can help us better understand how sin originates sorrow for others, even for the innocent, who thereby are mediators of salvation.

According to this tradition, the people formed one family and were all called in Hebrew *benê-yisrā'ēl*, the sons of Israel. This idea of being the one person Israel meant that each person was affected at once by the actions of every other person, whether good or bad. Religiously, the clan or tribal structure of Israel led to an understanding of God as a *gō'ēl*, a fellow tribesman. This idea led to the development of a theology of redemption. "Redeemer" is but a later translation of *gō'ēl*. Another theological development from this notion of the blood-bond of the Israelites shows up in St. Paul's appreciation of the Church as one living body in which Christ is the head and we are the members (1 Cor 12). Therefore, the idea of one person's sin harming all persons is readily understandable when seen in the context of its social and religious background. It also makes clear the correlative revelation that the perfect life will consist in complete reconciliation of all persons with one another and with God.

CONCLUSION

Now that we have seen it in its broader biblical context, it is possible to face the thorny question of original sin with more objectivity and greater equanimity. The story of the first Adam depicts in a gigantic way the condition of all people from their origins. It simply states a fact: all of us come into a sinful world and all of us repeat this pattern of sinfulness, originating a sinful world for the next generation. At the same time, the Bible, through its sages, presents the picture of a secret plan of God, a wisdom operating below the surface of the world which is cause for optimism.

Throughout history, Israel, through liturgical worship, emphasized the necessity for her people to depend totally on God so that he could fulfill hopes beyond anything they could imagine. Periodically the prophets came to remind Israel of these promises of extraordinary fulfillment. They also warned them about having any simplistic notions that God would keep these promises if they as individuals or as a nation did not take responsibility for their actions. Finally, the notion of the innocent suffer-

ing vicariously for the guilty and the idea of universal salvation
appeared in Isaiah's *Song of the Suffering Servant*. These notions
will be explored more fully in the next chapters.

Chapter Seventeen
Reconciliation:
Original Sin and Redemption

Ancient Israel lived the law of the desert whereby no individual could survive alone. Each person must shoulder the obligations of full community or tribal existence. The Hebrew word which designated the intimate bond and the mutual obligations intimately waiting all members of a tribe became one of the most important theological words of the Bible. *Gō'ēl* as it occurs in earlier biblical passages is normally translated, *kinsman*, and in later religious texts, *redeemer*.

Because the *gō'ēl* shared in the one blood of all his tribesmen, he could never be indifferent to any of their troubles. The Bible points out four major obligations of the *gō'ēl*:

(1) to redeem the life of a kinsman in slavery
    (Lv 25:47-55).

(2) to redeem property. So necessary was land for independent dignified life, that it could never be alienated from the clan (Lv 25:23-34).

(3) to redeem the life of a murdered kinsman by executing the guilty person, and so to protect other living kinsmen (Nb 35:31-34).
    Israel possessed no police force.

(4) to redeem the ongoing life of a husband who died without a male heir by marrying the widow and giving the name and property of the deceased husband to the first son (Dt 25:1-10; Book of Ruth). This law of the "levirate marriage" presumed polygamy.

9

Gō'ēl, then, included two principal aspects: the bond of life and the obligations to maintain and protect the common "blood" or life.

This social or political aspect of Israel's existence was applied to God for the first time seriously and consistently by Second Isaiah, the unknown author of chapters 40-55 in the Book of Isaiah. Once he perceived by faith the intimate love of God, supplying in Israel the life-blood of hopes, ideals and forgiveness, then Second Isaiah not only named God Israel's kinsman or *gō'ēl*, but he pointed out God's consequent obligation to save his people (see 43:1-7 and 54: 1-10). One of these passages can be translated:

> But now thus says the Lord, creating you, Jacob,
> and forming you, Israel:
> 'Do not fear, because I am your kinsman.
> I call you by your name; you are mine' (43:1, CS).

Unfortunately, when the Hebrew *gō'ēl* was translated into Greek, it became *ek-agorazō* (to buy back) and then passed over into the Latin *re(d)imere* (also, to buy back). From the force of the Greek and Latin words as well as through the influence of Greek pagan mystery cults, there developed a theology of redemption or reconciliation which stressed *substitution* instead of union. This new emphasis tended to overlook what was basic to *gō'ēl*. Christ was no longer considered a blood-brother suffering with us but a substitute taking all our sorrows upon himself. This "substitution-theory" even went so far with certain theologians that a "devil's right" explanation was offered: Christ purchased us back from the devil by the price of his blood. The few biblical texts which seem to support this hypothesis (Is 53:4-6; 1 P 1:19) must be interpreted within the *gō'ēl* obligation to obtain the kinsman's liberty. Another, later passage in 1 Peter 2:18-25 reinstates the passage in the larger concept of union.

By applying the Hebrew sense of *gō'ēl* to the question of penance and reconciliation, we see that unity is restored when men and women suffer the demands of family love. It was under these conditions that Jesus suffered and died with and in us, so that we rise from the dead with and in him. The consequences of the *gō'ēl* bond apply because God sees us as one family. St. Paul expressed this mystery of faith in as clear a language as possible:

> The proof that you are sons is the fact
> that God has sent forth into our hearts
> the spirit of his son which cries out,
> "Abba!" ("Father"). You are no longer a
> slave but a son. And the fact that you are
> a son makes you an heir, by God's design.
> There does not exist among you Jew or
> Greek, slave or freeman, male or female.
> All are one in Christ Jesus. Furthermore,
> if you belong to Christ you are the descend-
> ants of Abraham, which means that you in-
> herit all that was promised (Gal 4:6-7; 3:28-29).

If we share life, then we enjoy together its benefits and suffer together the guilt of one another, so that life can be revitalized for everyone. No one can be saved alone; reconciliation with the full people of God is an essential condition.

BIBLICAL GENEALOGIES AND RECONCILIATION

When St. Paul declared that all Christians without distinction "are descendants of Abraham" (Gal 3:29), the whole context of the epistle makes clear that Jews and Gentiles biologically are not from the same father and that Gentiles are not obliged to be "adopted" into the Jewish race ("genealogized" is the technical word) in order to be saved. Later in the same epistle, biology, in fact, was totally put aside by Paul in his allegorical style of argumentation. He was drawing theological conclusions out of the fact that Abraham had two sons. One of these, born of a slave girl, Hagar, was the father of those in bondage (i.e., Jews); the other, a child of promise begotten of his freeborn wife, Sarah, became the father of those in freedom (i.e., Christians). The theology given in the Bible is infallible but the biology is hopelessly tangled in historical error!

We might ask if there are any indications in the social structure of Israel, to show that genealogies need not be explained by strictly physical procreation. If the answer is "yes," then important observations can be made about the theology of reconciliation, reuniting people divided across color and other barriers, and about the very transmission of original sin from "first parents." The Bible at first gives the impression that everyone alive today can trace their generation back to a first couple called *Adam* and *Eve*. Various genealogical tables in the Bible seem to establish a strict line of procreation beginning with an original couple. In Genesis, chapter 5 presents the descent from Adam to Noah; chapter 10, from Noah's three sons, reaching out to all the nations of the world; chapter 11:10-26, a more limited view, from Noah's son Shem to Terah, the father of Abraham. At this point the family trees narrow down to the history of Abraham, Isaac, Jacob and the latter's twelve sons.

Important theological consequences can be drawn from these lists of strange names and people. First was the moment of truth for Israel when she realized she was included in a whole aggregate of nations without any special prestige or power (chapter 10); whatever place she acquired in world history was due to God's gracious choice of her. Second, Israel was to accomplish her mission in life only by thoroughly interacting with all nations of the world. Third, chapter 10, which followed upon the flood, also indicates a radical break with primeval history, and in chapter 11:10-26, a new beginning, made with Abraham, is presented.

A good case can be made for the hypothesis that chapter 10 of Genesis reflects, for the most part, the way by which the Jerusalem priests described the political alignment of nations around the little country of Palestine during the days of Isaiah, Jeremiah and Ezekiel (ca., 716-560 B.C.). If this majority view of scholars is true, then a serious rupture in continuous history occurred biologically and sociologically. The indications at this point are two. Negatively, we are led to conclude that the genealogical table from Adam to the twelve tribe system need not be accepted as biological succession. Positively, we find within the plan for Israel, a plan of salvation which has as its purpose the eventual uniting of all nations. The genealogies express theological hopes more than biological history.

Furthermore, there are many indications in the Bible that people entered the genealogies of the twelve tribes by means other than legitimate birth. We have the example of the history of Caleb, best known as one of the twelve spies whom Moses sent ahead "to reconnoiter the land of Canaan" (Nb 13:2). Older biblical passages trace his origin outside of Israel to the Kenizzites (Nb 32:12), an older brother of Kenaz (Jos 15:17; Jg 1:13), who in turn was an Edomite chief in the family line of Esau (Gn 36:10-11). Esau, we are told, was the twin brother of Jacob. Other biblical texts like the Priestly Tradition (Nm 13:6; 34:19) and the Chronicler (1 Ch 2:3-4, 18) consider Caleb as belonging to the tribe of Judah, and therefore trace his ancestry back to Jacob (Gn 29:35), not Esau.

Once a person was accepted as a full member of the twelve tribe system—whether by birth, adoption, marriage, conquest, treaties—they had to be "genealogized." In order to acquire rights to water, pasturage and land, or to the privilege of worshipping at the sanctuaries, a man or woman must inherit these titles from one's ancient forefather. A child, to be legally adopted, must be absorbed into the whole family tree and accepted as a son or daughter by all the ancestors.

Not only must rights and blessings be traced through inheritance to the ancestor of a family, but curses and disabilities were also read backwards. A good example is seen in the case of the Canaanites. These people opposed Israel's conquest of the land and later contaminated the people of Yahweh with their degenerate fertility cults in which male and female prostitutes serviced the devotees (Dt 23:18; 2 K 23:7). In the minds of the people, unnatural vice was possible only if Canaan's forefather had been cursed. The Bible offers an acceptable explanation for the people of the time by combining some folklore about the discoverer of wine with a play on words (Ham—Canaan):

Ham ridiculed his father lying drunk and naked
in his tent after innocently drinking the
wine he was the first to have fermented.
Canaan, therefore, is cursed by Noah as "the
lowest of slaves" (see Gn 9:18-23).

In the Bible, therefore, the relationship of Israel to the nations
was closely related to politics, geography and history as well as
to family and tribal bonds. If the overall plan of the Bible is God's
purpose of salvation, then the purpose of the genealogies is not
to be determined primarily by biology but by salvation-history.
At the base of sacred history is Israel's and, therefore, the world's
need for salvation by God's special intervention. This salvation,
whether for Israel as presented in the Hebrew Bible, or for all
nations as found in the New Testament, does not depend upon
one set of first parents but upon one universal plan of God.

CORPORATE PERSONALITY

Another important aspect of the closely knit tribal structure
of Israel must be considered: its corporate personality. According
to this generally accepted theory, extraordinary persons so dominated their own age and so determined the direction of future
ages, that a narrative of their life or times was considered inadequate unless it incorporated a description of the influence their
lives had for the future. Consequently, the words and achievements of future generations were read back and incorporated into
the person of the first leader. Except for the sapiential literature,
the Bible consists of the "biographies" of great heroes or corporate personalities: Abraham, Jacob, Joseph, Moses, Joshua and
so on.

Under scrutiny, these so-called "biographies" are seen to break
the bonds of any individual's lifetime and to transform the main
character into a type of model for all ages. Noah and Abraham
became the father of nations; Moses, the great law giver; Joshua,
the conqueror; David, the founder of liturgy and the composer
of psalms; Solomon, the wise man *par excellence.* The Bible, in

explaining the continuity of influence in various historical movements, projects back into the life-story of the leader those later actions carried out under their impulse and influence.

We may offer a conjecture about the corporate personality of *Adam*. In Genesis, chapters one through three, "Adam" is presented under various corporate personalities. In chapter 1 of the Priestly Tradition, Adam is the perfect human being, a copy of God upon earth or, better, a reflection of God's plans and activities. Genesis solemnly presents the mysterious origin of *'ādām* (humankind) with the triple use of *bārā:*

> God created *'ādām* in his image,
> in the divine image he created him;
> male and female he created them
> (Gn 1:27).

The Hebrew form of the first line insists upon this definite one humankind. Moreover, the text immediately adds that what was divided sexually into male and female will fulfill the divine work of ruling the earth only by being reunited as one:

> God blessed them, saying: "Be fertile and
> multiply, fill the earth and subdue it"
> (Gn 1:28).

Therefore, whether in terms of a more static image of divine nobility or of a more active expression of God's life, *'ādām* refers to both male and female.

In Genesis, chapters 2 and 3, *'ādām* remains a corporate personality, but representative exclusively of the male sex. It goes without saying that *'ādām* as male possesses a life closely intertwined with his female partner, *woman*, or as she is called later, *Eve*, (Gn 3:20). In Hebrew, Eve means "life." Each incorporated the eternal man or the eternal woman, the everlasting husband and the never-changing wife. The corporate personality of man and woman in the Yahwist Tradition took on still another dimension. The international and cultural aspects of the days of David and Solomon are reflected here, especially the impressive empire of David and the serious Canaanite contamination of Hebrew morals. Smaller details are also visible, like the parallel between Adam-Eve and David-Bathsheba.

A theological aspect was evident too. Even during his lifetime, David was considered the model king and his empire a type of God's kingdom. After his death the glorious ideals of God were read back into the image of David, and David became a corporate personality, uniting in himself all that God wanted a person to be, and so he was a good model for Adam, or humankind, in the Yahwist account of Genesis. David, however, committed serious sin, especially his adultery with Bathsheba. It lived on in their son Solomon, a sensual, cruel despot. Here lay the seeds of division and future sin. Because of Solomon's excesses the people of God split into hostile kingdoms, Judah and Israel, and were continually infested with Canaanite weakness. The serious, ongoing effects of David's sin was also read back into the sin of Adam and Eve, man and woman.

It is clear that the biblical account is not exclusively concerned with biology, history or sociology. Rather, it moves towards the master theological plan of salvation. Because all the sons and daughters of Israel are incorporated in the person of great leaders, the sin of any member at once released sorrow into the lives of all the people. The *gō'ēl* was committed to share these sorrows and thus to impart his own purified and strengthened hopes to others, until all became perfectly one in the image of God.

The "original" sin, which caused all sorts of troubles, happened the moment a person selfishly refused to share his God-given talents and powers with others and, instead, used these gifts against others. This self-centered act of separation refused the trust and the dependency so necessary for giving and accepting help. It resulted in keeping at hostile distance the talents intended by God for the enrichment of the entire human family.

No matter how one explains the historical setting of Genesis 2:4b-3:24 (initial human pair or David and Solomon's career), the religious or theological explanation of the first sin stresses a proud, then a jealous separation between human beings. Drawing conclusions from the symbols in the Yahwist account, we see a

wedge driven between woman and God, as she was induced to
become a mini-god, knowing good and evil, independently making her own decisions. The liberty of loving God now became a
declaration of independence from God. She took advantage of the
love relationship with her husband and easily prevailed upon him
to join her in revolt against God. Immediately, man and woman
began to suspect each other and set up defenses, symbolized in the
statement that "they sewed fig leaves together and made loincloths
for themselves" (3:7).

The division became more sorrowful and hostile: woman fear-
ful of childbirth, man angry against the soil; Cain the farmer
suspicious of Abel the shepherd; city people against the rural
folks; the sophisticated and cultured against the home-spun and
self-educated. This same source of trouble re-appeared in the episode of the second "original sin" at the Tower of Babel (Gn 11:
1-9), where men and women attempted to control their destiny
without God's direction; from this revolt there came about an
estrangement in which nobody spoke the language of anyone else.

Man and woman fell into sin precisely through the good qualities placed in them by God. Woman sinned through her womanly
nature—intuitive, careful about details, concerned with beauty;
man by his manly nature—logical and industrious, dependent on
a wife and desirous of pleasing her, impelled to control. God's
beautiful gifts became a source of division and trouble. When
anyone is at their best (i.e., woman as woman or man as man),
they are capable of their worst offenses, for here they possess the
talent to manipulate and offend others. Here, too, they can easily
become unbalanced. The good administrator will easily over-
administrate and lack the "milk" of human gentleness in his or
her stern, computer mind; the tender-hearted person can become
soft and overly dependent; the loving person can tend to love
too much or be overly sensual.

All sin, therefore, can be described as the excess of one's virtue,
unbalanced and harmful because the talent is not shared properly
with others, harmonized and steadied by the opposite virtue of
other people. Because these talents are inherited, this imbalance
and concomitant weakness is passed down through the gen-

erations. From one viewpoint, then, we should no longer speak of original sin, but of original virtues and talents. If these are not shared, they spoil at once. These must be given away to be kept properly. So many of the enigmatic statements of Jesus take on their true meaning in this context: "Give, and it shall be given to you" (Lk 6:38), "Whoever loses his life for my sake will save it" (Lk 9:24).

Once we admit that division is *the* sin originating all other sorrows, we can understand why chapters 3 and 4 of Genesis at once speak of the spiraling extent of evil in the human family. Division among people caused ignorance; from ignorance people easily moved to the next stage of jealousy and fear. These diseased attitudes induced aggression and war. The two concepts of *gō'ēl* and corporate personality remind us that every curse, like every blessing, not only belonged to an entire clan or tribe but also extended across the centuries backwards and forwards.

In the evil and sinful situation of society infants were conceived, born and reared. When the psalmist declared, "In guilt was I born, and in sin my mother conceived me" (Ps 51:7), he was stating the obvious: a people's prejudices and fears are immediately absorbed by an unborn infant from its father's seed and its mother's blood. Each community, moreover, has its own "original sins," its own set of weaknesses and prejudices, traced back again to its special gifts and talents held in defensive isolation. The Bible refers to the "original sin" of Ham inherited by the overly-sensual Canaanites. It also states that the northern kingdom continued "in the way of Jeroboam, son of Nebat, who made Israel to sin" (1 K 12:26-31; 13:34; 15:26, 34; 16:7, 19). The latter phrase is repeated all the way to 2 Kings 17:22 in which the obituary notice for the now defunct northern kingdom was written.

The separation of Israel from the nations eventually led to a theology of redemption and reunion. Yahweh separated his people from the Egyptians through the extraordinary intervention at the Red Sea and then settled them in their own promised land (Dt 32:10-14). Israel began to realize that she had been elected and chosen out of all other nations as God's very own people

(Dt 32:8-9). This belief about the election of the nation was purified by the prophets Amos and Isaiah and so evolved into the notion of the *remnant*. According to this new prophetic insight, "election" was not an automatic privilege conferred at birth but an interior disposition of holiness and fidelity. "Remnant" was not identified with the externals, such as fewer numbers, but with an intensity of interior faith. Through these insights, the door was being opened to a new universalism, so that the notion of "chosen people" could eventually include the Gentile nations. The Gentiles, too, were capable of faith.

The theology of election involved purification and revitalization. This was necessary to enable Israel to share her gifts with human dignity and purity of soul. She had to become strong and mature; otherwise, other nations would abuse her and plunder her riches. To develop a vibrant, fearless and mature purity of heart among the descendants of Abraham, God intervened as savior, bringing his people out of the slavery of Egypt and, later, out of the Babylonian exile. God had to send an extraordinary series of prophetic leaders, whom he inspired to see and articulate those things to which most men and women were blind. The last and greatest of these leaders was Jesus.

Separating a people as his chosen race and enabling them to realize their dignity and gifts through the experience of many centuries, God nurtured his image among the people of Israel. When that image came to its full perfection in Jesus, Israel was called upon to lose her "life" and separate existence by sharing these with the Gentiles. This was the way God brought to perfection the original unity he desired for his entire human family. The final redemptive act of God does not so much consist in the forgiveness of sin as it does in the reunion of God's scattered gifts among the human race in the one Christ.

SUMMARY

In this more detailed consideration of the subject of original sin, we see the purpose behind God's plan for his family. Despite the maze of biological and sociological confusions regarding the origins of the human race, the theological reality emerges: this plan concerns the unity of the human race. How this plan of moving from division to unity takes flesh will be the subject of the next chapters.

Chapter Eighteen
Reconciliation: In Jesus and in Us

The Old Testament is almost exclusively concerned with God's efforts to purify and redeem Israel, his chosen people. Only on rare occasions does the Old Testament reach out to the Gentile world with any universal redemptive hope. Normally, the Hebrew Scriptures reveal, at best, a neutral attitude towards foreigners. They are mostly concerned with a theology of "separation" in the themes of exodus and election. The double fact that Jesus ministered only to the house of Israel (Mt 15:24) and that the Jewish religion today maintains no missionary activity aimed at the conversion of the nations indicate the national or racial limits of Old Testament thought on redemption. There is no need to repeat here the traumatic struggles of St. Paul and the agony of the early Christian Church to accept Gentiles equally with the Jews into the ranks of full Christian discipleship.

Paul considered Jesus to be the new Adam. Jesus fully realized God's plans whereby all persons are united in the divine likeness, no longer divided as "Jew or Greek, slave or freeman, male or female. All are one in Christ Jesus" (Gal 3:28). Paul is not referring to any kind of biological or family unity, for he adds at once, "You are descendants of Abraham."

The classic statement of St. Paul on this subject occurs in Romans:

> Just as through one man sin entered the
> world and with sin death, death thus coming
> to all men inasmuch as all sinned . . . much
> more did the grace of God and the gracious

gift of the one man, Jesus Christ, abound
for all (Rm 5:12, 15).

Paul concerns himself with the biblical mystery of '*ādām*. The
reference here as well as in 1 Corinthians 15:45 is to the Adam
and Eve story in the Yahwist account of Genesis 2:4b-3:24, rather
than to the '*ādām* of the priestly tradition in chapter 1. In any case,
however, Paul made use of Scripture neither as a modern critical
scholar nor as a conservative fundamentalist. Paul's rabbinical
style showed itself most clearly in another passage (Gal 5:21-31)
where allusions to Sarah and Hagar, Isaac and Ishmael actually
rearranged, if not distorted, the details of the Bible historically
and biologically. The principle of interpretation for New Testament writers was to see all the scriptures fulfilled and therefore
understood in Jesus. They called upon them to enrich the full
meaning of Jesus. And in the tradition of the corporate personality, the image of Jesus was read back into Adam, Noah, Abraham, Moses, and other exceptional leaders.

Paul considers Jesus the new man, in whom all men and women
are united in a fullness of life (Rm 5:12 ff.). To appreciate the
meaning of this faith in Jesus, Paul referred to the role of Adam
in the first book of the Bible. Humankind as created by God bore
an image of goodness and fidelity. However, what was true and
good in the first Adam succumbed to treachery and evil. Humankind revolted from God and from others and so was doomed to
destructive jealousy, sorrow and death.

In the Bible, death meant separation from God, the source
of life. It not only included our idea of physical death, but it
imparted as well an almost hopeless fear. Without God, humankind could not fulfill its hopes for life, and so carried the marks
of lifelessness and decay. This punishment was clearly enunciated
to Adam and Eve in the biblical warning which read literally in
the Hebrew text, "the day that you eat of it [the tree of knowledge of good and evil], you shall surely die." That threat was not
carried out literally according to our modern sense of the word
death. Adam and Eve continued to live after they had sinned. But
it was only a make-believe life already in mortal struggle with

death. If God was the God of life, anyone cut off from him was immediately "dead."

The sin of the first Adam continued in the sin of every other 'ādām, or human being, and the spiraling effects of death spread through all humankind. Each person's death confirmed and intensified the results of the first human being's sin, as Paul testified in Romans 5:12. But this network of sin is shattered by the appearance of the new Adam. For Paul declares:

> . . . just as a single offense brought con-
> demnation to all men, a single righteous
> act brought all men acquittal and life.
> Just as through one man's disobedience
> all became sinners, so through one man's
> obedience all shall become just (Rm 5:18-19).

Thus, through Christ, the new Adam, the life of God's creation is restored.

To live, each one must ratify the bond of union with Christ, the new Adam, and reach out to all one's brothers and sisters in Christ. The reconciliation of all men and women in Jesus was achieved through the excruciating sorrow of the cross. The Epistle to the Ephesians expressed the cost of reconciliation:

> . . . you who were once far off have been
> brought near through the blood of Christ.
> It is he who is our peace, and who made
> the two of us one by breaking down the
> barrier of hostility that kept us apart.
> In his own flesh he abolished the law with
> its commands and precepts, to create in
> himself one new man from us who had been
> two and to make peace, reconciling both
> of us to God in one body through his cross,
> which put that enmity to death (Ep 2:13-16).

The suffering which achieved reconciliation resulted from the demands of charity and unity. The identification of a Christian with the sufferings of Christ, as developed already in chapter 16, is at the heart of St. Paul's theology of Christian asceticism (Gal 2:19-20) and of the Eucharist (1 Cor 11:17 ff.).

The unity of all men and women, divided and separated by sin, yet reunited in their true image and hopes through Jesus, can be seen in Luke's presentation of Jesus' baptism. The sequence of thought can be outlined as follows:

(1) A scene of men and women streaming down to Jericho and the River Jordan: "crowds . . . tax collectors . . . soldiers . . . people . . . full of anticipation" (Lk 3:1-19).

(2) Jesus, one with all the people, at the moment of his baptismal anointing as Messiah, hearing "a voice from heaven . . . 'You are my beloved Son. On you my favor rests' " (Lk 3:21-23).

(3) Jesus' genealogy being traced back beyond the days of Abraham to the origins of all mankind, back to "Seth, son of Adam, son of God" (Lk 3:23-38). What all men were from the beginning, "sons of God," but twisted and misshapen through generations of sin, they become once again in Jesus. For Luke, this genealogy was basically theological, a transmission of divine sonship.

(4) After the coming of the Spirit at Jesus' anointing in the Jordan he is tempted to accomplish the messianic task too quickly and too miraculously against the will of his Father (Lk 4:14-30).

(5) The temptation of the people of Nazareth, unlike that of Jesus in his trial, resulted in stubborn resistance and a demand for a quick miraculous messianic triumph for themselves (Lk 4:14-30).

Scenes four and five above indicate the nature of Jesus' baptism as a messianic anointing, linked to his temptation and the temptation of the Nazarenes. As an initiation into his messianic ministry, baptism not only plunged Jesus into the ranks of all humanity longing for salvation, but it also accomplished their hopes. What all men were from the beginning and continued to be only in a distorted and divided way, they became once again through their reunion with one another in Jesus.

If we see this in the light of the *gō'ēl* or kinsman relationship of the Old Testament, we have seen that redemptive reconciliation must be understood primarily as based upon a bond of love even greater than blood, and undertaken as a duty on the part of the kinsman. When an adult member of the family or tribe sold himself into slavery, or mortgaged his land, or died a violent death, or died without a son, he might have been sinless as far as guilt is concerned. *Gō'ēl* redemption never presumed sin, but it did always denote helplessness which only a blood-brother could and must remedy. It is important to remember this fact when we find the title "*gō'ēl*" applied to Jesus.

In some of the cures worked by Jesus, it was explicitly pointed out that no one had offended God; e.g., that neither the blind man nor his parents had sinned (Jn 9:3). At the same time, the miracles of Jesus were explained as a struggle against satan. This is clearly evident in the remarkable exorcism activity of Jesus, an aspect of his ministry given special emphasis by Mark. Jesus' mission is to rout the forces of evil and to restore a victimized and alienated humanity to wholeness. Thus both the healings and exorcisms of Jesus are ultimately a work of reconciliation.

As a result, several conclusions can be drawn from a study of the *gō'ēl* or kinsman bond: all men and women share the sin-situation of the human race; the removal of sin causes suffering among all persons, good and bad alike; no one can be totally at peace until all are saved or redeemed; all people share with Jesus the *gō'ēl* obligations of restoring the lost unity and of reuniting all the members of the human family. All suffer the evil effects of division. Where actual sin exists, the sorrow becomes greater for everyone. Jesus, in achieving the union of all men and women, suffered the trials and suffering of all persons across the ages. He incorporated all men and women in himself and so became the world redeemer or *gō'ēl*.

THE PATH OF RECONCILIATION

Jesus attempted no compromise to keep his disciples reconciled to himself when many of them remarked about his preaching,

"This sort of talk is hard to endure! How can anyone take it seriously?" Sadly he watched when "from this time on, many of his disciples broke away and would not remain in his company any longer" (Jn 6:60, 66). Though he came upon earth to reconcile all men and women among themselves with their heavenly Father, his conditions of reconciliation could and did have the opposite effect: "Do you think I have come to establish peace on the earth? I come for division. From now on, a household of five will be divided three against two and two against three; a father will be split against son and son against father, mother against daughter and daughter against mother, mother-in-law against daughter-in-law, daughter-in-law against mother-in-law" (Lk 12:51-53).

The Bible does not seek reconciliation at any cost, but only at the highest cost of total purification, and the sacrifice of one's life. Only the best, one's very life, can be accepted and shared, or at least one must be praying for that kind of charity and unity. Reconciliation is not achieved by piling all our sins and weaknesses together. For example, the sexes are not granted equality and reconciliation by allowing women the same double standard once tolerated among men. Nor is an ecumenical bond achieved among the churches by asking each one to be less Catholic, less Lutheran, less Presbyterian, and so on. Protestantism, several decades ago, would have blundered badly if it had weakened its energetic devotion to the Bible in the name of ecumenical dialogue with Roman Catholicism, and Catholicism would have much less to contribute to the reunion of the churches if her rich liturgical tradition or her mystical approach to prayer were allowed to disintegrate.

Reconciliation, then, does not consist in smoothing out differences and everyone becoming alike. Rather, we will be united by looking to Jesus as the source of each unique gift, by persevering long in prayer as each gift is purified and enriched, and by sharing these best gifts with all others. A charter of unity was composed for us in the Epistle to the Ephesians. It not only respects but demands diversity of gifts. At the same time, it enunciates faith in the one Lord and bestower of all gifts. It combines strength and compassion, challenge and invitation, aggressiveness and humility. It offers these directions:

(1) Reconciliation is a command from God. "Make every effort to preserve the unity which has the Spirit as its origin and peace as its binding force" (4:3).

(2) Recognize and perfect one's own gifts. "It is he [Christ] who gave apostles, prophets, evangelists, pastors and teachers in roles of service for the faithful to build up the body of Christ, until we . . . form that perfect man who is Christ come to full stature. Let us, then, be children no longer . . . Rather, let us . . . grow to the full maturity of Christ the head" (4:11-15).

(3) Reject evil and half-hearted efforts. "You must no longer live as the pagans do—their minds empty, their understanding darkened . . . You must lay aside your former way of life and the old self which deteriorates through illusion and desire" (4:17-18, 22).

(4) Be compassionate. "Be kind to one another, compassionate, and mutually forgiving, just as God has forgiven you in Christ . . . Defer to one another out of reverence for Christ" (4:32; 5:21).

(5) God is the source and final goal of reconciliation. "There is but one body and one Spirit, just as there is but one hope given all of you by your call. There is . . . one God and Father of all, who is over all, and works through all, and is in all . . . We are to become one in faith and in the knowledge of God's Son, and form that perfect man who is Christ come to full stature" (4:4-6, 13).

According to these conditions, then, reconciliation summons us in two different directions. Like Israel in Old Testament times, we are called out of the pagan nations, separated from them for a special covenant with God, and led to a promised land reserved for God's chosen people. God directs us into our "ghetto" where we learn who we are as his "special possession" (Ex 19:5), what gifts he has given us, how we are to purify and perfect them. God can also call us out of our promised land into the world, as

Jonah was commanded to preach to the Ninevites who turned out to be more humble and righteous than he was. This second call is heard as well in the words of Jesus, "Whoever would save his life will lose it, and whoever loses his life for my sake will save it" (Lk 9:24).

GOD'S SECRET PLAN

What the human race is to become, the Bible states, that it has been all along—mysteriously at the heart of its existence—*one family of God*. A proverb expresses this idea enigmatically but forcefully: the child is the parent of the adult, the boy is the father of the man, the girl is the mother of the woman. God's secret plan has been hidden in us like the substance of life from our father and mother. It demands to be heard in the evolution of life. It can be suppressed only so long before it explodes. It provides the motivation for life's greatest achievements.

God's kingdom, according to Jesus, ought not be confused with a point of time, nor with miracles perceptible of careful watching, nor with a geographical point of space. We already possess, Jesus states, what we are seeking to become. "The reign of God is already in your midst" (Lk 17:21). And God's choice of all persons in Christ happened "before the world began" (Ep 3:2-6). It followed that "mysterious design which for all ages was hidden in God, the creator of all . . . his age-old purpose carried out in Christ Jesus our Lord" (Ep 3:9-11). The "unfathomable riches of Christ . . . to enlighten all men" (3:8-9) pre-existed the universe.

The first page of the Bible introduces us to an exultant hymn resounding throughout the cosmos in honor of its creator. It is already evident that the earthly home created by God belongs to the family of humankind. God's love levels all distinctions of race or sex and rests equally upon all persons. Before there is any mention of racial or sexual differences in chapter 1 of Genesis, we are told that God created the human race. And both sexes equally reflect God. Races and nations also stem equally from God. We cannot deny who we are through God's creation. If we fight it, it will fight back with the most elemental force of life. If we suppress it, it will explode.

The first chapters of Genesis are more a historical-theological commentary on the relation of Israel to the nations than an explanation of the beginnings of the human race. Persons who explain them as strict history often overlook its theological implications for today. The impact of God's secret plan, hidden in us from the beginning, is lost on them. And when people who profess to be religious fail to respect the integral goodness of God's good earth and abuse it with all sorts of prejudice and pollution, the booming voice of an outraged Father is heard across the land through people marching for world peace, demonstrating for the dignity and equal opportunity of minorities, working for ecology and natural environment. This voice of God speaks from the lips of people who at times claim to be irreligious and non-church-goers!

Reconciliation is not a choice; it is our only hope for survival. Whether we are Jew or Gentile, black or any other color, male or female, rich or poor, educated or not, we have been created by God as one human family; and Christ who is already in our midst will never be revealed adequately or fully until we are all reconciled as brother and sister. These hopes of what we must be are fleeting intuitions which can scare us as much as they fascinate and attract us. We all know such ecstatic moments which evoke both wonder and fear and make us taste how weak we are and how courageous we ought to be. The difference between fear and wonder, between cowardice and heroic acceptance, comes in the presence of Jesus. He supplies for our weakness while sustaining the hope which may seem to be crushing us.

INTO THE GHETTO

Ghetto is a nasty word. Ghetto stands for forced segregation, minority status and caste system, the inability to mingle freely in society, little or no opportunity for advancement. The term,

"ghetto," goes back to medieval Europe and marks off that area
of a town where Jews had to live, crowded together in old tene-
ments, poorer than any other section, an object of hatred and
attack. Here the Jews were certain to be found. *Ghetto* was also
a glorious word, for here the Jew was free to be a Jew, to preserve and follow tradition, to be born, marry, bear children in
the name of the patriarchs and to die and be remembered forever
by the God of Abraham, Isaac and Jacob. Here the children of
the covenant preserved their identity as the object of God's loving
call and protection. Here God was certain to find his beloved
chosen people.

Ghetto continued the tradition of a chosen people, set apart
from all others and living in their separate land. At least the ghetto
made it possible, in God's mysterious providence, for the chosen
people to know who they were, so that they would be intact
when they returned to their promised land some day. Such became
their weekly Sabbath prayer. Ghetto symbolized the silent retreat,
the time to think and pray, the necessity of discovering one's
true self and identity, one's family and community, one's traditions and roots. Ghetto in this sense includes, for all people, that
stage of development in our youth when we must identify and
be at peace with our own proper sexuality as well as with our
major interests or vocation in life. Only then can we enter marriage, priesthood, or a religious community with any chance of
success.

Reconciliation, seen in this context, is a kind of "marriage"
uniting persons of different backgrounds and interests who are
liable to be suspicious and hostile towards one another. Such a
"marriage" has the odds stacked against it if any group is unsure
of itself and therefore defensive, jealous and aggressive. Persons
and communities must return "into the ghetto" and learn to
accept who they are, peacefully and contentedly, before they
can embrace the other person with dignity and unselfish love.
A family needs its privacy in order to entertain its friends. God
knew that the family of Israel yearned for its privacy and so he
called them out of the nations and preserved them intact as his
chosen people. During the Babylonian exile, Second Isaiah wrote

to the disheartened Israelites, far away from home and haunted by
the horrendous suffering of their recent past:

> Now, on the contrary,
> thus speaks Yahweh,
> your creator, O Jacob, and your
> fashioner, O Israel.
> Do not fear, because I redeem you,
> I call you by name. You are mine . . .
> I give Egypt as your ransom,
> Ethiopia and Seba in return for you.
> From the fact that you are precious in my eyes,
> that you are honorable, and that I love you,
> I give countries in return for you,
> and people in return for your life.
> Do not fear, because I am with you
> (Is 43:1-5, CS).

By living in her ghetto, Israel could develop a strong love and
obedience, gratitude and generosity. These interior attitudes could
then, and only then, be shared with all men and women.

The special lot of being God's chosen people, entrusted with
a promised land, made Israel the victim of jealousy and hatred,
persecution and oppression from foreign nations. The prophecy
of Daniel and the two books of Maccabees provide the tragic
account of such sorrow. It is no exaggeration to rank Israel among
the most persecuted people of all recorded history. Israel herself
at times took advantage of her privileged position. She showed
herself hateful and vengeful towards foreigners. Even the exquisite
beauty of chapter 7 of Deuteronomy reminding Israel that God's
choice of her was simply based on the fact that he had set his
heart on her, not because of any inherent worth in her, is marred
by sentences from the Holy War:

> When the Lord, your God, brings you into
> the land . . . and dislodges great nations
> before you . . . and when the Lord, your
> God, delivers them up to you and you de-

feat them, you shall doom them. Make no
covenant with them and show them no mercy
(Dt 7:1-2).

The Holy War was a violent excess of fervor and misdirected
zeal. Because Israel could become proud and self-complacent, soft
and sensual, God sent the prophets.

These prophets—Amos, Hosea, Isaiah of Jerusalem, Jeremiah
and Second Isaiah of the Babylonian exile—summoned Israel from
the ghetto of pride and injustice. They flung the gauntlet down
upon pride and false, superstitious security. They were called to
the most difficult task of telling good people they were not as
good as they thought! To people who kept the law of Moses
perfectly (at least, they thought so), these prophets called attention to a law of humanity which was also from God and always
came first. To sell a neighbor into slavery because he could not
pay his bills was declared immoral by Amos. Must laws be obeyed
when they destroyed one's brother? So unique were these prophets that the first of them, Amos, refused to be called one. He
almost spit the words into the eye of the high priest of Bethel:

> I am no prophet, nor do I belong to a
> company of [those charismatic] prophets;
> I am a shepherd . . . The Lord took me
> from following the flock, and said to me,
> 'Go! Prophesy to my people Israel'
> (Am 7:14-15, CS).

Thus, Amos inaugurated the series of religious reformers
which we usually think of when the word, "prophet," is spoken.
For this reason, they are called the "classical prophets" to distinguish them from the "charismatic prophets" (Samuel, Elijah
and Elisha) who became a powerful force not only sustaining
Israelite religion against the degrading influence of Canaanite
morality but also in anointing and destroying kings. This latter
type of prophet formed and worked out of religious communities

which anyone could join whether married or not. They tended toward the miraculous and the extraordinary.

The *classical prophets*, on the other hand, though remaining in their own communities, operated as individuals in striking out against the excessive concern of their people for looks and externals as well as against the rigid application of laws. They were reformers who went to the heart of things, or rather, to the heart of people, and there they found that everyone is pretty much the same. Amos began with the conviction that Israel was God's chosen family:

> You alone have I favored,
> more than all the families of the earth.
> Therefore I will punish you
> for all your crimes (Am 3:2).

He ended with the concept of a "remnant people," the few who were to be saved, strong enough to survive Israel's purification and sorrow.

Always the rough shepherd and sarcastic loner, Amos expressed this new theology in unforgettable language:

> Thus says the Lord:
> As the shepherd snatches from the
> mouth of the lion
> a pair of legs or the tip of an ear of
> his sheep,
> So the Israelites who dwell in Samaria
> shall escape
> with the corner of a couch or a
> piece of a cot (Am 3:12).

The "remnant" is not to be described by externals alone. Amos lashed against the custom of judging God's favor or disfavor by externals, be it wealth or numbers or the prestige of being the chosen race. The "remnant" idea might apply to those secret intuitions, inspired by God, which lift a person out of a routine and offer immense hopes for the future. The "remnant" gets to the heart of what it means to be an Israelite and recognizes this privileged position not in blood descent but in a personal love of God.

Another prophet, Hosea, a contemporary of Amos, carried the idea still further. From the experience of his own marriage, tragic because of the repeated infidelities of his wife, agonizing in the interior demand to take her back repeatedly, Hosea concluded, "Thus the Lord loves the people of Israel" (Ho 3:1). God is compelled to forgive over and over again. Not only that, but God's love transforms the adulterous Israel into the "virgin daughter" as she was at the moment of her first espousals with God, in the desert when she agreed to the Mosaic covenant. Again we see the prophet peering beneath the surface to the heart. Hosea did not delay over the externals of blood descent, special laws and promised land in order to state what makes an Israelite. He had a vision of God's extraordinary love for his creatures, to transform them into his "spouse." Men and women everywhere, no matter how sinful, can become Israelites through God's omnipotent love. Once the prophet could see beneath the externals and look into the heart of Israel, the prophets had left the ghetto and arrived at the common substance of all human life. Here they discovered a human creature, even in sin, loved for that reason all the more tenderly, by a God whose goodness can re-create the creature beyond its expectations.

The last of the prophets came in the person of Jesus who was born in the ghetto of Judaism to become the most perfect Jew of all times. This same Jesus ate and drank with sinners and even at times with foreigners, unashamedly forgave prostitutes and accepted their gratitude, and announced that the kingdom was within, not outside in externals (Lk 17:20-21). He died before his mission to the Gentiles could be undertaken. His death, within the heart of Judaism, meant a resurrection for all the world. Israel passed from the ghetto to the world.

We, too, must move in and out of our ghetto. Wherever we are secure and appreciative of God's gifts, we must go out to share; wherever we feel a loss of identity and an interior weakness, we must retreat back into prayer, counsel and privacy. If reconciliation is the sharing of our best with others, we need to step aside from life's distractions to recognize the special gifts God has given us. Nothing can take the place of time for these gifts to mature, and only the mature person is ready for the "marriage" of reconciliation. Life becomes a movement back and forth, of gaining and losing, of going in and out of the ghetto. People, moreover, are never completely in or completely out of their ghetto. In some ways they will find it necessary to withdraw into a retreat of thought and prayer, and at the same time in other ways they are reaching out to share with others. That part of themselves, however, which they have come to appreciate and prize, they must give away unselfishly. Only in this way will it remain their possession, transformed. In this sense we understand the mysterious statement of Jesus, "Whoever has [to give away], will be given more, but the one who has not [by selfishly retaining], will lose the little he has" (Lk 8:18, CS).

RECONCILIATION WITH GOD

As we search for God, we have the consolation of knowing that God is searching for us. When Zacchaeus, the tax collector, for instance, climbed the sycamore tree to get a look at Jesus, Jesus seized the initiative, "Zacchaeus, hurry down, I mean to stay at your house today" (Lk 19:5). When the prophet Habakkuk plied God with his questions, God knew that the time had come to close the conversation and so replied, "The just man lives by his faith" (Hab 2:4)—that is, wait until God finds you with *his* answer. So energetically is God searching for us, that he will, if necessary, send a whale to swallow us and take us back to where we refuse to go (Jon 2). When people complained against Jesus' going to the houses of sinners as a guest, Jesus replied, "The Son of Man has come to search out and save what was lost." Jesus was echoing God's searching question to the first man and woman in the garden, "Where are you?" (Gn 3:9).

To be reconciled with God, it is not sufficient, then, for us to search for God. Our eyes are not strong enough nor our hearts generous enough, to see and receive him. God is searching for us, to receive us within his heart. We must, therefore, look for God on his terms. We cannot tell God who he must be and what he must do. We wait and learn: "Lord! Who are you?" Everyone experiences the searching arm of God in the hopes which he inspires within us. God's hopes, deep within all creation, make the world groan in agony, like a woman in childbirth.

> Not only that, but we ourselves, although
> we have the Spirit as first fruits, groan
> inwardly while we await the redemption of
> our bodies. In hope we were saved. But hope
> is not hope if its object is seen; how is it
> possible for one to hope for what he sees?
> And hoping for what we cannot see means awaiting
> it with patient endurance (Rm 8:23-25).

What we seek, we already possess, like a mother carrying her unborn child within the womb.

Hope leads us beyond ourselves, beyond our vision and understanding. Hope represents the voice of God, calling us to be more prayerful, more forgiving, more appreciative, more obedient, more creative, more humble, more Godlike. Hope reconciles us to what we must become, by reason of the hidden dynamism breathed into us by God. Hope thus reconciles us with God who searches. The way towards God, inspired by godly hopes within us, turns out to be difficult and demanding. Great leaders, who have suffered much, started out with great hopes. Jeremiah's first preaching, rebounding with expectations (Jr 30 and 31), pointed the prophet toward his way of the cross. Not only must he himself, even in his understanding of these hopes, submit to a vigorous purification, but he was also persecuted by his fellow Israelites, those, in fact, of his own family (Jr 12:6). They could silence the challenging and condemnatory voice of these hopes only if they muzzled Jeremiah.

God never frustrates us with unreachable desires in our search for him. Whatever he calls us to seek, he helps us to attain. Hopes indicate his presence and his search for us. That presence makes him known as a Savior who empowers us to accomplish what would otherwise be impossible. His assistance comes in the most intimate or personal way possible, at that point of ourselves where we think and love and cherish and hope. These personal hopes can be discerned as good and holy, not as selfish and abusive, when they reconcile us with more and more of our brothers and sisters. In this union with others we learn that our God is a God for all the world. He himself answers our question: "Lord! Who are you?"

RECONCILIATION AND PATIENCE

If we are to be reconciled in a truly redemptive and sanctifying way, then we must be like God, taking our time. We seek a reconciliation, one with another, in God according to his hopes for all of us. These expectations reach beyond our normal energy and even beyond our sharpest vision. God must take over and intensify our effort. Even so, after intervening some four thousand years since the call of Abraham and sending his own Son, God still needs more time.

Reconciliation could be achieved much more quickly if we could simply lock arms and accept each other just as we are. God, however, has much more ambitious plans for us than a pooling together of our selfish desires, vague ideas, and very tolerant attitudes. Such a self-indulgent independent spirit—to get as much pleasure out of life without bothering anybody else—ends up with a tower of Babel. People no longer talk anyone else's language and everybody is scattering to their more selfish corner of the universe. Immediately after the Tower of Babel fiasco (Gn 11:1-9), God summoned the family of Abraham on the long difficult path through salvation history in the Bible, until the "designated time had come [when] God sent forth his son born of a woman" (Gal 4:4). There is then the necessity of time, a long time of waiting, for us to be reconciled with God. But as we see also, reconciliation requires that we carefully discern the "designated time" and take action, lest it pass us by. God prepares us by prophecy to recognize the right moment, but we need to know how to explain prophecy. Prophecies can often be very puzzling and open to many interpretations. The Bible can divide as well as reconcile.

Perhaps the most important image for salvation in the Bible is the *exodus* or *the way*, leading from oppression to freedom, from sin to goodness, from scattered disunity to harmony in prayer. Within the way of the exodus we meet some of the greatest moments of salvation-history, such as the time of Moses' leadership, the sealing of the covenant, and the revelation of the commandments. But the biblical account of the *exodus* came to include much more than the achievement of Moses. So central, in fact, was the Mosaic accomplishment to all future generations, that it intended to absorb more and more of that future which it dominated. Not only did future legislators formulate their laws to keep the Mosaic law alive, but they inserted their new laws into the *Torah*. The exodus led by Moses assimilated the way of life of many future leaders; Kings David and Solomon are reflected in many sections of Genesis, and the religious reforms of Kings Hezekiah and Josiah are united with the work of Moses in Deuteronomy. These are examples of how the time of the first exodus, forty long years in itself, was extended more and more over the centuries of time leading up to Jesus.

God called Israel to respond in special ways during this very long time. The most important of all these divine interventions came when God "sent his son born of a woman, born under the law [of Moses], to deliver from the law those subject to it." Jesus' ministry was itself absorbed into the way of the "exodus." That is exactly the word used by St. Luke, when at the Transfiguration two great leaders of Judaism, who themselves journeyed to Mount Sinai, conversed with Jesus about his mission:

> (Jesus) took Peter, John and James, and went
> up onto a mountain to pray. While he was
> praying, his face changed in appearance and
> his clothes became dazzlingly white. Suddenly
> two men were talking with him—Moses

> and Elijah. They appeared in glory and spoke
> of his passage [in Greek, his *exodus*], which
> he was about to fulfill in Jerusalem
> (Lk 9:28-31).

Not only does Luke describe the greater part of Jesus' ministry as a journey or exodus, but the way of the Cross, which must be followed by everyone who would come after Jesus and share his glory (Lk 9:25), is itself an "exodus." Our life, therefore, must be folded into that of Jesus', just as his was into that of his Jewish forebears who, in turn, walked in the steps of Moses. This way was and is a long one over centuries of time. Reconciliation is not an instant achievement.

Moreover, God wants us to be healed and united in all parts of our life, individually and as community. Reconciliation must begin interiorly at the heart of life. Here is where we function as persons and respond to a personal God, seeking a personal response from us. It takes time to reach the depths necessary for such interior dialogue. Many biblical passages, especially among the prophets, stress the interior, healing, transforming presence of the Spirit. Understandably enough, Jeremiah announced the Mosaic Covenant transformed in this way:

> This is the covenant which I will make with
> the house of Israel after those days [note
> the reference again to the necessity of time],
> says the Lord. I will place my law within
> them, and write it upon their hearts;
> I will be their God, and they shall be my
> people (Jr 31:33).

Even the more legalistic prophet, Ezekiel, insisted that God's bestowal of the Spirit must precede obedience of the law. We cannot even know, much less accomplish, what God really wants of us, unless God fulfills the prophetic promise:

> I will sprinkle clean water upon you to
> cleanse you from all your impurities . . .

> I will give you a new heart and place my
> spirit within you, taking from your bodies
> your stony hearts and giving you natural
> hearts. I will put my spirit within you
> and make you live my statutes, careful to
> observe my decrees (Ez 36:25-26).

It is important to notice the sequence or development of Ezekiel's thought. First, the individual must be a part of the community at liturgical prayer. Next, an interior conversion is accomplished by God's holy spirit, remaking the person with a "new heart." Finally, obedient observance of the laws is expected of the individual within the community. God wants to heal emotions and prejudices, whether in individuals or in society. For a long time he put up with the two separate kingdoms of Judah and Israel. Even in the time of Jesus the Lord's own disciples tended to despise and fear the northern Samaritans (Lk 9:51-56) and the Jerusalemites looked down on those other northerners, the Galileans (Mt 26:69-75). As if by divine reversal these "inferior" people of the north were among the first to receive the gospel after Jesus' death (Ac 8:1, 4, 25). But how long God waited!

RECONCILIATION AND LIBERATION

The Bible surprises us, too, with its long tolerance of slavery and male chauvinism. The Ten Commandments, even in their more moderate and more humanitarian version, were addressed to men, not women; nothing is said about coveting a neighbor's husband. Slavery, too, was accepted (Dt 5:21). Deuteronomy, however, explicitly legislated that slaves were not to work on the Sabbath (5:12-15). This more considerate understanding of a slave reaches great intensity in Paul's letter to the slave-owner Philemon. Paul's letter is carried to Philemon by his run-away slave:

> It is he I am sending back to you— and that
> means I am sending my heart . . . that you

might possess him forever, no longer as
a slave but as much more than a slave, a
beloved brother, especially dear to me;
and how much more than a brother to you,
since now you will know him both as a man
and in the Lord (Phm 12-16).

God's plan was to free slaves, not quickly by a divine edict,
but slowly by inducing love for one's "brother to you" whom
you must respect "as a man and in the Lord." Reconciliation was
to be a total reunion, internally and externally. Nothing takes the
place of time for healing and for learning. God's life is eternal,
without past or future. He is always totally alive, but he respects
our human need for time as he gradually transforms us according
to his own image into a relationship of love. Humankind must
learn this lesson all over again from God, who practices it with
such exquisite patience and sturdy hopes. The way to reconciliation will be the long one of the exodus through salvation history,
the deep one through the ways of the spirit in the human heart,
the surprising one through the sudden fulfillment of prophecy.

Reconciliation, the Bible maintains, must happen on God's
terms or it will never happen at all, or at least it will not last!
God's conditions summon us to be holier, more patient and more
understanding, not only than we are, but even than what we
think possible. Those expectations are made of us, at times directly
through God's Holy Spirit within our conscience and at other
times indirectly through our family, friends and even our enemies.
Within our ghetto of thought and prayer we struggle with these
divine hopes for ourselves. It is a struggle for no other reason
than the simple fact that hopes will not let us alone. A child
with great hopes is usually a personality kid always straining at
the leash, getting into more trouble than other children, until
the energy is harnessed. Later, the child who reaches adulthood
must make a more than special effort at patience. Like God, they
must follow the long way of time towards that "designated moment" of reconciliation when hopes are fulfilled because they
are shared with others.

No prophet began his ministry with greater, more spontaneous hopes than the prophet Jeremiah. As the world-tyrant, Assyria, was falling apart, Jeremiah bounded with hopes that his own people would return from exile and resettle their own country. That was in the year 627 B.C. Decades of time passed and not only did the northern tribes never come back, but a new tyrant Babylon reached out to grasp the southern tribe of Judah and to squeeze out its lifeblood through taxation, hostages, and religious interference. The Judean officials were weak. As Jeremiah appealed to conscience and national morale, they wanted only their governmental posts and power. The long agony of Jeremiah ensued, from 609 until 587 B.C.

Jeremiah prayed, but the only prayer possible for him consisted in questions and more questions. He wrote some of his prayers on a separate scroll, hidden away from others. Was he ashamed of himself or afraid of others that he kept it secret? After he died, his secretary Baruch found this scroll and inserted the prayers where he thought they originated in Jeremiah's tumultuous life: 12:1-5; 15:10-21; 17:14-18; 18:18-25; 20:7-18. They are now known as Jeremiah's *Confessions*. They record no answers. All they seemed to accomplish by their questions was a sustained attitude of faith. They enabled Jeremiah to continue remembering the presence of God, but not a God who capitulated to second-rate hopes. God kept the hopes of Jeremiah strong. He even made these hopes more demanding in terms of forgiveness and practical application. Jeremiah, who pre-figured Jesus, was to be reconciled with the world only on God's terms, and he left us an example in his prayers of faith, how to wait in God's presence until our hopes equal the prophet's.

Jeremiah began and ended with faith. His reconciliation with God was consummated in total darkness. The love and hopes of God were so overpowering as to blind the prophet's eyes. These hopes included a world beyond Israel, stretching out to include the Gentiles. This seemingly impossible hope—that Jews and Gentiles be one chosen people—was expressed in one of Jeremiah's last compositions. This piece was placed at the beginning of the book because it explained the meaning of the prophet's vocation (1:4-10). There is good reason to think, however, that it was actually written much later and represented the prophet's attempt as an old man to understand the strange development of his life, from vaulting hopes as a youth to almost total collapse at the end. Jeremiah could find peace only by concluding that God knew and planned it that way. Even before his conception and birth, God had determined the mission of this child. This mission would extend long after his death. God summoned him to be "a prophet to the nations," something Jeremiah never was during his lifetime. Jeremiah's life reminds us that hopes reach beyond the present moment, that they even extend beyond one's lifetime. Hopes are given to some great people, not to be fulfilled and enjoyed, but to be transmitted to the next generation. Moses died before setting foot on the good earth of the Promised Land. Jesus was cut down and buried without seeing the Church.

And so, we can come to many important conclusions about the biblical call to reconciliation, but the most important ones are those secret inspirations given by the Holy Spirit to each person. Some less secret expressions of the Spirit might be the following:

(1) We are called upon to persevere long enough to pass on salvation to the next generation under the aspect of hope. This confidence in the future is the basic ingredient of all life as well as the rallying point of reconciliation between the dead and those yet to be born. Waiting upon God is necessary, because we will be united only in God's terms, conditions which reject mediocrity, vagueness and easy acceptance of one another's faults.

(2) We must manifest our hope now in meaningful symbols. We must go out of our ghetto and choose from contemporary culture those signs of divine goodness which summon us into the future. Hope, we are told, is the memory of the future. Good symbolism must be achieved especially in the performance of the sacred liturgy. If people are rejecting the Church and its sacraments, the Church must ask itself whether or not the symbolism

of the altar speaks the presence of a hidden God and the mystery of the future to youth today in order to present a realistic challenge for goodness.

(3) The ghetto where one learns the meaning of being God's chosen people and the prayer of a prophet like Jeremiah totally alone with God demand simplicity of life. All baroque clutter must be stripped away. Is it too outlandish to be reminded that nakedness is an important symbol of paradise? Through simplicity of life-style, one manifests a total dependence upon God as savior and at the same time one cleanses the mind for contemplative prayer. Simplicity in the apostolate expects us to seek out the real problems and real values of the contemporary age and never to allow Church energy to be dissipated on clergy problems and religious life issues or on problems of jealousy and personalism.

(4) Reconciliation presumes the God-given grace to forgive, and forgiveness means that the other person has sinned willfully. Reconciliation presumes a love so personal and so total as to die for the other. To lose oneself within the hopes of another reveals the one God, who has personally saved his people through us and so there is manifest the full glory of God's secret plan, no longer secret and no longer a hope. It is reconciliation.

Chapter Nineteen
From Chaos to a New Creation

Two men of our day, Dr. Martin Luther King and Pope John XXIII, were spokesmen for peace and unity: Dr. King with the goal of one nation of equal opportunity for all its citizens, Pope John with the hope of one Christian community drawn together by the attractiveness of its Christ-like goodness. Yet, as each man died, chaos was erupting in our land and throughout the Church. Does the Bible show any necessary connection between proclaiming peace and precipitating turmoil and chaos?

Are people like Dr. King or Pope John to be censored as tragically incompetent leaders because of their failure to provide a plan for implementing their intoxicating dreams and because of the unnecessary suffering they have thus fomented in the world? All of us, especially religious educators, need to face this question in a very personal way. For, if we are trying to educate Christians to become peacemakers, they will often find that they are stirring up conflict in families, in the parish, in the diocese and in the community.

To make peace, in the biblical sense of fullness of human life, both personal and social, means trying to change institutions and forces that are stifling and crippling human life. But many good Christians hotly resent the idea that efforts to bring about social change are an essential aspect of the Christion vocation. However tactfully and charitably this idea is proposed, they will not accept it and will oppose those who do. To what kind of peace and unity, then, should we be dedicated—to the existing kind of order with which so many people are content, or to the kind of peace that the gospel proclaims which seems only to stir up conflict and confusion?

The Bible has no pre-cooked answer for this, nor indeed, for any question. But it does prod us to think and ponder and so to approach the kind of solution which enables us to live and carry out our work courageously and with interior serenity. And it does this in a moment of history wrenched into violence apparently by the champions of peace. We see a parallel to these men in the New Testament image of Jesus Christ who went about announcing peace and charity but in so doing threatened the tranquility of his nation. The keen mind of Caiaphas had sized up the situation correctly: "Can you not see," he insisted, "that it is better for you to have one man die [for the people], than to have the whole nation destroyed?" (Jn 11:50).

Nor did the Old Testament prophets offer a detailed plan for safeguarding the freedom and prosperity of their country as they denounced oppression and condemned war. These prophetic forebears of Jesus possessed too much confidence in the impelling goodness of ideals to worry about the outcome. When goodness, peace and unity are announced clearly and perseveringly, the chips can fall where they may, the future will be godly and ever more worthy of the divine image in each person. When one of the prophets, Habakkuk, hesitated for a moment and questioned God's seemingly incompetent handling of Israel's national affairs, the answer took shape in his mind: "The just man lives by faith" (Hab 2:4)—by faith in the goodness of God, not by the vision of clearly worded solutions.

When chaos ensued and nothing was left of the old order, the "Great Unknown" of the Babylonian exile penned this mysterious definition of faith, too genuine to be ignored:

> Though young men faint and grow weary,
> and youths stagger and fall,
> They that hope in the Lord will renew
> their strength,
> they will soar as with eagles' wings;
> They will run and not grow weary,
> walk and not grow faint (Is 40:30-31).

These lines, especially the words, "They that hope in the Lord will renew their strength," became the classic Old Testament formulation of faith. Hope is the direct opposite of possession and vision. Hope is faith in the exalted ideal which sweeps one off one's feet into the mysterious future.

Biblical leaders, then, released a redemptive force of overwhelming ideals, which disrupted into chaos for nations prepared only for mediocre compromise. But through the sustaining power of absorbing faith, a new creation began to emerge. Biblical theology calls this phenomenon *creative redemption*—redemption into chaos towards a new creation. From the biblical perspective, Yahweh approaches his people as a redeemer, who ends up creating their life, their country, even their universe. God, moreover, meets his people as a personal redeemer. "I am Yahweh your God, who brought you out of the land of Egypt, that place of slavery" (Ex 20:2). He redeems them so magnificently that he creates them anew:

> I am Yahweh your God . . .
> because you are precious in my eyes . . .
> from the east I will bring back your
> descendants,
> from the west I will gather you . . .
> everyone who is called by my name
> for my glory I create, form and make
> (Is 43:3-7).

The final outcome of Yahweh's redemptive effort, according to the prophet Jeremiah, will be "a new covenant [inscribed] . . . upon their hearts [when] I will be their God, and they shall be my people," a new wonder which "the Lord has created" (Jr 31:31-33, 22). Again the sequence follows the biblical way of redemption: through chaos into a new creation.

God, accordingly, accomplishes his redemptive task by imprinting ideals of peace and charity in the conscience of his leaders, ideals at times so exacting that Jeremiah cried out in agony:

> It becomes like fire burning in my heart,

> imprisoned in my bones;
> I grow weary holding it in,
> I cannot endure it (Jr 20:9).

Yet, for Jeremiah to cry out his word of faith brings a reaction of violence against himself. And in this rejection the entire country comes crashing down. Yet because of the prophet's persevering faith through darkness, the nation emerges out of the chaos of exile as a new creation of Yahweh. Divine ideals destroy the sinful situation and out of the shambles these same ideals of God's continuing concern create the new, resurrected people.

Three important links, leading to the fulfillment of biblical promises, can be noted. First, redemption and at the conclusion, the new creation. In between lies the dark chaos wherein life is sustained solely by faith in the goals announced by Yahweh-Redeemer through his prophets and leaders. That most important link, joining redemption with creation, is faith—faith in the goals and ideals inspired by God.

Several factors of this biblical theology of creative redemption must be examined still more closely. Most important is the scriptural understanding of God as personal redeemer (cf. ch. 1). This idea restates what has been said about the role of faith linking redemption with the creation. This intimate, personal bond between Yahweh and his people envelops redemption in the mystery of a sweep into the future. The resulting creation is triggered by hope, sustained by faith, and achieved by charity.

As redeemer, God is determined to rescue us from our accumulated weakness, frustration and sin; but as a personal redeemer, God always respects us as persons, free, responsible individuals within our community. He never pushes or shoves or violates our freedom. Neither does God "form" us with plaster casts poured on us from outside. We are not broken arms to be patched up. In his redemptive undertaking, God touches us where we are persons, that is, where we think, ponder and love, reach decisions and plan their execution. God is with us throughout this entire human process, and precisely as God, aflame with desire for our well-being, empowered with irresistible energy already alive in the moment of fulfillment. God, nonetheless, does not do the thinking for us, nor does he force decisions on us independent of our judgment. He, our savior, is a personal God.

Biblical leaders reached major decisions only at a slow, steady pace. But God must have been there all along the way, for the end product is announced as "The Word of God." However, the steps along the way must have been human steps as well, because the way was long and sometimes lost and almost always controversial. At least 292,000 days crawled along to make eight hundred years before the law code of Moses reached its definitive form in the Bible. God might have burned it upon rock with the swiftness of lightning—a most sensational way for the cinema but most impersonal for human beings. Instead, God allowed each word of the law to rise to the surface of community consciousness slowly and painfully in the seething cauldron of human life. The law of Christ could have been formed according to a quick, easy formula of Jesus speaking a sentence and the inspired evangelists writing it down. But a personal God would not do it that way.

Those passages of the Bible describing the moment when Moses received the two tablets of the law from Yahweh on Mount Sinai (Ex 31:18; 34:1 ff.), or portraying Jesus on the Mount of the Beatitudes as he proclaims the charter of the new kingdom to his select disciples (Mt 5:1 ff.), enunciate the scriptural faith that Israel, or the Church, could do nothing of itself. But they also declare that with God's or Jesus' continuing presence and sustaining hope, the results of the Mosaic code or the evangelical law of "blessedness" would surpass the people's abilities and even their desires.

God's presence was as irresistible as lightning. It was also as hidden and mysterious as the wind blowing at night across the countryside. It "blows where it will. You hear the sound it makes, but you do not know where it comes from or where it goes. So it is with everyone begotten of the Spirit" (Jn 3:8). Though it is mysteriously present at the heart of each believer, God does not relieve Israel, or the Church, from its own thinking, studying, pondering, praying, discussing, changing, rewriting, and deciding.

In the Old Testament, God accepted the people as he found them: orientals of desert nomadic background, highly independent, united under Moses by means of a broadly based legal and cultic norm, always applying this norm to immediate circumstances, thereby revising and adding to it. Only in the late fifth century before Christ is the document finalized in its present written form. God, therefore, did not meet Moses and the people with a "take it or leave it" attitude and a ready-made law envisioning any and every eventuality. Nor did he expect passive subservience to its legislation. Perhaps all that God provided for Abraham, Moses, Samuel and the later leaders was the intuition of himself as a personal God, always there with his people. Such is the meaning of the divine name Yahweh, "He who is always there."

By means of this personal covenant, the people were enabled to glimpse a future far happier than anything at the moment, to which they must strive with the best of their ability as they experimented with existing laws, adapting them and rewriting them. This future appeared exhilarating as the sky, hopeful as an open door to the universe. It was also stern in its demand for courage and faith. And all the while it promised a new creative redemption—redemption seen as a cooperative venture between persons.

When people lost their vision and consequently their courage, they settled for a legal interpretation of law. They did just what was required for the moment—proceeded to the temple, offered sacrifice, maintained order in the land. It led them also to think how pleased God must be with them. In this type of religion, God was not a person but a code to be obeyed. Religion no longer inspired the courage to seek a divine ideal; rather, it sanctioned the smugness of having done all that was humanly possible.

When this happened, the prophets shouted from the mountains and their words resounded across the land. Their shouting was so thoroughly human as to be as sarcastic as Amos, as sensitive as Hosea, as regal as Isaiah, as brilliant as Nahum, and as introspective as Jeremiah. At the same time, the shouts were as divine as God, because the words pulsed with a hope breathed by God within the soul of Israel. Without working a single miracle, each prophet began his speech in a most daring way, solemnly stating, "Hear the word of God." If you think that is not daring, try it some time.

The prophet had no detailed plan; he respected the intelligence of his audience too much to do their thinking for them. As the Syro-Ephraimite forces were moving south against Jerusalem, Isaiah announced this word of God: "Take care that you remain tranquil and do not fear." His only plan was: "Unless your faith is firm, you shall not be firm." Such idealism was too impractical for King Ahaz of Jerusalem who had already made an alliance with Assyria and was preparing for war against his northern neighbors. When Ahaz rejected Isaiah's advice against foreign entanglements, the prophet proceeded to announce doom. Yet he also assured his fellow countrymen that, as the wars roared destructively through the land, God would be present as Emmanuel, cleansing the country and preparing for the great messianic moment. "Emmanuel"—God with us—was with his people, as the chaos swept deluge-like across the land, sustaining them with a mysterious hope and keeping them alive for that day of the new creation when

> A shoot shall sprout from the hidden
> stump of Jesse [David's father],
> and from his [seemingly dead] roots a
> bud shall blossom.
> The spirit of the Lord shall rest upon
> him . . . (Is 11:1-2).

The way of salvation was becoming evident: from divinely inspired hopes for peace to a hardening, sinful reaction favoring war. This stance was followed by a renewed prophetic announcement of ideals, into chaos, with a new creation emerging in the future. And always God was present, not on the surface but at the heart, as Israel's personal redeemer and gradually becoming Israel's creator of a blessed future.

Ideals thrust Israel into chaos and the nation was left divided between those who rejected and those who accepted the prophetic ideals demanding super-human courage. But the prophet's continuing faith in these ideals sustained the nation as it moved into the new creation. This faith lived in them to such a degree as to lead them to a situation of identification with the nation's chaos and total tragedy. This concrete sharing of the people's loss and destruction is exemplified in Jeremiah's call to celibacy.

> Do not marry any woman; you shall not have
> sons or daughters in this place, for thus
> says the Lord concerning the sons and daugh-
> ters who will be born in this place, the
> mothers who will give them birth, the fathers
> who will beget them in this land: of deadly
> disease they shall die. Unlamented and un-
> buried they will lie like dung on the ground,
> sword and famine will make an end of them . . .
> (Jr 16:1-4).

Not only was Jeremiah to experience the lonely desolation of Israel, but he was also destined to be plunged into their doubting, hesitating, even apostasizing reaction towards Yahweh. In one of his "Confessions" he complains with God against the tide of events:

> Woe to me, mother, that you gave me birth . . .
> Tell me, Lord, have I not served you well? . . .
> You know I have . . .
> Under the weight of your hand I sat alone . . .
> Why is my pain continuous . . . ?
> You have indeed become for me a treacherous
> brook,
> whose waters do not abide (Jr 15:10-18).

Jeremiah is almost, if not already, sucked into apostasy. Yahweh has not kept faith with him, the prophet cries out bitterly. The Lord has become a dry river bed, a Palestinian wadi, once flowing with fresh water but now a bursting sweep of sand, encrusted with salt and pockmarked with scrub bushes.

Yet God's reply, presented in the language and style of Jeremiah, calls upon the prophet to "repent" or "turn," in one of the words he often repeated in preaching to apostate people. What follows are the most radical lines in the entire Bible:

> If you bring forth the precious without
> the vile,
> you shall be my mouthpiece
> (Jr 15:19).

The phrase is radical because some of the inspired word of God in the scroll of Jeremiah is denounced as "vile" stuff, which must yet be purified like gold in fire in order to become the pure, energetic thrust of God's word. Here again is an extraordinary instance of Yahweh as personal redeemer. So close is the Lord to the person of Jeremiah, so much respecting his vocabulary and even his mental distress and seeming apostasy, that Jeremiah's complaint and God's reply both rank as the inspired "word of God"! What preserves Jeremiah from suicide or collapse is the intuitive realization that "I [Yahweh] am with you, to deliver and rescue you" (Jr 15:20). This presence of Yahweh keeps alive the ideal of God in Jeremiah's deepest heart and is able also to transform the entire world of Jeremiah from an alloy of precious and vile material to a pure, precious "word."

This faith not only sustained Jeremiah, but it also kept his words alive in the community of Israel. After the prophet's death, the goals and ideals, which had precipitated excruciating suffering for Jeremiah as well as for people who rejected them, continued to live, announcing the grandest future possible: a new covenant, inscribed upon the heart, to be fully realized in the messianic community (Jr 31).

This same theology of redemptive creation appears in the creation passages of the Bible. Psalm 8 is a good example principally because the New Testament interprets the psalm in a way authentically true to its Old Testament meaning. It reads:

> O Lord, our Lord,
> How glorious is your name over all the earth!

... When I behold your heavens, the
work of your fingers,
the moon and the stars which you set in place—
What is man that you should be mindful of
him ... ?
You have made him little less than the angels,
and crowned him with glory and honor.
You have given him rule over the works of
your hands ...

Psalm 8 certainly presents the Creator-God in terms of a very
personal God, concerned about the human family. In fact, the
only way by which the Bible distinguishes human beings from
the animals derives from the more excelling love which Yahweh
has for men and women. Such love announces a unity and a
friendliness stretching throughout the universe. The ideal is too
demanding for many people. Their struggle with it and initial
rejection of it are enunciated in the line which we omitted from
our quotation of the psalm. The verse reads:

Out of the mouths of babes and sucklings you have
fashioned praise because of your foes,
to silence the hostile and the vengeful.

This note of hostility and struggle in a psalm about creation
deserves attention. If the psalmist were celebrating Yahweh's first
act of making the world out of nothing, there would be no
struggle to announce, for there was no enemy to combat. But if
the psalmist is anticipating the new creation, the dream of
Yahweh's redemptive transformation of a sinful world, then conflict is to be expected. Yahweh's plan of one world in which all
persons belong to one family and willingly invite everyone else
as a brother or sister to the family dinner table—such love demands
too much forgiveness and loss and humiliation to be accepted
without struggle.

Psalm 8 is found again during the Palm Sunday procession of
Jesus in Matthew's Gospel, and the Epistle to the Hebrews. In

Chapter 21 of Matthew's Gospel, Jesus has triumphantly "entered Jerusalem [with] the whole city stirred to its depths." Going into the Temple, Jesus cleanses it of buying and selling, repeating Isaiah's thought that "My house shall be called a house of prayer." Then he cures the blind and the crippled who were brought to him in the Temple. When the chief priests and the teachers of the law complain against Jesus' curing those unlettered poor people and receiving the joyful songs of the children, he responds to them with Psalm 8:

> From the speech of infants and children
> you have framed a hymn of praise.

As Jesus approaches the full goal of his messianic work, which he anticipates by the triumphal procession of Palm Sunday, he is challenged with violent opposition. This, his last week on earth, will destroy him in agonizing death. Yet, on Palm Sunday, as titanic forces close in upon him, he announces the new creation, the full achievement of his messianic mission: not only he but all the just will be cured of every infirmity and the world will be remade. At this moment, Jesus offers no elaborate plan for the Church to come, no provision for saving the Jewish nation from collapse before the Roman armies.

Jesus has only a goal and an ideal, the personal love of God-redeemer for all persons, Jew and Gentile, slave and free. Yet his death united everyone to himself, not only because nothing is so human as dying, but because never was such love as this manifested for all people. This divine love could never be quenched; it brought him through death to the new creation of his resurrection, a pledge that all persons would arise from the dead, provided they would die with Christ, that they may live with him (Rm 6:3-11, Gal 2:20).

Again in the Epistle to the Hebrews, Psalm 8 is quoted in a context of suffering and death. The author of this richly theological document wrote:

> . . . we do see Jesus crowned with

> glory and honor because he suffered
> death: Jesus who was made for a little
> while lower than the angels, that through
> God's gracious will [some manuscripts read,
> "without God"] he might taste death for
> the sake of all men (Heb 2:9).

But immediately after these verses about the redemptive death of Jesus, when he shared the deepest personal problems of his brothers and sisters of the human race, the author of the epistle turns to the idea of a new creation in Jesus and through Jesus.

> Indeed, it was fitting that when bringing
> many sons to glory God, for whom and
> through whom all things exist, should
> make their leader in the work of salvation
> perfect through suffering (Heb 2:10).

The sequence again is the same—from redemption which inspires ideals, through darkness and chaos and death, into a new creation.

CONCLUSIONS

Redemption, then, is the most personal act of God, so personal as to make the overwhelming demand that everyone be a brother or sister to everyone else. This demand is so great that society is thrown into chaos. Some people violently reject it while others wholeheartedly accept it. Faith is sustained by great leaders who are often martyred. Their sufferings keep them within a suffering and struggling community, which, in turn, enable that community to maintain its ideals and to continue towards its new creation. The sequence of God's action then would seem to be: first, redemption proclaimed through the enunciation of God's personal love for each person within the community; then, chaos as such ideals are opposed and the community appears to be rent apart; finally, the emergence of a new creation, already achieved in Jesus and which is on its way for us.

Out of this sequence, some conclusions can be proposed.

(1) Redemption does not mean that the child begins life purely and innocently, then sins; and so tarnishes and breaks asunder this initial goodness, and eventually is forgiven by God who somehow puts the parts back together again for heavenly purposes. Heaven is not a patched-up situation, but a full and new creation. Biblically, each person begins from a sinful condition. God meets each individual not with laws about everything that must be done, but with his personal presence, where a person ponders and prays and makes decisions. Here is where the commandments (and plans for their implementation) emerge as a response to God's goodness in which people have a share. This goodness stirs up many struggles and failures, much darkness and chaos. When the entire world seems collapsing, one can lay claim only to faith in God's abiding presence. In the depth of this complete consecration to Jesus, a new creation of goodness and innocence is achieved.

(2) This sequence of creative redemption alerts us to treat one another with the same kind of personal respect shown to each individual by God. We should not seek to transform other people by insisting upon ready-made plans of redemption. Rather, we can encourage each other to think, ponder and pray in God's presence. Then, in a gradual and deeply personal way, God will work the transformation of a new creation. Unfortunately, we often demand too much perfection (really, a false external perfection) before we allow God's personal redemptive power to reach others.

(3) Finally, the Bible does not tolerate the condemnation of ideas for the specious reason that they are too great for the community. Nor does it countenance the objection that these ideals can be proclaimed only if the prophet has a detailed plan for implementing them. Nonetheless, our positive response to the prophetic word must include conversion, reflection, decision-making and action, intelligently and responsibly directed toward preparing for the new creation. This means that we must be

prepared both to suffer and die and to live and work for the ideals of true non-violence and peace.

The biblical idea of creative redemption needs to be applied by each of us, both as individual persons and as a community of persons. We can have confidence in our decisions to the extent that we think and ponder and pray in union with our brothers and sisters. Where two or three are gathered together in his name, Christ is with us—with his explosive ideals of peace for everyone.

Chapter Twenty
Death to Life

Our last chapter is a kind of epilogue. It is related to the preceding chapter, but its point of reference is from a more personal perspective. The final chaos which we must face as individuals is death. Nothing is more certain about life than death. It poses a traumatic problem for both the old and young. Even Jesus begged his Father to be spared "this hour" (Mk 14:35). The real dilemma which confronts us is not so much the act of dying as in living with the prospect of inevitable death. Yet no one, it seems, can capably handle the stresses and worries of life if they attempt to suppress the thought of death. Death, in fact, may not be nearly as severe a trial as many other frustrations encountered in the course of living. At the actual time of death, God grants his special assistance, as we see in Hebrews:

> In the days when he was in the flesh,
> he offered prayers and supplications
> with loud cries and tears to God, who
> was able to save him from death, and he
> was heard because of his reverence. Son
> though he was, he learned obedience from
> what he suffered; and when perfected, he
> became the source of eternal salvation
> for all who obey him (5:7-9).

At the moment of death, most of us will be so comatose if we are elderly or so taken by surprise if we are young, that we will be unaware of what is really happening. How we face the other trials of life will determine our attitude at the trial of death. In the Old Testament, we discover in Israel's attitude of faith in times of personal affliction and national disaster, a scriptural approach to the problem of death. This answer remained very intuitive, always eluding the conscious grasp of the mind, because up until the second century before Christ, the Israelites did not possess a clear belief in personal immortality or bodily resurrection. Death seemed to stop all human activity.

Unlike the Israelites, we explicitly accept conscious survival after death and bodily resurrection. And yet, despite our knowledge of the resurrection, death still terrifies us, as it did Jesus. Therefore, Israel's answer has an important message for it enables us to put the enigma of the modern agnostic and atheist in perspective, for in the Old Testament we find an example of people intuitively or subconsciously accepting what they explicitly or consciously denied.

Israel did not possess explicit belief in personal immortality all the way up to the second century before Christ. Only in Daniel 12:1-3 and in the Pharisaic document of 2 Maccabees (ch. 7) is the bodily resurrection of the just announced as an object of faith within the community of Israel. Within the largest sections of the Hebrew Scriptures, death seemed to silence all contact with the living God and even at times to negate God's fidelity. We are told: "For among the dead no one remembers you [O God]: in the nether world who gives you thanks?" (Ps 6:6). Preserved from a premature death, King Hezekiah sang a hymn of thanksgiving which reflected Israel's frightened attitude before such an early end of life:

> Once I said,
> 'In the noontime of life I must depart!
> To the gates of the nether world I shall be
> consigned
> for the rest of my years.'
> I said, 'I shall see the Lord no more
> in the land of the living.
> No longer shall I behold my fellow men
> among those who dwell in the world.
> My dwelling, like a shepherd's tent,

is struck down and borne away from me;
You have folded up my life, like a weaver
who severs the last thread.
Day and night you give me over to torment;
I cry out until the dawn . . .'
(Is 38:10-13).

Even while chanting a joyful cry of gratitude at being cured
from his mortal illness, Hezekiah could not help but reveal his
fearful attitude before the possibility of an untimely death. He
continued:

For it is not the nether world that
gives you thanks,
nor death that praises you:
Neither do those who go down into the pit
await your kindness [in Hebrew, 'emeth].
The living, the living give you thanks,
as I do today.
Fathers declare to their sons,
O God, your faithfulness [in Hebrew,
'emeth] (Is 38:18-19).

The abode of the dead (Sheol is the Hebrew name) seemed to
be outside of God's 'emeth, the Hebrew word which signifies the
kind of fidelity to be expected among kinsmen as they rally
around a relative in need. Those who were in Sheol were generally
thought to be abandoned or forgotten by God and they themselves exercised no activity. Too many biblical passages reflect
this attitude to think that Hezekiah was voicing a popular superstition or a particularly melancholic disposition of his own (see,
for example, Psalms 31; 35; 88; 115; 143).

These passages, separating the deceased from the presence of
God and declaring the corpse to be an unclean object (Nb 19:
11-22), express their thought too explicitly to say that Israel was
taking a neutral position and simply denying any knowledge
about the future life. Nor may we infer that Israel was rejecting

only bodily activity on the part of the deceased, leaving open the possibility of a spiritual activity by the "liberated" soul. Israel did not know of a soul independent of the body; she had not arrived at the Greek philosophical distinction of matter and form, body and soul.

If death posed a problem for Israel, it was not simply because each man and woman died. Nor was suffering a totally enigmatic question. Pain and eventual death were accepted as the common lot of humanity (2 S 14:14). These facts of life flowed quietly through the delicate pen of an artist and created one of the most exquisite portraits of old age and death in world literature:

> Remember your Creator in the days of
> your youth,
> before the evil days come
> And the years approach of which you will say,
> I have no pleasure in them;
> Before the sun is darkened,
> and the light, and the moon, and the stars,
> while the clouds return after the rain;
> When the guardians of the house tremble,
> and the strong men are bent,
> And the grinders [at the mill] are idle
> because they are few,
> and they who look through the windows
> grow blind;
> When the doors to the street are shut,
> and the sound of the mill is low;
> When one waits for the chirp of a bird,
> and all the daughters of song are suppressed;
> And one fears heights,
> and perils in the street;
> When the almond tree blooms [with the white
> color of old age],
> and the locust grows sluggish
> and the caper berry is without effect,
> Because man goes to his lasting home,

and mourners go about the streets;
Before the silver cord is snapped
and the golden bowl is broken,
And the pitcher is shattered at the spring,
and the broken pulley falls into the well,
And the dust returns to the earth as it once was,
and the life breath returns to God who gave it.
Vanity of vanities, says Qoheleth,
all things are vanity (Ec 12:1-8).

The final statement, "the life breath returns to God who gave it," seen in the context of the entire Book of Ecclesiastes, does not announce anything more than the presence of God at the final moment of human existence on earth.

Despite a bleak prospect for the deceased person, Israel could even speak about a "happy death" if three conditions were realized: a long life (Gn 6:3; Ps 90:10); many descendants (Gn 22:17; Ps 90:16); and burial in the family sepulchre (Gn 23; 50:25). Death, consequently, was not always considered a punishment for sin; that idea, clearly proposed in Genesis 3, is not generally reflected in the rest of the Old Testament. Premature death and a long, painful illness were attributed to sin, but not death itself. Some death scenes, in fact, breathe peace and serenity (Gn 25:7-8; 49:33; 50:24-26).

But Israel never had a completely satisfying answer to the question of suffering and death. The Book of Job defies any such oversimplification as that. Israel was sustained in peace and sometimes in joy by an intuition of personal immortality, an intuition which did more than enrich the formal statements of its sacred tradition. A mystical contemplation of God's goodness and fidelity exploding the rigid confines of rationalization and sentence structure corrected what was erroneous in the explicit or obvious meaning of Israel's theology of the afterlife. Here is an instance where a biblical statement must be interpreted not only within the evolving context of the entire Bible, but especially according to the prayer of the people in their holiest moments of faith.

It is worthwhile to reflect on Israel's attitude of faith as she confronted the trials of life in order to discover how she could face the trial of death, at least in the subconscious or mystical depth of its experience. The prayer of Israel drew its warp and woof from the great redemptive acts of God within her history. These acts included not only his fatherly concern to assure off-spring to Abraham and Sarah despite the seeming sterility of their marriage, or to bring the slave people Israel out of Egypt and to care for them during their wandering through the vast and fear-ful desert (Dt 1:19); but his greatest acts appeared in his repeated forgiveness of their sins. Though experiencing the sorrowful effects of sin, Israel still always felt confident to pray for pardon. Whenever she cried out to Yahweh for help, "the Lord took pity on their distressful cries of affliction under their oppressors" (Jg 1:18), and sent a deliverer in the person of a judge or a King David or a series of prophets.

From one of the prophets, Hosea, came a cry of divine com-passion breaking the bonds of human restrictions yet humanly communicating the extraordinary mystery of God's love and fidelity:

> How could I give you up, O Ephraim,
> or deliver you up, O Israel? . . .
> My heart is overwhelmed,
> my pity is stirred.
> I will not give vent to my blazing anger,
> I will not destroy Ephraim again;
> For I am God and not man (Ho 11:8-9).

True, Hosea, the prophet of delicate, fragile, and explosive emo-tions, could swing from one extreme to another. A little later he has God exclaim, "My eyes are closed to compassion!" Still, the overall tone of the book is divine forgiveness. Only thus could Hosea explain his own compulsion to pardon his wife throughout her repeated adulteries. He could unravel the mystery of himself by remembering the history of God's forgiveness of Israel. Then from this new knowledge about himself he could leap anew into the mystery of God's continuous love towards Israel:

I will espouse you to me forever;
I will espouse you in right and in justice,
in love and in mercy;
I will espouse you in fidelity,
and you shall know the Lord
(Ho 2:21-22).

Could such a divine espousal with Israel be broken by death?
Faced with the overwhelming inability to reject and divorce his
wife and marry someone else more worthy, Hosea intuited the
mysterious, persevering love of Yahweh. God would always be
there with his people. Such, in fact, is the better explanation of
the divine name Yahweh: "He who is always there." Faith such
as this left the mind in darkness by the brightness of its love.
Could it also enable the Israelite to react to the darkness of death
in a way beyond explication? Was the darkness so black because
the light of God's goodness was shining so brilliantly?

While Hosea discovered a partial answer in the persevering
love of Yahweh for Israel, other prophets could do no more than
simply survive in darkness. God provided no answer whatsoever;
he even intensified the problem. God closed the conversation
abruptly, much in the same way that death slams the door on life.
Typical of this manner of divine-human dialogue are the first two
chapters in the book of Habakkuk. Habakkuk introduced an
entirely new style into prophetic preaching. Up until his time,
the prophets announced God's word to Israel. Habakkuk reversed
the pattern. He put the human questions to God—and this, too,
was considered equally the inspired word of God. Habakkuk
began with an interrogation of God:

How long, O Lord? I cry for help
but you do not listen! (Hab 1:2).

God answered this question in verses 5 to 11; he would punish
the wicked Jerusalemites by summoning the Chaldeans (or Babylonians) to invade and conquer the city. This reply did not
satisfy Habakkuk, and again he dared to question God:

> Why, then, do you gaze on the faithless in silence
> while the wicked man devours one
> more just than himself? (1:13)

God then indicated that his reply would be so important that it ought to be inscribed with letters on a billboard that anyone could read on the run: *"The just man lives by his faith."* God refused to answer directly the question put to him; he left Habakkuk dangling in darkness. The prophet must wait.

> For the vision still has its time, presses on to
> fulfillment, and will not disappoint;
> If it delays, wait for it, it will surely come,
> it will not be late.
> The rash man has no integrity;
> but the just man lives by his faith (Hab 2:3-4).

Habakkuk's style of dialogue shows up in a still more unique, inimitable way in the preaching of Jeremiah who put his question squarely before God with exquisite delicacy yet with impetuous argumentation:

> You are just, O God, but I must argue with you ...
> Why does the way of the godless prosper (Jr 12:1, CS).

Before recording God's reply, Jeremiah already had an answer in one of the most tender lines of the entire Old Testament: "You explore my heart within you" (Jr 12:3). The word "explore" (in Hebrew *bahan*) means to test, to experiment, to move into the black unknown. Jeremiah was admitting before God in paraphrased form: As I plunge into the darkness of my questioning mind, you are there, exploring it with me. What greater reassurance was possible than this secret sense of God's presence? (Could this statement be the mystic's answer to death, and will death always have to be a mystical experience for everyone?).

In replying to Jeremiah, God did not answer his question but addressed himself to the prophet's faith:

> If running against men has wearied you,
> how will you gallop against horses?
> And if in a land of peace you seek your confidence,
> how will you fare in the jungle of the Jordan?
> (Jr 12:5, CS).

In other words, God was saying to him: Things are going to get much worse before they get better. This present situation is peaceful compared with what is to come! You will have to run all the faster to keep up with horses. God expected his Chosen People to persevere in their faith as they moved through the darkness of any and every human barrier. Did this expectation, which God's love induced within the heart of Israel, implicitly include death? Why not, especially when death might have seemed a blessed relief to Jeremiah when it would have ended the harrowing frustrations of his forty-year ministry? Although he cursed the day of his birth (20:14-18), Jeremiah continued to live in faith. Here, then, was a power reaching beyond the decisions of life and death.

Jeremiah's curse for the day of his birth is echoed in the laments of Job (3:1-10; 10:18), who also took his flesh between his teeth and demanded an audience with his Maker (Jb 13:14). God, this time replying out of the whirlwind, gave the same kind of response. He answered by asking further questions beyond those of Job:

> Who is this that obscures divine plans
> with words of ignorance?
> Gird up your loins now, like a man;
> I will question you, and you tell me the answers!
> Where were you when I founded the earth?
> Tell me, if you have understanding (Jb 38:2-4).

Only another deity can question God! At this majestic speech of God, Job could only "repent in dust and ashes" and abide in his faith. Such faith enabled him to do what the wisest men in the world—Eliphaz, Bildad and Zophar—could not do. Job prayed for his enemies and false comforters (Jb 42:7-9). Another act beyond the wise man's competence to explain was the very human experience of death. Job would be capable of it by his faith, not by his answers.

This exposition of Israel's attitude toward death leaves many questions unanswered. It silently passes over many important and relevant aspects of Old Testament theology: the liturgical piety of the psalms in the face of death; the adumbrations of personal immortality in the very early traditions about Henoch (Gn 5: 24) and Elijah (2 K 2:11-12), whom God took to himself without their seeming to die; the miracle stories about the prophets Elijah and Elisha, who raised dead men to life (1 K 17:17-20; 2 K 4:18-37; 13:20-21).

What is most surprising is the way Israel resisted foreign theologies about the future life. Both Egypt and Mesopotamia possessed some kind of belief in personal immortality. Egypt especially expressed this religious conviction rather clearly. In rejecting the polytheism and magical superstition of Egyptian future life, did Israel overreact? In any case, Israel's opposition remained strong, even at such a late date as the second and first centuries before Christ and way into the Christian era. Neither the authors of such late books as Sirach, Judith, Baruch and First Maccabees nor the Sadducean priesthood at Jerusalem accepted the new theology of bodily resurrection.

For most of her history, then, Israel rejected any clear theology of life after death and in fact denied any kind of human activity, much less joyful experience, in the shadowy abode of the dead. Still her strong, persevering faith in God's fidelity implicitly inferred something more positive and attractive. If it is true that the trials of living are more intense than the sorrow of dying, then Israel's faith during life was saying something about death. If God remained at the side of his faithful ones, despite the darkness and agony of the prophets or Job, then would he not stay with his people as they confronted the barrier of death? The inability to explain God's presence during agonizing problems of life, all the while remaining true to God, implies an ability to maintain faith in God when facing the inexplicable fact of death.

Mystical prayer seemed to be the solution to death, as ecstasy is the truest response to life in God.

> While you wrought awesome deeds
> we could not hope for,
> such as they had not heard of from of old.
> No ear has ever heard, no eye ever seen,
> any God but you doing such deeds
> for those who wait for him (Is 64:2-3).

Waiting is the attitude of faith and the language of contemplative prayer. Only those who trust in God during life can wait for divine life in death.

INDICES

General Index

Biblical Index